OXFORD WORLD'S CLASSICS

CAN JANE EYRE BE HAPPY?

JOHN SUTHERLAND is Lord Northcliffe Professor of Modern English Literature at University College London, and is the author of a number of books, including *Thackeray at Work*, *Victorian Novelists and Publishers*, and *Mrs Humphry Ward*. He has also edited *Vanity Fair*, *Pendennis*, *The Woman in White*, *The Moonstone*, Trollope's *Early Short Stories*, *Late Short Stories*, and *The Way We Live Now* and written *Is Heathcliff a Murderer?* and *Who Betrays Elizabeth Bennet?* in Oxford World's Classics.

OXFORD WORLD'S CLASSICS

*For almost 100 years Oxford World's Classics have brought
readers closer to the world's great literature. Now with over 700
titles—from the 4,000-year-old myths of Mesopotamia to the
twentieth century's greatest novels—the series makes available
lesser-known as well as celebrated writing*

*The pocket-sized hardbacks of the early years contained
introductions by Virginia Woolf, T. S. Eliot, Graham Greene,
and other literary figures which enriched the experience of reading.
Today the series is recognized for its fine scholarship and
reliability in texts that span world literature, drama and poetry,
religion, philosophy and politics. Each edition includes perceptive
commentary and essential background information to meet the
changing needs of readers.*

OXFORD WORLD'S CLASSICS

—

JOHN SUTHERLAND

Can Jane Eyre Be Happy?

More Puzzles in Classic Fiction

—

OXFORD
UNIVERSITY PRESS

Oxford University Press, Great Clarendon Street, Oxford OX2 6DP

Oxford New York

Athens Auckland Bangkok Bogota Bombay
Buenos Aires Calcutta Cape Town Dar es Salaam
Delhi Florence Hong Kong Istanbul Karachi
Kuala Lumpur Madras Madrid Melbourne
Mexico City Nairobi Paris Singapore
Taipei Tokyo Toronto Warsaw

and associated companies in
Berlin Ibadan

Oxford is a trade mark of Oxford University Press

Reissued as an Oxford World's Classics paperback 2000

British Library Cataloguing in Publication Data
Data available

Library of Congress Cataloging in Publication Data
Data available

ISBN 0-19-283603-X

1 3 5 7 9 10 8 6 4 2

Printed in Great Britain by
Cox & Wyman Ltd., Reading

Contents

Preface and Acknowledgements

The poor fictionist very frequently finds himself to have been wrong in his description of things in general, and is told so roughly by the critics and tenderly by the friends of his bosom. He is moved to tell of things of which he omits to learn the nature before he tells of them—as should be done by a strictly honest fictionist. He catches salmon in October; or shoots his partridges in March. His dahlias bloom in June, and his birds sing in the autumn. He opens the opera-houses before Easter, and makes Parliament sit on a Wednesday evening. And then those terrible meshes of the law!

(Anthony Trollope, *Phineas Finn*, chapter 29)

Can Jane Eyre be Happy? is a follow-up to *Is Heathcliff a Murderer?* As in the earlier book the poor fictionist's seeming errors, anomalies, illogicalities, and contradictions are investigated—tenderly rather than roughly, I trust—for the light they shed on the complexities of fiction and its power over us. Although the books are similar in method I have extended the chronological range in *Can Jane Eyre be Happy?* beyond the Victorian period, starting with Daniel Defoe's *Robinson Crusoe* and finishing with Virginia Woolf's *Mrs Dalloway*. Doubtless by straying outside my strict area of expertise I shall find myself, like Trollope, in some terrible meshes.

Writing *Is Heathcliff a Murderer?* was enjoyable and the book received friendly reviews (with a rather two-edged compliment *The Economist* observed that if this kind of thing went on, literary criticism would get a good name). Most gratifying to me, however, was the unusual number of personal letters I received from readers of World's Classics. Some courteously pointed out errors I had made. Judith Stokes wittily undermined my contention (in 'What

Preface and Acknowledgements

does Edward Hyde look like?') that Spencer Tracy's por-
trayal of Hyde was horrific. 'In fact', she commented,
'Tracy was famous for not using any "shock" make-up—
other than a pair of false teeth—to show Dr Jekyll's trans-
formation to Hyde. So subtle was the effect that Somerset
Maugham, on visiting the set, is said to have asked,
"which one is he now, Jekyll or Hyde?"' In a letter on the
same lines Donald Weeks suggested, tactfully, that I must
have been thinking of Fredric March's earlier version of
the character. In a less corrective letter the author Wolf
Mankowitz recalled that in his screenplay of Stevenson's
novel (*The Two Faces of Jekyll*) some years before, he 'presented the idea that to the Victorians an evil, elegant (if
small) man (if evil enough) would probably look like a
possessed and deformed Byron (and would certainly
limp!)'. His vision, Mr Mankowitz recalls, 'suffered from
bad casting . . . but I was glad to read in your analysis that
I was nearer to the original than most other adaptations'.

Marianne McLeod Gilchrist wrote in a similar spirit of
solidarity:

to express gratitude and delight for *Is Heathcliff a Murderer?* It is
giving a great deal of pleasure to myself, friends and family send-
ing us scurrying back to much-loved books in search of clues to
some of the puzzles you have highlighted. We had never doubted
Heathcliff's guilt: there are clues to his sadism even when, in
boyhood, he wired the lapwings' nest to kill the chicks (chapter
12, as Catherine recalls in her delirium). We also welcomed your
defence of a favourite Hardy tragic hero, Alec d'Urberville:
Simon Gatrell's comments about him in the introduction to the
World's Classics edition of *Tess* are outrageous ('cardboard cut-
out, two-dimensional rapist and bounder', p. xxii, sticks in my
mind as particularly unjust!) Your contribution to this debate is
appreciated.

Ms Gilchrist and her family are obviously formidable
readers, and I am glad to have them on my side. But lest I

rest on my laurels she goes on to instruct me (in reference
to the chapter, 'How much English blood, if any, does
Waverley spill?') that 'to refer to the opposing sides in the
1745 Jacobite Rebellion as "the English army" and "the
Scots" is a mistake . . . So please note that Edward Waverley bears a commission in the *British* army or *government*
forces, while the rebels with whom he fights at Preston-
pans are *Jacobites*, not exclusively Scots.' Point taken.

Simon Levene sent me a letter about *Frankenstein*
whose trenchancy I relished:

Without seeming ragingly pedantic, may I mention p. 27, where
you refer to a 'metallic bolt attaching [the monster's] head to its
body'? in fact, it is not a bolt but the ends of the electrodes
through which the electricity flows into the monster. More to the
point, why should Victor Frankenstein ever *construct* a body?
Why wouldn't *one* body have done quite as well?

I wish I had thought of that first. With a truly Holmesian
acuteness Paul Jenkinson noted: 'If I may be permitted
one minor cavil, it is with your description of Sherlock
Holmes as having "the best brain in England". As other
readers may have reminded you, Holmes himself took
pains to point out that his mental abilities were inferior to
those of his brother, Mycroft.' Crushingly precise chapter
and verse citation followed.

Academic readers of literary texts, since they do it for a
living, tend to think they are more scrupulous than the
general public who merely read for pleasure. One deduction I draw from the response to *Is Heathcliff a Murderer?*
is that, for many World's Classics readers, the pleasure
itself comes from an extraordinarily fine-toothed combing
of the text. In another letter to me Mr Jenkinson outlined
no less than five possible chronologies of the central
events of *Pride and Prejudice*. Having, by ruthless logic
and recourse to the perpetual calendar, eliminated two of

them, he concluded his letter: 'It would greatly please me if you could determine which of these three [remaining] scenarios is the "real" one.' I can't. For those who are interested, the conundrum pivots on whether Elizabeth and the Gardiners visit Pemberley and unexpectedly encounter Darcy on 21 July, 28 July, 4 August, 11 August, or 18 August. It is, I warn you, a brain-stretching puzzle not to be followed up unless you have a week or so's wholly undistracted time and a very good head for figures.

Sir Geoffrey Wardale outlined a similarly close investigation into the chronology of Jane Austen's fiction (something which, henceforward, will protrude fatally into my own reading of the six novels). I took great delight—as would Trollope himself; I believe—in John Kahn's description of the Chronicler of Barsetshire's incorrigible 'nonchalance about small details':

His slipshod chronology can't often be rationalized away as smartly as in your account of *Rachel Ray*'s two-timing. Harding was warden for twelve years or nine years; Silverbridge [in *The Duke's Children*] is 22 when he should be 16; Amelia Gazebee is 'the happy mother of many babies' after just one year of marriage, etc. . . .

Dr Kahn's entertaining catalogue of Trollopian blunders continues for a close-packed page. He concludes with a 'challenge for your next set of essays. Having reconstructed the seduction scene of *Tess*, how about reconstructing the seduction scene of *The Scarlet Letter*. Try penetrating *that* silence!' I have duly tried in the Hawthorne chapter in this volume (see 'What are the Prynnes doing in Boston?').

Briefer thanks to Eleanor Barraclough (who questioned a certain callousness, as she saw it, in my comments on Tess), Nora Crook (who queried, learnedly, among much else, my assumption—*vis-à-vis* Thackeray's allusion to it—

that *Peter Wilkins* was a well-known text in the nineteenth century), E. E. Duncan Jones (who directed me to an exasperated earlier critic, complaining about Wilkie Collins's abysmal ignorance about the niceties of marriage registers), Claire Lamont (who wrote perceptively about the habits of grazing sheep and the likelihood of kitchen fires in June), Charlotte Mitchell (who shrewdly suggested Mr Hart in *Rachel Ray* may have been based on Sir Massey Lopes), Valerie Grosvenor Myer (who disagreed, persuasively, with my contention that Hetty's lovemaking with Arthur in the woods was 'fumbled'), P. K. Samant (who appended to a letter on Jane Austen a query which floored me, 'What, exactly, are Mr Hale's "doubts" in *North and South?*'), Margaret I. MacPhee Smith (who wrote informatively about the journalistic career of E. S. Dallas), George Watson (who pointed out that Sir Thomas's 'deep silence' when Fanny asks him about the slave trade may simply arise from the fact that 'Fanny was something of a conversation-stopper'; he has 'always felt glad not to have known her', Dr Watson adds).

A number of friends and correspondents have looked at the proofs of chapters of *Can Jane Eyre be Happy?* I cannot resist quoting at some length Kenneth Fielding on the question of Esther's (ill-)treatment of her mother-in-law in *Bleak House* (for the Ian Botham reference, see the opening paragraphs of the chapter 'What happens to Mrs Woodcourt?'):

As to Ian Botham being averse to mothers-in-law—it is either a joke, or perhaps he means it but does not take a politically correct view. Neither did Dickens who detested his mother-in-law, I suspect, and packed his own mother off to Exeter or wherever he sent her. One is not obliged to admire one's mother-in-law, even in fiction. Who is to say whether they are right or wrong?

If the reader detects a firmness of tone in the above, it

probably originates in the fact that Professor Fielding
was, many years ago, my Ph.D. supervisor. As always I kiss
his rod.

Mr R. Worrall, who took issue with my depiction of Tess
in *Is Heathcliff a Murderer?*, offered a contradiction of my
concluding words in this volume's *Tess* essay, about
Angel's sexlessness ('One of the favourite conundrums of
medieval theologians was whether angels had sexual
organs and if so whether they used them. This one has,
and doesn't'). Mr Worrall's refutation constitutes a succinct puzzle ('Do Angel and Tess make love after the death
of Alec?') which I am happy to pass on:

> I much enjoyed the witty ending—but is it strictly true? It is
> Angel's confession of '. . . eight and forty hours' dissipation with
> a stranger' that precipitates Tess's own confession and the sub-
> sequent disasters that follow. What are Angel and Tess doing
> during the five days and nights they spend at Bramshurst Court,
> following Alec's murder? Darkness and seclusion are emphasized
> and time seems to pass by without them noticing . . . I don't think
> they were playing scrabble! Polanski is surely faithful to the
> understated spirit of Hardy's narrative when he inserts a scene
> into his film version, showing Angel undressing (and venerating)
> Tess, and another showing them in bed together.

I am indebted to a number of friends and fellow academ-
ics for suggestions as to possible puzzles. My colleague
John Mullan suggested the *Tom Jones* conundrum (who is
the hero's father?) and pointed me to the '*caro sposo*' problem in the text of *Emma*; Michael Slater proposed the
Fagin and Pip puzzle (why is one hanged and the other not
punished?); Fred Schwarzbach suggested the intriguing
question about Pickwick's earlier career, or lack of it;
David Lodge pointed out the odd anachronism in *The
Woodlanders* which he came across when editing the
novel; Rosemary Ashton pointed me to the oddities about
Maggie's handling of the boat in the climax of *The Mill on*

the Floss; Tony Tanner, in an amusing review of an earlier book of mine in the *TLS*, drew my attention to the minuscule 'error' about Pug's sex in *Mansfield Park* (in justice to Dr Tanner, I should say that his point was that such things do *not*, in his view, justify the amount of space I like to devote to them); my colleague Keith Walker has been entertaining students for some years with his account of Mrs Dalloway's odd peregrination round the West End—and I am indebted to him in my Woolf chapter; as will be evident in the 'Is Daniel Deronda circumcised?' chapter, I am much indebted to Ken Newton (Professor Newton writes 'I enjoyed it . . . though I'm sure you don't expect me to agree with your line').

For help in preparing this book I should also like to thank Jonathan Grossman, Mac Pigman, Jane Dietrich, Ann Totterdell, Alison Winter, and—for much encouragement and constructive criticism—Judith Luna.

Daniel Defoe · *Robinson Crusoe*

Why the 'Single Print of a Foot'?

J. Donald Crowley is amusingly exasperated about Defoe's many narrative delinquencies in *Robinson Crusoe*. 'Perhaps the most glaring lapse', Crowley says in his edition of the novel,

> occurs when Defoe, having announced that Crusoe had pulled off all his clothes to swim out to the shipwreck, has him stuff his pockets with biscuit some twenty lines later. Likewise, for the purpose of creating a realistic effect, he arranges for Crusoe to give up tallying his daily journal because his ink supply is dangerously low; but there is ink aplenty, when, almost twenty-seven years later, Crusoe wants to draw up a contract. . . Having tried to suggest that Crusoe suffers hardship because he lacks salt, he later grants Crusoe the salt in order to illustrate his patient efforts to teach Friday to eat salted meat. Crusoe pens a kid identified as a young male only to have it turn into a female when he hits upon the notion of breeding more of the animals. (p. xiii)

Such inconsistencies convince Crowley that 'Defoe wrote too hastily to control his materials completely'. His was a careless genius.

Haste and carelessness could well account for some baffling features in the famous 'discovery of the footprint' scene. It occurs fifteen years into Robinson's occupation of his now thoroughly colonized and (as he fondly thinks) desert island. At this belated point the hero is made to describe his outdoor garb. He has long since worn out the European clothes which survived the wreck. Now his coverings are home-made:

1. Frontispiece from the first edition, 1719

I had a short Jacket of Goat-Skin, the Skirts coming down to about the middle of my Thighs; and a Pair of open-knee'd Breeches of the same, the Breeches were made of the Skin of an old *He-goat*, whose Hair hung down such a Length on either Side, that like *Pantaloons* it reach'd to the middle of my Legs; Stockings and Shoes I had none, but had made me a Pair of somethings, I scarce know what to call them, like Buskins to flap over my Legs, and lace on either Side like Spatter-dashes; but of a most barbarous Shape, as indeed were all the rest of my Cloaths. (p. 149)

This sartorial inventory has been gratefully seized on by the novel's many illustrators, from 1719 onwards (see fig. 1). The salient feature is that Robinson goes barefoot. And it is to rivet this detail ('Shoes I had none') in our mind that at this point Defoe describes Crusoe's wardrobe. In the preceding narrative, if it crosses the reader's mind, we assume that Crusoe has some protection for the soles of his feet (the island is a rough place). Oddly, Robinson seems not to have taken a supply of footwear from the ship's store nor any cobbling materials with which to make laced moccasins from goatskin. Shortly after being marooned he found 'two shoes' washed up on the strand, but they 'were not fellows', and were of no use to him. Much later, during his 'last year on the Island', Robinson scavenges a couple of pairs of shoes from the bodies of drowned sailors in the wreck of the Spanish boat. But, when he sees the naked footprint on the sand, Crusoe is barefoot.

The footprint is epochal, 'a new Scene of my Life', as Crusoe calls it. He has several habitations on the island (his 'estate', as he likes to think it) and the discovery comes as he walks from one of his inland residences to the place on the shore where he has beached his 'boat' (in fact, a primitive canoe):

It happen'd one Day about Noon going towards my Boat, I was exceedingly surpriz'd with the Print of a Man's naked Foot on the Shore, which was very plain to be seen in the Sand: I stood like one Thunder-struck, or as if I had seen an Apparition; I listen'd, I look'd round me, I could hear nothing, nor see any Thing. I went up to a rising Ground to look farther, I went up the Shore and down the Shore, but it was all one, I could see no other Impression but that one, I went to it again to see if there were any more, and observe if it might not be my Fancy; but there was no Room for that, for there was exactly the very Print of a Foot, Toes, Heel, and every Part of a Foot; how it came thither, I knew not, nor could in the least imagine. (pp. 153–4)

2. Lynton Lamb, cover design for Oxford University Press, 1957

Two big questions hang over this episode. The first, most urgent for Robinson, is 'Who made this footprint?' The second, most perplexing for the reader, is 'why is there only one footprint?' In the above passage, and later, Crusoe is emphatic on the point. We are not much helped by illustrations of the scene, such as that above by Lynton Lamb to an early World's Classics edition, which shows the footprint, on a flat expanse of beach, with nothing else for yards around. (It's a lovely picture; but Lamb has erroneously given Crusoe a pair of Scholl sandals.[1])

Was the single footprint made by some monstrous hopping cannibal? Perhaps Long John Silver passed by, from *Treasure Island*, with just the one foot and a peg leg? Has someone played a prank on Robinson Crusoe by raking over the sand as one does in a long-jump pit, leaving just the one ominous mark? More seriously, one might surmise that the ground is stony with only a few patches of sand between to receive an occasional footprint. This is the interpretation of G. H. Thomas in the next version of this scene (note the shoes, again). The objection to the thesis of this illustration is that Crusoe would scarcely choose such a rocky inlet as a convenient place to beach his boat.

Robinson has no time for investigation of the footprint. He retreats in hurried panic to his 'Castle', not emerging for three days. Is it the mark of the Devil, he wonders, as he cowers inside his dark cave? That would explain the supernatural singularity of the footprint, since the devil can fly. In his fever vision, years before, Robinson saw the Evil One 'descend from a great black Cloud, in a bright Flame of Fire, and light upon the Ground' (p. 87)— presumably leaving an enigmatic footprint in the process, if anyone dared look. But if the mark in the sand is the devil's work it would seem lacking in infernal cunning or even clear purpose: 'the Devil might have found an

3. Illustration by George Housman Thomas, from an edition of 1865

abundance of other Ways to have terrify'd me than this of
the single Print of a Foot', Robinson concludes.[2] Similar
arguments weigh against the footprint's being a sign from
the Almighty. It is more plausible, Robinson finally concludes, 'that it must be some of the Savages of the main
Land over-against me, who had wander'd out to Sea in
their *Canoes*'. Will they now come back in force, to
'devour' him?

Fear banishes 'all my religious Hope' for a while. But
gradually Crusoe's faith in Providence returns, as does his
trust in rational explanation. 'I began to perswade my self
it was all a Delusion; that it was nothing else but . . .the
Print of my own foot' (p. 158). He emerges from his hole
and, stopping only to milk the distended teats of his goats,
he returns to examine the print more carefully. In three
days and nights one might expect it to have been covered
over by the wind, but it is still there, clear as ever. Crusoe's
rational explanation proves to be wrong: 'When I came to
measure the Mark with my own Foot, I found my Foot not
so large by a great deal.' Panic once more.

We are never specifically told who left the print, nor why
it was just the one. But the experience changes Robinson
Crusoe's way of life. No longer supposing himself alone,
he adopts a more defensive ('prudent') way of life. He is
right to be prudent. Some two years later, on the other side
of the island, he sees a boat out at sea. That far coast, he
now realizes, is frequently visited—unlike his own: 'I was
presently convinc'd, that the seeing the Print of a Man's
Foot, was not such a strange Thing in the Island as I imag-
in'd.' Providence, he is grateful to realize, has cast him
'upon the Side of the Island, where the Savages never
came' (p. 164). Never? Who left the print then—friendly
Providence, as a warning that there were savages about?

Gradually Crusoe comes, by prudent anthropological
observation, to know more about the Savages—a process

that culminates ten years after the footprint episode with
the acquisition of his most valuable piece of property, Man
Friday. The savages are, as Robinson observes, opportunist
raiders of the sea—black pirates with a taste for human
flesh. When they find some luckless wrecked mariner, or
defenceless fellow native in his craft, the savages bring
their prey to shore to cook and eat them. Then they leave.
In their grisly visits they never penetrate beyond the
sandy beach to the interior of the island (perhaps, as in
Golding's *Lord of the Flies*, there are legends of a terrible
giant, dressed in animal skins, with a magical tube which
spurts thunder). It is likely that the footprint must have
been left by some scouting savage making a rare foray to
the far side of the island. He noticed Crusoe's boat, concluded on close inspection that it was flotsam, and went
off again. Luckily the hero's residences, livestock, and
plantations were some way distant and could not be seen
from this section of the shore.

But why the single footprint? Before attempting an
answer one needs to make the point that although careless
in accidental details (such as the trousers and the bis-
cuits), Defoe usually handles substantial twists of plot
very neatly. A good example is the corn which Crusoe first
thinks is providential manna but which later proves to
have a rational origin. Defoe sets this episode up by
mentioning, on page 50, that Robinson brought back
some barley seed from his wrecked ship, 'but to my great
Disappointment, I found afterwards that the Rats had
eaten or spoil'd it all'. He threw it away in disgust. Then,
twenty-eight pages later, the seed sprouts. Robinson at
first believes the growing barley to be a miracle. Then he
puts two and two together and realizes it is the result of
his thoughtlessly shaking out the bags of spoiled chicken-
feed some months earlier. It is an accomplished piece of
narrative.

A few pages before the episode of the footprint Defoe
has Crusoe describe, in great detail, the tides which wash
the island and their intricate ebbs and flows. Many
readers will skip over this technical and unexciting
digression. Ostensibly, Crusoe's meditation on the 'Sets of
the Tides' has to do with navigation problems. But the
ulterior motive, we may assume, is to imprint in the
reader's mind the fact that the island does have tides and
that they are forever lapping at its shoreline.

What we may suppose happened is the following. Crusoe
has beached his boat, not on the dead-flat expanse which
Lamb portrays, but on a steeply inclined beach. The
unknown savage came head-on into the beach and pulled
his boat on to the sand. He investigated Crusoe's canoe, all
the while walking below the high-tide line. Having satisfied himself that Crusoe's vessel had no one in it, he
returned to his own craft. Coming or going, one of his feet
(as he was knocked by a wave, perhaps, or jumped away
from some driftwood) strayed above the high-water mark.
This lateral footprint (i.e. not pointing to, or away from,
the ocean) was left after the tide had washed all the others
away together with the drag marks of the savage's boat.

Robinson Crusoe's discovery of the footprint is, with
Oliver Twist's asking for more, one of the best-known episodes in British fiction—familiar even to those who would
scarcely recognize the name of Daniel Defoe. It is also one
of the English novel's most illustrated scenes—particularly in the myriad boys' editions of *Robinson Crusoe*.
Most illustrations I have seen make one of three errors (as
does Lamb above): they put the footprint too far from the
waves; they picture Robinson as wearing shoes; they show
the beach as too flat. These errors, I think, reflect widespread perplexity at the scene and a fatalistic inclination
not to worry too much about its illogical details. But there
are, as I have tried to argue, ways of making sense of the

single footprint. And at least one illustrator has interpreted the scene as I have. Despite its rather melodramatic *mise en scène*, the most persuasive pictorial interpretation I have seen is this by George Cruikshank (although he too gives Robinson shoes).

The Oxford World's Classics *Robinson Crusoe* is edited by J. Donald Crowley.

Illustration by George Cruikshank,
from an edition of 1890

John Cleland · *Fanny Hill*

Where does Fanny Hill keep her contraceptives?

I first read *Fanny Hill* (or, more properly, *Memoirs of a Woman of Pleasure*) in the 1950s, when it was still a banned book. A friend loaned me a much-thumbed copy, vilely printed in Tangiers, and evidently smuggled in by a merchant sailor. Any bookseller handling Cleland's 'erotic masterpiece' in 1955 would have faced prosecution. British schoolboys caught with the book might expect instant expulsion. Adults found in possession would probably receive a formal police warning[1] and summary confiscation of the offending object (which, one guesses, would be eagerly pored over at the station). *Fanny Hill* was a much less exciting text after it—along with *Lady Chatterley's Lover*—was 'acquitted' and became a legal high street commodity.[2] It was elevated to classic status by Penguin in 1985 and by OUP as a World's Classic in the same year. Doubtless some of the more adventurous A-level boards will soon be prescribing *Fanny Hill* as a set text and the BBC will chip in with a 'Book at Bedtime' version.

Fanny Hill was, one suspects, a subversive presence in English literature during its long career as an 'underground' text—particularly in the moralistic Victorian era. It seems likely that Dickens read it, and at a number of points one can plausibly detect its mark in his fiction. Mr Dick, the amiable, kite-flying idiot in *David Copperfield*, conceivably owes his name—and possibly more—to the idiot in *Fanny Hill:* 'The boys, and servants in the neighbourhood, had given him the nickname of *Good-natured Dick*, from the soft simpleton's doing everything he was bid to do at the first word, and from his naturally having no turn to mischief' (p. 160).

In a spirit of lascivious mischief Fanny and Louisa undress Good-natured Dick. His *membrum virile* amazes them: 'prepar'd as we were to see something extraordinary, it still, out of measure surpassed our expectation, and astonish'd even me, who had not been us'd to trade in trifles' (p. 162). Modest Fanny merely looks but the wanton Louisa must sample the aptly named Dick's 'maypole'. And so, we learn, do other women, inflamed by Louisa's 'report of his parts'. As a sexual toy, Dick has the advantage that since he remembers nothing he can be trusted to be discreet. He is no more likely to blab than a king-sized, battery-operated vibrator. Obviously Miss Trotwood would not, like Louisa, misconduct herself with her Dick—whose 'King Charles's head' keeps poking in everywhere (Fanny's true love is called Charles, we recall; he too is a great one for poking). But a spinster living alone with an adult man would surely give rise to bawdy speculation among the locals. It was Victorian folklore that all idiots had massive penises (something that features in depictions of the age's favourite mascot, Mr Punch, and his phallic truncheon). Every schoolboy would have a sniggering awareness of the *double entendre* in Mr Dick's name.

Joss Lutz Marsh, in a perceptive article,[3] notes another interesting echo from *Fanny Hill* in Dickens's *Dombey and Son*. When Florence Dombey loses her way in London she is abducted by a horrible crone who calls herself 'Good Mrs Brown'. 'A very ugly old woman, with red rims round her eyes', Mrs Brown deals in rags and bones in a small way. She incarcerates Florence in a filthy back room in a shabby house in a dirty London lane. Mrs Brown then strips off all Florence's clothes and gives her rags to cover herself with. For a few moments we picture the little girl either in her underclothes or stark naked. Suddenly Mrs Brown catches sight of Florence's head of luxuriant hair under her bonnet and is gripped by the lust to clip the tresses off and sell them. She obviously has further plans to make money out of the child's body which are happily forestalled when Florence escapes to be rescued by Walter.

Mrs Brown's predatoriness should be read metaphorically, Marsh suggests. With a little adjustment we can see 'Good Mrs Brown' as a procuress of underage girls for immoral purposes, one of the suppliers of the 'tribute of Babylon'. When she has stripped and shorn Florence, Mrs Brown will sell what is left to some expensive London brothel specializing in juvenile virgins. As Marsh is apparently the first to notice, there is an echo here from Cleland's novel. When 15-year-old Fanny Hill comes to London the first of the procuresses she falls in with is Mrs Brown. A 'squob-fat, red-fac'd' woman of 'at least fifty', possessed of Messalina's appetites, Cleland's Mrs Brown is not an attractive personage, if not quite as revolting as her Dickensian namesake. Cleland's bawd tries to sell Fanny's maidenhead to the odious Mr Crofts but when that fails (Fanny having heroically kept her legs crossed) Mrs Brown treats the young virgin not at all badly. She is put in the charge of a kind-hearted trull, 'Mrs' Phoebe Ayres, 'whose business it was to prepare and break such young Fillies as I was to the mounting-block' (p. 9). Phoebe is Fanny's 'tuteress'. By cunning (and gentle) lesbian caresses the older woman stimulates Fanny's latent sensuality and by voyeuristic spectacles she instructs the child in the mechanics of sex and its repertoire of 'pleasures'. Phoebe also inducts her pupil into 'all the mysteries of Venus'. They probably include, as we deduce from Fanny's later career, planned parenthood.

Having benefited from Phoebe's tuition, Fanny is now
ready for the next phase of her career. She elopes with her
19-year-old 'Adonis', Charles, to a convenient public house
in Chelsea, where she finally surrenders her maidenhead.
The young lovers enjoy each other many times and with
excesses of mutual 'pleasure'. Physically Charles is both a
man of wax and a man of means. The only son of a prosperous revenue officer, he is also the favourite of a wealthy
grandmother. Charles rescues Fanny from Mr Brown's
clutches and promptly sets her up as his mistress in
apartments with another bawd—Mrs Jones. Fanny, looking back on events, expresses a strong dislike for this new
protector. Mrs Jones is a 'private procuress . . . about forty
six years old, tall, meager, red-hair'd, with one of those
trivial ordinary faces you meet with everywhere . . . a
harpy' (pp. 51–2). On the side she engages 'in private pawn-
broking and other profitable secrets' (abortion, as we
apprehend).

Fanny resides under Mrs Jones's uncongenial roof for
eleven months, at which point she is, as she tells us, 'about
three months gone with child'. One deduces that she is
pregnant by policy not accident. Over the months Charles
has been 'educating' her—expunging her rusticity, making her a lady 'worthier of his heart'. His love, she protests, is of 'unshaken constancy', and he 'sacrificed to me
women of greater importance than I dare hint' (p. 53). It is
clear that Fanny fondly expects to marry Charles—despite
the class difference and the fact that he found her in a
London brothel. It is to this end that she has allowed herself to become pregnant—to force his hand.

What follows in Fanny's account is highly suspect. She
herself confesses that she will 'gallop post over the par-
ticulars' (p. 54). According to her skimped version of
events, Charles (who has just learned that Fanny is with
child) is kidnapped by his father and put on a boat leaving

that hour for the South Seas where a rich uncle has just died. He is not allowed to dispatch any messages (or money) back to shore. Although it is said that he later sends letters, they all 'miscarry'. Implausible, one might think.

Fanny learns from a maid that Charles has left the country and that any attempt to communicate with him is hopeless. She is alone again in the world, penniless and pregnant. Her ruse, if ruse the pregnancy was, has backfired. What actually happened seems clear enough, if we discount (as probability suggests we should) Fanny's version of events. Charles confessed to his father that he had made a woman of the town pregnant. Her bawd would swear the child was his. It would be very embarrassing for the revenue officer—and expensive. Aged 20, Charles could not marry without paternal consent even if he wanted to, and he probably does not intend to ruin his prospects by setting up house with a reformed whore. He is sent abroad for a couple of years until the whole thing blows over. The traditional solution for young men of good families who got into this kind of pickle was to send them away—preferably as far and for as long as possible.

According to Fanny she swoons when she hears the news of her lover's disappearance and, after 'several successive fits, all the while wild and senseless, I miscarried of the dear pledge of my *Charles*'s love' (p. 56). What seems more likely is that Mrs Jones aborted the child. Fanny now has only one resource—to sell herself, preferably as a 'virgin' newly up from the country. She owes Jones a huge sum for rent (over £23), and unless she can go on the game she will find herself in prison—as her landlady unkindly reminds her. Carrying Charles's 'pledge' to term is out of the question unless she wants to enter motherhood in Bridewell.

Under Mrs Jones's guidance, Fanny for the first time

takes paying clients. Some welcome stability enters her
professional life when she becomes the mistress of Mr
H—. But, after seven months, in sheer boredom, she surrenders to her protector's massively endowed footman,
Will. When she is discovered *in flagrante*, Mr H— turns
her into the streets with 50 guineas (he is not a hard-
hearted man, we apprehend). Thus Fanny, still only 16,
comes under the care of the third and most amiable of her
bawds, Mrs Cole. Mrs Cole is not only good-natured, but
conscientiously instructs her whores in 'prudential economy'. She is a skilled madame. 'Nobody', Fanny says, had
'more experience of the wicked part of the town than she
had [or] was fitter to advise and guard one against the
worst dangers of our profession' (p. 88). One main danger is
disease; the other, we guess, is pregnancy.

Enriched by three years' service with Mrs Cole, Fanny
('not yet 19') finds herself possessed of a fortune and,
thanks to her patroness, knows how to look after her nest-
egg. She is now an independent woman and has been making desultory enquiries about the whereabouts of the
errant Charles. On a triumphant trip to show herself off in
her native Lancashire village she is finally reunited with
her lover by accident. He has been shipwrecked coming
back from the South Seas. More to the point, he is now a
poor man. The tables are turned but Fanny's heart is true.
She accepts him as her husband and they go on to have
'those fine children you have seen by this happiest of
matches'.

Over the five years of our acquaintance with her, Fanny
avoids pregnancy when it would be professionally
inconvenient. She becomes pregnant when (as she wrong-
ly thinks) it will coerce Charles into marriage. She has
legitimate children after marriage. How does she control
her reproductive functions so efficiently? *Fanny Hill* is
unusual among works of popular pornography in that it

does not assume that the sexual act has no consequences—
venereal disease and pregnancy are always darkening the
edge of the heroine's 'pleasures'. The house of accom-
modation under the supervision of a knowledgeable bawd
offers invaluable prophylaxes for someone in Fanny's position. It is clear that Mrs Cole screens clients to eliminate
the grosser disease carriers.[4] It is only slightly less clear
that the Cole establishment is furnished with an efficient
contraceptive apparatus for the working girls. The nature
of the apparatus is obliquely described in the scene where
Fanny has to fabricate a broken hymen for the benefit of
Mr Norbert.

In each of the head bed-posts, just above where the bed-steads are
inserted into them, there was a small drawer so artfully adapted
to the mouldings of the timber-work, that it might have escap'd
even the most curious search, which drawers were easily open'd
or shut, by the touch of a spring, and were fitted each with a
shallow glass tumbler, full of a prepar'd fluid blood; in which lay
soak'd, for ready use, a spunge that requir'd no more than gently
reaching the hand to it, taking it out, and properly squeezing
between the thighs. (p. 135)

The defloration of a virgin would be a relatively rare
event in Mrs Cole's house. Rich fools like Mr Norbert are
not come by every day. But the sponge and the tumbler
would have a more quotidian usage, justifying the expensive alterations to the bedroom furniture. As Peter Fryer
records in his history of birth control, there were in the
eighteenth century five approved forms of contraception:
coitus interruptus, anal intercourse, primitive condoms,
exotic prophylactic potions (spermicides or abortifa-
cients), and vaginal sponges—usually dipped first in a
tumbler of some such spermicide as brandy or vinegar.[5]
There is no coitus interruptus in *Fanny Hill*—the 'bal-
samic fluid' is invariably 'inspers'd' in the woman's 'seat of
love'. Fanny, her fellow whores, and her bawds have a holy

horror of sodomy. There is no mention of condoms—which in this period are associated less with the class of whore-mongers who patronize Fanny than with virtuoso libertines like Casanova (whose 'English overcoat' was made of sheep's gut). Vaginal sponges, however, would seem to be quite at home in the world of *Fanny Hill*, conveniently available on every bedpost.

The Oxford World's Classics *Memoirs of a Woman of Pleasure (Fanny Hill)* is edited by Peter Sabor.

Henry Fielding · *Tom Jones*

═══

Who is Tom Jones's father?

═══

According to the scholar John Mullan, even readers who
know Fielding's novel well will struggle with the above
question, without recourse to the book. One can see why
Tom's paternity should be something of a poser. The crucial information is held back until the very last pages and
then passed over quickly. Maternity is something else.
That young Jones is Bridget Allworthy's offspring will be
picked up early by astute readers. It is implicit in Miss
Allworthy's instant partiality for the foundling—a partiality which continues even after she has a legitimate
child of her own (whom she evidently hates as his father's
son)—and her refusal to join in the persecution of Jenny
Jones. Fielding sows a number of such hints in the early
chapters. But the author tantalizingly withholds the identity of Tom's father—even from the characters themselves
at crucial junctures. It was, as Jenny tells Mr Allworthy,
always Bridget's intention 'to communicate it to you'. But
when she sends her deathbed confession via Dowling, it is
frustrating (particularly for Blifil, who intercepts the
message) that Bridget does not, even on the brink of
eternity, name Tom's father. 'She took me by the hand,'
Dowling recalls, 'and as she delivered me the letter, said, "I
scarce know what I have written. Tell my brother Mr
Jones is his nephew.—He is my son.—Bless him," says she,
and then fell backward, as if dying away. I presently called
in the people, and she never spoke more to me, and died
within a few minutes afterwards' (p. 840). Her son, and who
else's?

Finally, at the denouement of the novel, Mrs Waters
(formerly Jenny Jones) enlightens Allworthy Tom's father,
we at last learn, was 'a young fellow' called Summer. We
never learn his Christian name, nor is his surname mentioned before this point. Allworthy remembers the young
fellow well: 'he was the son of a clergyman of great learning and virtue, for whom I had the highest friendship.'
Apparently Summer was orphaned and there was no
immediate family. Allworthy 'bred the young man up, and
maintained him at university'. He came to reside at Mr
Allworthy's house on graduation—beating the trail later
followed by Square and Thwackum. Allworthy treated
Master Summer like a son.

Young Summer 'was untimely snatched away' by smallpox leaving Miss Allworthy pregnant. For reasons which
are not entirely clear, Bridget then confided her plight to
Jenny Jones and to Jenny's mother—but not to her own
brother. Jenny had recently been dismissed from service
with the Little Baddington schoolmaster, Partridge (later
one of Tom's putative fathers), on grounds of sexual
looseness—not, one would have thought, a strong recom-
mendation for her to be taken into the moralistic Miss
Allworthy's service. But the lady had her reasons.

It is a stroke of fortune for the conspirators that Mr
Allworthy is away on a three-month sojourn in London.
When Bridget's time comes the unreliable Deborah
Wilkins is sent off on a wild-goose chase to Dorset to
investigate the character of a prospective servant (Bridget
has dismissed her personal maid three months earlier—
clearly the girl knew too much about the affair with Summer). As Jenny recalls, 'It was . . . contrived, that my mother
and myself only should attend at that time'. The plan was
that Jenny should 'own' Bridget's child—in return for a
handsome sum of money 'The child was born', Jenny tells
Allworthy, 'in the presence only of myself and my mother,

and was by my mother conveyed to her own house, where it was privately kept by her till the evening of your return, when I, by the command of Miss Bridget, conveyed it into the bed where you found it' (p. 833). Thus begins the novel.

There is little encouragement for us to go back and reread the early chapters in the light of Jenny's last-page revelation. Bridget is a shadowy presence in the narrative after the death of Captain Blifil. Any residual curiosity we have about her is deliberately damped down. There are only a few offhand references to Miss Allworthy in the last seventeen years of her life. She dies, as she has largely lived, off-stage.

If, however, we do make the effort to go back and insert Jenny's information about Summer into the early chapters an interestingly enigmatic subplot can be reconstructed. At the time of Tom's birth Bridget Allworthy is 'past the age of thirty' (p. 32)—a euphemism for nearly 40, as we learn at the time of her courtship by Captain Blifil. She is a woman 'whom you commend rather for good qualities than beauty' (p. 32). Since her good qualities are headed by religious hypocrisy, duplicity, and sexual incontinence, her beauty must be small indeed. She is not quick-witted (as Jenny is). Why would Summer, almost twenty years her junior, and university educated, be attracted to Bridget? He was, as Jenny recalls with suspicious warmth: 'the handsomest person I ever saw, he was so genteel, and had so much wit and good breeding.'

The Allworthy fortune, of course, may add a golden lustre to Bridget's otherwise meagre attractions. Some five years earlier Allworthy's three children and his wife were wiped out in a previous smallpox epidemic, as we assume. Bridget, much younger than her brother, is now his inheritrix. Who, then, seduced whom? What deduction should we draw from Bridget's sordid liaison, a few months after giving birth to Tom, with Captain Blifil? Rather than announce his suit to Mr Allworthy (whom he fears would not approve the match) Blifil methodically sets out to seduce Bridget Allworthy into a clandestine marriage. To this end, he assaults her virtue on three occasions. Twice she responds, *'nolo episcopari'* ('I do not want the bishopric'—with the stress on the last syllable). On the third occasion, it emerges she does want the bishopric. A month later they are secretly married. Eight months after the marriage, Blifil is born (p. 69). Did young Summer, like Blifil, impregnate the spinster with a view to guaranteeing Allworthy's acquiescence to an otherwise unpropitious match?

Summer leaves no residue in the early part of the narrative—although he must have died shortly before the story opens and as an adoptive 'son' to Allworthy must have been a heavy loss. The secret birth of Tom Jones is just plausible, given the absence of Allworthy, Wilkins, and the personal maid. But there are a number of contingent puzzles. Why did Bridget choose to confide in Jenny? Why, when Jenny was examined before Allworthy as magistrate, was evidence not taken as to her pregnancy? While a gentle-lady with private apartments like Bridget might keep her interesting condition secret, a servant like Jenny could surely not, any more than Molly Seagrim can, twenty years later. If Jenny were pregnant, that would be known; if she were not pregnant that would be known too. The foundling Tom would need a wet-nurse—why was Jenny not offered the position? If she were, it would be very suspicious if she said she was unable to suckle because she had no milk.

These puzzles should be taken in conjunction with the piece of news that, a few months later, inflames Anne Partridge to physical violence on her luckless spouse, precipitating his ruin and exile from Little Baddington. One of Anne's gossips tells her, in response to a casual

inquiry after Jenny Jones: 'You have not heard, it seems
that she hath been brought to bed of two bastards; but as
they are not born here . . . we [i.e. the parish] shall not be
obliged to keep them.' The two bastards must none the less
have been begotten in the parish, Mistress Partridge calculates, 'for the wench hath not been nine months gone
away' (p. 77). What provoked the series of events that led to
her going away, many months earlier, was a dinner-table
contretemps in the Partridge household:

the husband and wife being at dinner, the master said to his maid,
'Da mihi aliquid potum', upon which the poor girl smiled, perhaps at the badness of the Latin, and, when her mistress cast her
eyes on her, blushed, possibly with a consciousness of having
laughed at her master. Mrs Partridge, upon this, immediately fell
into a fury, and discharged the trencher on which she was eating,
at the head of poor Jenny, crying out, 'you impudent whore, do
you play tricks with my husband before my face?' (p. 73)

Where, or from whom, has Jenny learned better Latin
than the schoolmaster who taught her the language? What
seems possible is that Summer, having got Bridget pregnant, fell in with the precociously clever Jenny Jones and
put her in the family way as well. Jenny, having raised
herself above Partridge's level of scholarship, willingly
succumbed to the 'handsomest person I ever saw', with his
university Latin, his 'wit', and 'gentility'. Tom Jones, it
would seem, has inherited his cheerfully polygamous
instincts. As Tom can be in love with Sophia Western and
simultaneously lust after Mrs Waters (i.e. Jenny Jones), so
could Summer with Bridget and Jenny. Like father, like
son.

It was, one may hypothesize, their common plight that
created the unlikely bond between Miss Allworthy and
Miss Jones. The fact that Jenny was pregnant herself
would make it easier for her to take charge of Miss Bridget's baby; both children could be looked after by old Mrs

Jones until they were disposed of in their different ways. Hence the gossip about the girl having *two* bastards—a piece of garbled information that must have leaked out via Jenny's mother. There were two bastards in the Jones household for a while—but only one of them was truly Jenny's.

Obviously, in these unhappy circumstances, Miss Allworthy could not marry the promiscuous Mr Summer (a foreshadowing of Sophia's problems with the similarly promiscuous Tom Jones). This impossibility would also explain her vehement reaction to Mr Allworthy's suggestion that she might consider marrying Summer—a vehemence that still mystifies the good old gentleman, two decades later:

I confess [he tells Jenny] I recollect some passages relating to that Summer, which formerly gave me a conceit that my sister had some liking to him. I mentioned it to her: for I had such a regard to the young man, as well on his own account as on his father's, that I should willingly have consented to a match between them; but she expressed the highest disdain of my unkind suspicion, as she called it, so that I never more spoke on the subject. (p. 833)

Why would Bridget not consent to such a suitable arrangement, with a comely, clever, supremely eligible young man; not consent, moreover, when she was carrying his child? Because she did not want to be linked in scurrilous gossip with Jenny Jones who was also carrying Summer's child—thus making herself a figure of ridicule in her community.

The Oxford World's Classics *Tom Jones* is edited by John Bender and Simon Stern.

Slop Slip

'Has anyone noticed that Sterne seems to have over-reached himself and slipped in Volume Two, Chapter 8 of *Tristram Shandy*?' Barbara Hardy asks, in *Notes and Queries*.[1] Her query, and the explanatory note she offers, lead into a beguiling Shandean brain-twister. The 'slip' (which is chronological) is the more remarkable in that Sterne is a writer obsessively concerned with time in his novel. But is it, in fact, a slip?

The passage in question is found on page 83 of the World's Classics edition. At last the hero, Tristram, is about to be born. It has been a long wait for would-be readers of his life and opinions. A commotion has been heard upstairs, where a very pregnant Mrs Shandy is confined with women attendants. Downstairs, Uncle Toby and Mr Shandy anxiously wait on natal events. On hearing the tell-tale noises and bustle above their heads, Uncle Toby has summoned the servant Obadiah by ringing the bell. It is not clear exactly when he performed this act—there have been so many Shandean digressions. But, at some point previously, Obadiah has been sent off post-haste to fetch the man midwife, Dr Slop.

Chapter 8 begins: 'It is about an hour and a half's tolerable good reading since my uncle *Toby* rung the bell, when *Obadiah* was order'd to saddle a horse, and go for Dr. Slop, the man-midwife.' Just a few lines higher up the page, at the end of chapter 7, 'a devil of a rap at the door' has been heard, which has caused Mr Shandy to snap his pipe in two—an event of great significance in the little

world of Shandy Hall. The pipe-shattering rap, of course,
betokens the arrival of the man midwife (much beslopped,
as it will appear, from having fallen in the stable-yard,
just outside the house). How did Slop get to Shandy Hall
so quickly? It is an eight-mile ride, a sixteen-mile round
trip.

Sterne side-steps what the reader really wants to know
at this point (has Tristram been born?) for a character-
istically subtle disquisition—apropos of Slop's miracu-
lously prompt journey—on real and imaginary duration,
which ultimately becomes a cogitation on the nature of
fictionality. The issue can be simplified as follows: (1) The
'real' time which has intervened between the ringing of
the bell and the knock on the door betokening the arrival
of Slop is very short—'no more than two minutes, thirteen
seconds, and three fifths', as Sterne 'hypercritically' calculates;[2] (2) in between describing the ringing of the bell
and the arrival of Slop, Sterne has digressed to give us a
mass of antecedent information: 'I have brought my
uncle *Toby* from *Namur*, quite across all *Flanders*, into
England ... I have had him ill upon my hands near four
years; and have since travelled him and Corporal *Trim*, in
a chariot and four, a journey of near two hundred miles
down into *Yorkshire*' (p. 84). In these digressions, Sterne
has chronicled large tracts of imaginary historical time—
four years, at least; (3) reading about Uncle Toby's history,
in the interval between ring and knock, will occupy the
average reader, as Sterne estimates, an hour and a half.
The clock time (two minutes, odd) is too short, the narrative time (four years plus) is too long, the reading time (an
hour and a half) is just right for the sixteen-mile gallop at
ten miles an hour.

The paradox is familiar from films which centre on a
long flashback or dream. For example, at the beginning
of *The Wizard of Oz* Dorothy is knocked out during a

tornado which strikes her family farm in Kansas. She is unconscious, as we reckon, for a few hours at most. During this real time (shown in black and white) Dorothy has a vivid and lengthy Technicolor dream. She and her dream companions make a long journey to the land of Oz which takes several weeks, as we reckon. The film itself lasts an hour and a half in the watching. So when Dorothy, the Tin Man, the Cowardly Lion, and the Scarecrow skip up the yellow-brick road, how long does it take? In Dorothy's unconscious mind, it can occupy only a microsecond or two. In implied narrative time, the journey will take several days. On screen, the yellow-brick road sequence is abbreviated into ten or so minutes. Which is the 'right' answer?

Having posed a similar problem in *Tristram Shandy*, Sterne rudely knocks it down by informing the reader that 'Obadiah had not got above threescore yards from the stable-yard before he met with Dr Slop'. In other words, Obadiah was not, after all, obliged to travel the eight miles to fetch the man midwife. Slop was already on his way and almost arrived at Shandy Hall (all that remained was for him to fall in the stable-yard mire). It's a typical piece of Sterneian one-upmanship. He sets up an elaborate intellectual puzzle, draws the reader into it, and then lets him/her down, like Slop, with a terrific bump.

It's nicely done. But, as Barbara Hardy points out, Sterne spoils the effect of his little ambush on the reader by what looks like a clumsy slip. This slip stands out prominently from the opening sentence of volume II, chapter 8: 'It is about an hour and a half's tolerable good reading since my uncle *Toby* rung the bell.' In fact, as Hardy notes, it is at the beginning of volume II, chapter 6 (only a couple of pages earlier) that the bell was rung. There (II.6) we are given a vignette of Uncle Toby 'taking as I told you, his pipe from his mouth, and striking the ashes out of it as he began his sentence;—I think, replied he,—it would not be amiss, brother, if we rung the bell.' As Hardy points out, 'all that comes between the ringing and the rapping is a two-chapter conversation' between Uncle Toby and Mr Shandy. For even the most primitive reader, this couple of pages would not require more than ten minutes. Where, then, did Sterne get his 'hour and a half' from? It is, Hardy observes, 'a strange lapse since it involves forgetting what happened only two chapters ago'. It is, for a writer as attentive to details of time as Sterne, more than strange— grotesque, even. Hardy surmises that even Sterne, like Homer, can nod, and that an uncharacteristic error has been made.

To return to Hardy's opening query ('has anyone noticed'); another critic, H. K. Russell, thirteen years earlier, noticed the same 'slip'.[3] But Russell picks up that when Sterne writes 'taking *as I told you*, his pipe from his mouth . . . as he began his sentence', the phrase 'I told you' refers to something a long way back in the text, as far back as volume I, chapter 21, in fact (page 51 of the World's Classics edition). There it was that the narrator first told us about the sudden commotion among the ladies upstairs, and (prefiguring the opening of II.6) we find the following passage: 'I think, replied my Uncle *Toby*, taking his pipe from his mouth, and striking the head of it two or three times upon the nail of his left thumb, as he began his sentence,—I think, says he:—but to enter . . .' (Sterne embarks on the long series of digressions that will take us to Namur, Uncle Toby's wound, the journey to Yorkshire, etc.). Clearly, the 'I think' was to be followed (as it finally is in II.6) by 'it would not be amiss, brother, if we rung the bell'. Getting from the interrupted sentence in I.21 to its completion in II.6 and II.8 will certainly take most readers an entertaining hour and a half.

So, what happened? Did Sterne momentarily forget that

in 1.21 Uncle Toby failed to complete his sentence? It is plausible. But there is, I think, another explanation which exonerates Sterne from the charge of having made a slip so injurious to his text (and not correcting it in proof—which seems a strange oversight). To demonstrate that there may not, after all, be a slip, consider the following pairs of sentences:

1. 'I think it is time for a drink,' he said, and poured himself a whisky.
2. He poured himself a whisky; 'I think it is time for a drink,' he said.

1. 'This bottle is empty,' he said, raising it up to the light.
2. He raised the bottle up to the light. 'This bottle is empty,' he said.

Sequentially, the act and the description of the act in the above sentences are reversible. In formulation (1), the utterance is predictive or proleptic (he will imminently pour himself a drink, check the contents of the bottle). In formulation (2), the utterance is explanatory of what has just happened (he has poured himself a drink, he has checked the contents of the bottle).

Consider, in the same light, the following pair of statements, as they apply to *Tristram Shandy*:

1. Uncle Toby rang for Obadiah, and began knocking the ashes out of his pipe. 'I think it would not be amiss, brother, if we rang the bell,' he said.
2. Uncle Toby began knocking the ashes out of his pipe. 'I think it would not be amiss, brother, if we rang the bell,' he said, and rang it.

To my eye and ear, the first of these is if anything more natural than the second. It is natural for masters summoning servants to act peremptorily, then pronounce on their act ('he kicked the footman down stairs: "You are dismissed", he muttered'). Nor is it easy to picture Toby scraping the ashes out of his pipe *then* pulling the bell-cord. The natural order would be to pull the bell-cord and occupy the fidgety moments until the arrival of Obadiah by nervously tapping one's pipe. The strongest support for the hypothesis that Uncle Toby rings, then fiddles with his pipe, then speaks, is that Sterne does not specifically say when the bell was rung. Had he written, for example, as opening to 11.6, the following there would be no grounds for argument:

—What can they be doing, brother? said my father.—I think, replied my uncle Toby,—taking as I told you, his pipe from his mouth, and striking the ashes out of it as he began his sentence;—I think, replied he,—it would not be amiss, brother, if we rung the bell. *He duly rang the bell.*

But Sterne did not add the italicized comment, or anything equivalent. Nowhere, in fact, is the statement 'he rang the bell' to be found. It floats un-narrated, wherever we choose to place it. It is as logical to place it in I.21 as in II.6. In these dubious circumstances, and with the author's chronic punctiliousness in mind, it seems reasonable to assume that there is no error here, or at most an ambiguity within which 'hypercriticks' can muddle themselves.

The Oxford World's Classics *The Life and Opinions of Tristram Shandy* is edited by Ian Campbell Ross.

Jane Austen · *Mansfield Park*

Pug: dog or bitch?

If there was ever an inconsequential quibble in Austen scholarship, the changing sex of Lady Bertram's lap-dog would seem to be it. Tony Tanner, who has done more than any living critic to instruct us how to read the six novels, sees it as a litmus test, dividing what is useful to discuss from what is irredeemably petty.[1] Quixotic as it may appear, there is something worthwhile to be dredged up from this, admittedly picayune, detail in *Mansfield Park*'s background. It does not substantially alter our reading of the novel, but it does offer a sharper outline of one of its principal characters.

The core of the puzzle is an incidental reference in volume I, chapter 8, as the Mansfield Park party depart in their carriages to visit Sotherton. Whether or not Fanny is to be one of the party is the main preceding issue. Mrs Norris is adamant she shall not go; Mr Rushworth gallantly wants her included; it is left to Edmund to find a solution. In the minutes before departure, there is some fierce skirmishing between Julia and Maria as to who shall be on the barouche-box seat, alongside Henry Crawford. The younger sister wins. Lady Bertram, who is too 'fatigued' to make the trip, sees the company off: 'Happy Julia! Unhappy Maria! The former was on the barouche-box in a moment, the latter took her seat within, in gloom and mortification; and the carriage drove off amid the good wishes of the two remaining ladies, and the barking of pug in his mistress's arms' (p. 72). It's a vivid tableau. Our eyes are firmly on the carriage and the sexual warfare seething within it (in her quiet way, Fanny is just as much a combatant as her cousins). But the little dog's bark may momentarily catch our attention. And, we may note from the use of 'his', it is a dog not a bitch.

Pug does not reappear until the third volume. Sir Thomas and Lady Bertram have by now resolved that Fanny must marry Henry. They are using every carrot and stick at their disposal to induce the unexpectedly stubborn young woman to conform to their wishes. 'You must be aware,' Lady Bertram tells her niece, 'that it is every young woman's duty to accept such a very unexceptionable offer as this.' The narrative continues by throwing the spotlight back on the mistress of Mansfield Park:

This was almost the only rule of conduct, the only piece of advice, which Fanny had ever received from her aunt in the course of eight years and a half.—It silenced her. She felt how unprofitable contention would be. If her aunt's feelings were against her, nothing could be hoped from attacking her understanding. Lady Bertram was quite talkative.

'I will tell you what, Fanny,' said she.—'I am sure he fell in love with you at the ball, I am sure the mischief was done that evening. You did look remarkably well. Every body said so. Sir Thomas said so. And you know you had Chapman to help you dress. I am very glad I sent Chapman to you. I shall tell Sir Thomas that I am sure it was done that evening.'—And still pursuing the same cheerful thoughts, she soon afterwards added,—'And I will tell you what, Fanny—which is more than I did for Maria—the next time pug has a litter you shall have a puppy.' (p. 302)

The episode perfectly catches Lady Bertram's moral obtuseness and her selfishness. But, out of the corner of our eye, we may note that 'pug' would now seem to be a bitch—the proud mother of puppies.

Pugs are 'toy dogs' (miniaturized bulldogs—the plucky mastiff peculiarly associated with John Bull) and, although they are short-coated, their sex may not be immediately apparent without indecently close inspection. Narrators are only human and may make the same mistakes as all of us do about such things. A devious reader might further argue that highly strung thoroughbred dogs like pugs are carefully mated, with their owners in watchful attendance as the deed takes place. Typically, the sire's owner takes an agreed share (as much as half) of the subsequent litter. So when Lady Bertram says 'the next time pug has a litter' she could conceivably mean that the next time 'he' sires one, Fanny shall have one of pug's offspring.

Pug makes two other fleeting appearances in *Mansfield Park*. In the first chapter, when it is agreed that Fanny will come to the Park House, not the Rectory, Lady Bertram observes: 'I hope she will not tease my poor pug . . . I have but just got Julia to leave it alone' (p. 8). Pug is here the neuter 'it'. There is a follow-up reference a few pages later in Chapter 2, when we are told that Lady Bertram is 'a woman . . . of little use and no beauty, thinking more of her pug than her children'. Pugs are ugly beasts like their full-sized ancestor. Unlike bulldogs, however, they are entirely useless—there being no miniature bulls for them to bait. We are to assume that the un-beautiful and useless Lady Bertram, like other dog-lovers, has come to resemble her pet. The dates implied by these early references are perplexing. Fanny, we are told, is 'just ten years old' when she comes to Mansfield Park, where—we may be sure—she will never tease Lady Bertram's pet. Assuming that pug was housebroken before Lady Bertram took possession of 'it', and that it has been in the family some time (otherwise how could 12-year-old Julia have been in the habit of teasing it?) the animal must be going on 11 or 12 years old when Lady Bertram promises 19-year-old Fanny one of its puppies—if she consents to accept Crawford. I am no dog-breeder, but this seems rather late in the day for thinking

of future litters. It might be, that as with other small
dogs (miniature poodles, King Charles's spaniels) it is chic
to have more than one. The consistent lower-casing ('pug'
not 'Pug') suggests a generic rather than an individual
beast. But descriptions such as that of Lady Bertram as 'a
woman . . . of little use and no beauty, thinking more of her
pug than her children' (pp. 16–17)[2] make it clear that she
has just the one pet dog. Otherwise it would be 'thinking
more of her pugs than her children'. One might hypothesize that the old (male) pug died and a younger (female)
pug was acquired in the interval between the Sotherton
and Portsmouth episodes—but this would be very far-
fetched.

One assumes that Jane Austen did make a tiny error
and—as Tanner says—it matters not a jot to any sensible
reader. The *de minimis* rule applies to literary criticism as
it does to law. But once our attention is drawn to the dual-
sexed pug with its unusually long sex life, some other useful points can be made. First, about pugs themselves. As
the *Oxford English Dictionary* notes, the little dogs 'came
into fashionability in 1794'. They are supposed to have
come across with William III, and are among the most
venerable of 'toy dogs'. Their tininess made them peculiarly useful as women's accoutrements, as did their placid
temperament. The placidity went with a tendency to obes-
ity ('Has anyone ever seen a thin pug?', asks one history of
the English dog). By the early decades of the nineteenth
century pugs were commonly 'ornamentally' mutilated
(ears cropped, tail docked) and the species was generally
felt to be almost bred out. It was revived, in the mid-
nineteenth century, by enterprising pug-breeders.

Pugs, then, were cherished fashion accessories because
they were *petite*, docile dogs which could be held in the
arms by women as a kind of canine muff. Essentially
they were 'masculine' beasts—mastiffs—genetically re-

modelled as ornaments for the weaker sex. The pug's miniaturized 'bulldog' lineaments rendered it not just fashionable in the late eighteenth century but—at a period of war with France—patriotic. Like the 'Blenheim spaniel' which Tory Mrs Transome has in *Felix Holt*, the pug made a political statement, in an acceptably feminine way.

The main events of *Mansfield Park* are commonly taken to be set between 1805 and 1811, during the Napoleonic Wars,[3] and the novel opens with the dating phrase: 'About thirty years ago . . .' It would seem that Lady Bertram (who after the birth of her children never can be troubled to go to London during the season) has retained the tastes of her youth, when she was the belle who captivated Sir Thomas Bertram of Mansfield Park. The pug, so fashionable when she was Miss Maria Ward, is a Miss Havisham-like attempt to stop the clock which has rendered her middle-aged and *fade*.

It is also relevant that pugs were the outcome of a strenuous and artificial breeding programme. In this they make another statement about the attitude of Lady Bertram's class to the all-important question: who should marry whom? Lady Bertram's sister, Frances, marries, 'in the common phrase, to disoblige her family . . . fixing on a Lieutenant of Marines'. The Prices' breeding is thereafter undisciplined in the highest degree. When she implores Lady Bertram to take Fanny, Mrs Price 'was preparing for her ninth lying-in'. Since they have been married eleven years (a period of frigid estrangement between the sisters), one wonders when it was that Lieutenant Price ever went to sea. On his part, the lieutenant is in the habit of cursing his unruly pack of children as 'young dogs' (p. 348)—mongrels all.

As elsewhere in *Mansfield Park*, Jane Austen sets up a thought-provoking opposition. Too much attention to breeding results in the odious pug, a useless, ugly, 'inbred'

fashion accessory. Too little attention to breeding leads to
the jungle of the Price household at Portsmouth—with its
stravaiging pack of 'ill-bred' young dogs. None the less,
Portsmouth—for all its undisciplined breeding—produced
William and Fanny. Mansfield Park has produced Julia
and Maria. Austen would seem to endorse the principle
known to all dog breeders and eugenicists—that breeds
must be regularly reinvigorated from outside the pedigree
line. The aristocratic Bertrams, on the verge of inbreeding
(as was the pug in 1810), need an admixture of mongrel-
ized Price blood.

The Oxford World's Classics *Mansfield Park* is edited by James
Kinsley, with an introduction by Marilyn Butler.

How vulgar is Mrs Elton?

In 1994 Pat Rogers published an elegant article on a small piece of fashionable (or perhaps not) slang in *Emma*, entitled: ' "Caro Sposo": Mrs Elton, Burneys, Thrales, and Noels'.[1] The Italian endearment ('dear husband') is associated indelibly in the reader's mind with Mrs Elton (née Augusta Hawkins)—heiress of Bristol, whose money is very new and breeding rather dubious. We first hear her favourite phrase when she returns, victrix, with the Revd Elton ('Mr E.') in tow as her newly wed husband.

Among the flood of offensive things which Mrs Elton pours out to Emma (whom she regards as a bested opponent in love) one remark causes unforgivable offence. Mrs Elton is talking of the descriptions her husband has given her of his circle at Highbury. ' "My friend Knightley" had been so often mentioned,' she tells Emma, 'that I was really impatient to see him; and I must do my caro sposo the justice to say that he need not be ashamed of his friend' (p. 250). Fuming after their meeting, Emma thinks savagely that her new neighbour at the vicarage is 'A little upstart, vulgar being, with her Mr. E., and her *caro sposo*, and her resources, and all her airs of pert pretension and underbred finery'.

As Rogers points out, Mrs Elton's slangy speech, particularly her 'easy application of a cant Italianate phrase . . . is a strong pointer towards her affectation and vulgarity'. But *caro sposo*, he further suggests, may be something more than 'a mark of pretension'. Arguably it carries a subtler satirical load. He goes on to survey the rise and fall of the phrase (in the mouth of the middle- and upper-class English) as something fashionable. Its heyday was in the 1770s and 1780s, when it was often used in the conversation and correspondence of younger members of noble and literate families, such as the Noels, Burneys, and Thrales. It was less commonly used in the 1790s, largely because it had become hackneyed. The latest non-ironic usage Rogers can find is 1808 (used by an elderly member of the Burney family). By this date, also the putative period of *Emma, caro sposo* would be very vieux jeu—rather like someone in the 1990s resurrecting trendy jargon from the swinging sixties ('Cool, man!'). Such cultural infelicities make the sensitive listener's skin crawl. Rogers's history of the currency of *caro sposo* is learned and wholly convincing. He concludes that 'Mrs Elton's attempts at "smart talk" reveal her not just as uncultivated, but as badly out of date with fashionable slang . . . people were not saying *caro sposo* any more'.

It's a satisfying demonstration of the value of historical philology to the general reader. Unfortunately textual bibliography steps in to complicate things. Rogers relies on the R. W. Chapman text (on which the 1988 World's Classics edition is also based). When he prepared *Emma* (initially for the Clarendon Press in 1923) Chapman made some silent alterations to the original 1816 text which materially affect the *caro sposo* business. In the first (1816) edition the offending words of Mrs Elton read as follows: ' "My friend Knightley" had been so often mentioned, that I was really impatient to see him; and I must do my cara sposo the justice to say that he need not be ashamed of his friend. Knightley is quite the gentleman.' Not *caro sposo*, that is, but the ungrammatical *cara sposo*.

The next time Mrs Elton uses the jarring term is after having received some routine courtesy from Emma's father over dinner. If anything, the notion that her aged

parent might be sexually interested in Mrs Elton infuri-
ates the heroine even more than the gross impertinence
about 'my friend Knightley'. 'I wish you had heard his gallant speeches to me at dinner,' Mrs Elton tells a frozen-
faced Miss Woodhouse. 'Oh! I assure you I begin to think
my cara sposa would be absolutely jealous. I fancy I am
rather a favourite.'

Now it is 'cara sposa' which Chapman again silently
emends to 'caro sposo'. His editorial judgement was evidently that these linguistic lapses were printer's errors
which might be cleaned up without distracting comment.
English printers often make errors with foreign phrases,
particularly when working from handwritten copy-text.

Not all editors and readers (when it is pointed out to
them) agree with Chapman's correction, on the grounds
that what Austen is trying to get across—with sly wit—is
Mrs Elton's blundering ignorance of Italian. Such is the
line taken by the Penguin Classic and the 'Norton Critical
Edition' editors, who religiously retain the misspelled ver-
sions of 1816. These lapses from strict grammatical cor-
rectness, it is assumed, are intended satire on Austen's
part. She knows, Emma knows, we know, Mrs Elton has
got *caro sposo* wrong. The only person who doesn't know is
Mrs Elton herself.

What, then, are the arguments in favour of Chapman's
emending all the usages to 'caro sposo'? First, Mrs
Elton— incorrigibly tactless as she may be—is a woman of
the world. She has seen more of that world (specifically
Bath, as she incessantly points out) than Emma. She has
almost certainly been to the theatre. Much slang and cant
Italian would be heard in these places. Bristol, where Miss
Hawkins originated, is a large cosmopolitan city (it was
also the centre of the British end of the African slave
trade, from which we may assume the Hawkins money
came—Sir John Hawkins was a well-known slave-trader

and Austen presumably intends us to pick up the allusion).
From her comments on music, the young Augusta
Hawkins evidently had the services of an expensive governess. She is obnoxious, but no fool. It is quite clear in the
above exchange about Mr Woodhouse's gallantries that
she knows she is galling Emma: she *wants* to gall her rival
and does it with malicious and practised expertise. The
phrase 'caro sposo', as Pat Rogers demonstrates, was
extremely well known by the early nineteenth century—so
well known that people of real *ton* took great care not to
use it any more. One would have to be very vulgar and very
ignorant to misquote or mispronounce it in 1810. And, as
even Emma grudgingly admits, Mrs Elton does have a
modicum of 'accomplishment'. She quotes Gay and
Gray from memory (reasonably accurately) and uses
French terms like *carte blanche* and *chaperon* correctly.
Mr Elton is a conceited man; but an educated clergyman
like himself who has been to university would not marry a
complete ignoramus, and if his wife were consistently
misusing Italian to his public embarrassment he would
have a quiet word with her *('caro sposo*, my love, *caro
sposo!')*.

There is also some textual support for the correction.
Immediately after the first 'caro sposo' insult, a furious
Emma inwardly passes the irreversible verdict: 'Insuffer-
able woman ... A little upstart, vulgar being, with her
Mr E., and her *cara sposo*, and her resources, and all her
airs of pert pretension and under-bred finery'. It could be
argued that Emma is spitefully mimicking the gross error,
or that she does not register it as an error. But if she did
mark 'cara' as a mistake, surely Austen would have indicated her heroine's contempt for the solecism a little more
clearly for the duller reader's benefit. It is not, on the face
of it, an Austenish kind of humour. It seems more likely
that the printer was unsure of the spelling from the

author's manuscript and hopefully reproduced what he had printed a few lines up.

There is a third use of the phrase which, I think, lends further support to Chapman's decision to correct and regularize. In volume III, chapter 6, during the planning for the picnic, a relentlessly talkative Mrs Elton—whose proposals are becoming more and more impractical—declares: 'I wish we had a donkey. The thing would be for us all to come on donkeys, Jane, Miss Bates, and me—and my caro sposo walking by (p. 331)' (the 1816 text has 'caro sposo'). Now it seems she can get it right. Why then did she butcher the phrase two different ways a few weeks earlier? One could argue that Mr Elton has finally had a word in her ear, or she may have been tactfully instructed by her dear Miss Fairfax, who knows quite a lot about Italy.[2] But if that were the case, Mrs Elton would surely have avoided 'caro sposo' altogether in these latter days, embarrassed at the awful gaffes she had made earlier.

This is a very tiny puzzle. Its value is that it obliges readers to determine for themselves just how vulgar they think Mrs Elton is, and what kind of vulgar. Is she the kind of grossly uneducated woman who would mangle a well-known Italian phrase? Or is she merely someone who would use a once-fashionable phrase correctly, but long after it had ceased to be fashionable, and in provincial company where it would strike her listeners as disgustingly 'slangy'? Is she coarse; or merely egotistic and insensitive to social nuance? Readers will determine the issue for themselves; myself, I tend towards Chapman's view of Mrs Elton—she is vulgar, but not so ignorantly vulgar that she would say 'cara sposo'.

The Oxford World's Classics *Emma* is edited by James Kinsley, with an introduction by Terry Castle.

James Fenimore Cooper · *The Last of the Mohicans*

Whose side is Hawk-eye on?

The first half of *The Last of the Mohicans* is taken up with
the perilous journey through the Indian-infested wilder-
ness which lies between Fort Edward and Fort William
Henry in the war-torn summer of 1757. There is much mystery attaching to this section of Cooper's tale. Why does
Colonel Munro want his daughters to join him at the very
moment that the poorly defended fort under his command
is about to be attacked by an overwhelming force of
French soldiers and their savage Huron allies? Does he
want his daughters to be scalped, or worse? Why does he
release one of his senior aides, Major Duncan Heyward, to
bring his daughters to him instead of a junior officer? It is
the more mysterious since Heyward, as it emerges, does
not know the route and gets hopelessly lost. Why does
Heyward employ as scout the treacherous Magua, whom
he knows to have a burning grudge against Colonel
Munro? If ever a trip through the woods was destined for
disaster, this is it.

Such questions fade with the series of exciting events
which ensue—particularly after Heyward's little band
picks up with the frontiersman Hawk-eye (Natty Bumppo)
and his two Mohican comrades, Chingachgook and Uncas.
Thanks to Hawk-eye's cunning, Heyward's party finally
fights its way through to Fort William Henry at precisely
the same time as the encircling French set up their siege.

It is what happens next, between chapters 15 and 19,
that I want to explore here. It seems that almost as soon as
he arrived with Heyward and the Munro girls, Hawk-eye

was dispatched back to Fort Edward, to implore the commander, General Webb, to send reinforcements. Some 1,500 men have been promised and they are desperately needed. There are 20,000 enemy with superior artillery surrounding Fort William Henry. The defenders' provisions, ammunition, and morale are running low.

A few days later, Heyward, now commanding an entrenched forward position beyond the fort's wall, sees a prisoner being escorted back to William Henry, under flag of truce. It is Hawk-eye:

[Heyward] walked to an angle of the bastion, and beheld the scout advancing, under the custody of a French officer, to the body of the fort. The countenance of Hawk-eye was haggard and care-worn, and his air dejected, as though he felt the deepest degradation at having fallen into the power of his enemies. He was without his favourite weapon, and his arms were even bound behind him with thongs, made of the skin of a deer. (pp. 168–9)

Hawk-eye is uninjured. It seems that he was captured on his return journey and that a letter from Webb to Munro was taken from him. Montcalm now has it. It is of the utmost importance that Munro should know what is in the letter. If reinforcements are on their way, the commander must, at all costs, hold out—to the last man and the last bullet, if necessary. But, equally, he must know *when* Webb's relief column will arrive. We learn in passing from Munro that Hawk-eye was returned unharmed as a gesture of Montcalm's 'accursed politeness'. It seems an odd kind of politeness, to return such an accomplished warrior to the ranks of your enemy. It is even odder since Hawk-eye will have useful verbal information to impart to Munro.

It emerges that Webb's letter, now in Montcalm's possession, instructs Munro to surrender. No reinforcements are on their way. It also emerges that, from some spy, Montcalm knows exactly the state of the opposing army:

'twenty-three hundred gallant men', as he serenely informs the fort's commander. How did he come by this valuable information? With the knowledge from the letter that no battle may now be necessary, the French general is disposed to be generous. Munro bows to the inevitable and capitulates. Montcalm has offered generous terms and may intend to keep them. But he cannot control his Indian irregulars, who run amok and massacre up to 1,500 of the defenceless British soldiers (who have surrendered their ammunition), their wives, and children.

We do not see Hawk-eye (or his Mohican comrades) again until three days after this atrocity. Where he has been we do not know. He reappears on the scene to help Heyward and Munro track Cora and Alice, who have once more been abducted by Magua (who lusts to make Cora his squaw). It is striking that at this point in the narrative Hawk-eye again has his formidable rifle, 'Deer-slayer', by his side and ammunition. It is manifestly the same weapon that he had before.

A first question is: how did Hawk-eye, a disarmed prisoner of war, get his rifle back? He did not have it when he was returned to the fort. It would have been madness for the French to have allowed the best marksman in North America to retain his *longue carabine* with which to take pot-shots at them from the fort's battlements. Deer-slayer would surely have been snatched by some Indian chief as a trophy. How, then, did Hawk-eye repossess it?

This leads on to other questions. How was it that Hawk-eye was taken uninjured by the French? Did he not put up a fight? Why did he not destroy the letter he was carrying before he was captured? We never know the details of how he was taken, nor is it easy to picture the event, knowing the man as we do. Where was he during the massacre?

We can work out possible answers to these questions from Hawk-eye's behaviour at other hazardous moments in the narrative—moments when he has to balance prudence against his frontiersman's code of chivalry. It is never Hawk-eye's practice to risk his life foolishly. In the siege at Glenn's Cave Uncas and Chingachgook—realizing that further resistance is useless—elect to save themselves by allowing the rapid current to carry them downstream to safety (or death by drowning; it's a desperate remedy). Their thinking is eminently practical: a live Mohican warrior is more use to his nation than a live white squaw. As a white officer and a gentleman, Heyward elects to stay with the ladies even though he knows it will be death for him, will not help them, and that he is needed to help defend Fort William Henry. His and the women's scalps (unless they are taken as concubines) will be dangling from some Indian's belt within a few hours. *Noblesse oblige*. White men act one way in these crises, red men another way.

Hawk-eye seems to allow himself to be persuaded by Cora's argument that he can leave the cave with the Mohicans, get to the fort, and bring back help. In acquiescing, however, he says something to his Indian comrades in the Delaware tongue which they listen to 'with deep gravity'. Of course Cora, Heyward, and the scout himself know that there is no hope that even someone as fleet-footed as Hawk-eye can bring back aid in time (assuming that British soldiers could battle their way through hostile Indian country). They are simply giving their friend a pretext for saving his skin which the more gallant Heyward scorns to avail himself of.

Hawk-eye duly jumps into the flood with the two Mohicans. It later turns out, however, that the three men do not—once out of the clutches of the enemy—make their way to safety. They secretly return to observe the capture of Heyward and the white women—intending to intervene if they can be of use, but to do nothing if intervention will

be hopeless. As it happens, they are able to save Heyward
and the women as, bound to the stake, they await fiendish
Indian torture.

Hawk-eye, one deduces, is shrewd and pragmatic about
such matters. He does not take unnecessary risks. If he
has to lie or deceive in order to save his skin, he will.
Better a live dog than a dead lion is his motto. There is
another illustrative moment in the second half of the
novel which highlights his pragmatism. On the track of
Magua and the abducted maidens (if Cora is still such),
the white men are pursued in their canoe. The Hurons fire
on them. Hawk-eye tells Heyward and Munro to lie down
on the floor of the canoe, so as to present a smaller target.
With a dare-devil smile, Heyward demurs: 'It would be but
an ill example for the highest in rank to dodge, while the
warriors were under fire!' This officer's bravado provokes a
blistering retort from the scout:

Lord! Lord! that is now a white man's courage . . . and like too
many of his notions, not to be maintained by reason. Do you
think the Sagamore [Chingachgook], or Uncas, or even I . . . would
deliberate about finding a cover in a skrimmage, when an open
body would do no good! (p. 207)

Like a good poker player, Hawk-eye knows when to
stand and when to fold. What, then, may we assume happened when he (and his letter) were 'captured'? On his
mission to Fort George he evidently perceived that there
was to be no relief column from the pusillanimous Webb.
Hawk-eye was aware of the massive ten-to-one superiority
of the attacking force of French, having passed through
their lines a few hours earlier. For the occupants of Fort
William Henry fighting 'would do no good'. Why then
fight? It would be 'white man's courage' and red man's
foolishness. Hawk-eye, no white fool, calculated that the
best thing was to collaborate with the French to minimize

the bloodshed. He surrendered himself, gave up the letter to Montcalm, and requested that—as a cover—he be taken back as a prisoner. His weapon 'Deer-slayer' was taken on the understanding that it would be returned to him at some later point. He slipped out of the fort during the surrender negotiations, retrieved his beloved rifle, and watched events. He could not prevent the massacre, so he did nothing. He could help Munro and Heywood rescue the Munro women, so he rejoined them, fully armed again.

Cooper inserted a clue to this interpretation—namely, that Hawk-eye is playing his own game during the siege. Heyward's first question to Munro after Hawk-eye has been escorted back is: 'I hope there is no reason to distrust his fidelity?' (p. 150). Heyward—who has recently had the opportunity to observe Hawk-eye in action—has his doubts. Munro, not a perceptive commander as we apprehend, blankly refuses to believe Hawk-eye has betrayed them, 'though his usual good fortune seems, at last, to have failed'. The reader will probably concur with Heyward's scepticism in this matter.

The Oxford World's Classics *The Last of the Mohicans* is edited by John McWilliams.

Charles Dickens · *The Pickwick Papers*

What does Mr Pickwick retire from?

This is a short puzzle because it is about something that seems not to exist, twice—namely, Samuel Pickwick's occupation in life. At the end of the novel, in which 'everything is concluded to the satisfaction of everybody', Mr Pickwick announces to his club *confrères* that events have:

rendered it necessary for me to think soberly and at once upon my future plans. I determined on retiring to some quiet, pretty neighbourhood in the vicinity of London; I saw a house which exactly suited my fancy. I have taken it and furnished it. It is fully prepared for my reception, and I intend entering upon it at once, trusting that I may yet live to spend many quiet years in peaceful retirement. (p. 714)

Retirement from what? At the beginning of the novel it is clear that Mr Pickwick is a gentleman in late middle-age, already retired from the hurly-burly of whatever sector of professional life he was previously engaged in. For two years he conducts his 'Club'—which is not an occupation as such, but an amateur society, or hobby. So, it would seem, Mr Pickwick retires to his haven at Dulwich from retirement.

This relates to a larger perplexing aspect of the novel, Mr Pickwick is a man entirely without a *curriculum vitae*—rather like those aliens who fall to earth in Hollywood science-fiction stories. Readers will search in vain for clues as to what Samuel Pickwick has done, been, or experienced in life before 12 May 1827. He has, apparently, no family; no parents; no siblings; no married relations;

even no personal servant until Sam Weller comes along to
look after him. We do not know what occupation Mr
Pickwick followed—if indeed he has ever done a day's
work—nor how he came by his evidently substantial
source of personal wealth (pretty houses in Dulwich village, if not as expensive as they are now were not cheap in
1829).

Is Pickwick's money earned, inherited, won, counter-
feited, or stolen? He is clearly not a military man, from his
comical ignorance of firearms; he is not a lawyer, as we
may guess from his ineptitude in Bardell versus Pickwick.
Was he in business? Trade? The 'Exchange'? We do not
know from which part of the country or the metropolis he
originates. His incompetence with horses suggests he is a
townee. He lives in London, but his ignorance of nearby
Stroud, Rochester, Chatham, and of suburban Brompton
make one wonder under what stone he has spent his fifty
or so years of life previous to 12 May 1827. He has no
house, but 'rooms' in Goswell Street (apparently a non-
existent address in 1827—although honorary Goswell
Streets sprang up all over the English-reading world with
the popularity of the *Papers*). In the case of Bardell versus
Pickwick we learn a lot about the plaintiff, his landlady,
the custom officer's relict. All we learn about Pickwick is
that he has rented rooms on her first floor for three years
and that he likes tomato sauce with his chops. He has no
political affiliations. He apparently has no friends or
acquaintance until the formation of the club—which
also gives him his only known occupation, G. C. M. P. C.
(General Chairman: Member Pickwick Club). He claims
the title 'Esquire', which indicates at least gentry status.
He can write and speak correctly which argues education.
But we do not know if Mr Pickwick went to university or
what other professional or learned societies he may
belong to. He has no detectable regional accent and uses

no dialects or specialized jargons in his speech which would help us place him.

There are other men of mystery in Victorian fiction. We do not, for example, know Heathcliff's Christian name nor his parentage. But we do know that he was found in a gutter in Liverpool. It's not much of a pedigree—but more than we know about Samuel Pickwick, Esq. According to Dickens, 'I thought of Mr Pickwick, and wrote the first number'. Was Mr Pickwick so brilliant an invention that everything around him was obscured? At only one point in the text does Dickens relent about the blank context of nothingness surrounding his hero. In his farewell speech, Mr Pickwick vouchsafes that 'Nearly the whole of my previous life having been devoted to business and the pursuit of wealth . . .' It's a tantalizing fragment ('Goodbye for ever: oh, by the way, I used to be in business'). What business? Import-export, retailing, finance?

We shall never know. What we can usefully ask is why Dickens created Pickwick as a man without a past. As he recalls in his preface to the first book edition of the novel, when he began the *Papers* he had no idea of what the novel would grow into. In the early numbers he was working within various 'machineries'—such as the 'Club' gimmick—which were eventually outgrown. It seems likely that Dickens initially devised his hero as an antithesis to Mr Jingle. Mr Jingle is a man with many pasts—too many. In the first few minutes of his encounter with the astonished club members it emerges that he has written an epic poem of 10,000 lines on the July 1830 Revolution (interesting, since it is 1827 and the Parisian uprising is three years in the future); he was the owner of a literate dog called Ponto; and he has conducted a passionate *affaire de coeur* with the Spanish beauty, Donna Christina. The joke is, that for all the wealth of biographical information that keeps spewing out, we know as much about

Mr Jingle's real past as we know about Mr Pickwick's—
precisely nothing. Unlike the 'Club' (and the ominous
'Posthumous Papers') this opposition between Pickwick
(man with no past) and Jingle (man of a hundred pasts) is
a joke that Dickens chose to keep running to the end of his
novel.

The Oxford World's Classics *The Pickwick Papers* is edited by
James Kinsley.

Why is Fagin hanged and why isn't Pip prosecuted?

The Dickens scholar Michael Slater reports that two of the questions most often asked him by lay readers are those above. First, why is Fagin hanged? Everyone is familiar with Cruikshank's great illustration of the prisoner in his death cell, 'the night before he was stretched'. Like his illustrator, Dickens rises to the occasion, both in the accompanying description of the Jew's last night in Newgate, and in the preceding trial with its nail-biting suspense as the jury returns with its verdict:

At length there was a cry of silence, and a breathless look from all towards the door. The jury returned, and passed him [Fagin] close. He could glean nothing from their faces; they might as well have been of stone. Perfect stillness ensued—not a rustle—not a breath—Guilty.

The building rang with a tremendous shout, and another, and another, and then it echoed deep loud groans that gathered strength as they swelled out, like angry thunder. It was a peal of joy from the populace outside, greeting the news that he would die on Monday.

The noise subsided, and he was asked if he had anything to say why sentence of death should not be passed upon him. He had resumed his listening attitude, and looked intently at his questioner while the demand was made; but it was twice repeated before he seemed to hear it, and then he only muttered that he was an old man—an old man—an old man—and so, dropping into a whisper, was silent again.

The judge assumed the black cap, and the prisoner still stood

Fagin in the condemned cell

with the same air and gesture. A woman in the gallery uttered
some exclamation, called forth by this dread solemnity; he looked
hastily up as if angry at the interruption, and bent forward yet
more attentively. The address was solemn and impressive, the sentence fearful to hear. But he stood, like a marble figure, without
the motion of a nerve. His haggard face was still thrust forward,
his under-jaw hanging down, and his eyes staring out before him,
when the jailer put his hand upon his arm, and beckoned him
away. He gazed stupidly about him for an instant, and obeyed.
(pp. 428–9)

It is magnificent. But a number of awkward thoughts
suggest themselves. On a legal technicality, it is Friday—
two weekend days would hardly seem to give the remotest
chance of the appeal to which Fagin surely has a right.
And how does the crowd outside *know* that Fagin will be
hanged on Monday, before the judge has put on his black
cap and pronounced sentence? Are they deciding the matter? Is the bigwig judge dancing to the mob's savage tune?

More importantly, what capital offence has Fagin committed? He has, we know, trained boys in pickpocketing
and appropriated their daily haul. He has received stolen
goods and keeps a secret store of them in his den. He has
been an accessory before and after the crime of house-
breaking. Fagin has connived with Monks to keep Oliver
out of his patrimony. He has verbally provoked Sikes to
murder Nancy. None of these is, in the context of the mid
1830s (when the novel must be set, to justify its passionate
assault on the 1834 New Poor Law) a hanging crime. As
Philip Collins notes, 'from 1832 onwards . . . murder was
virtually the only crime for which capital punishment was
exacted'.[1] The Bloody Code, by which fences might conceivably be hanged for handling stolen goods, was—since
Peel's 1828 reforms—a thing of the past. Fagin richly
deserves punishing: but a longish term of imprisonment or
a term of transportation (such as his original, Ikey Solo-

mon, received in 1831) would seem a condign sentence. 'What right have they to butcher me?' he plaintively asks his jailer. It is a good question.

Fagin's most heinous offence is complicity in the beating to death of Nancy—a character who has been raised from the status of burglar's moll to sanctified heroine during the course of the novel. Fagin's involvement in this 'worst' of deeds is, however, equivocal.[2] Morris Bolter (i.e. Noah Claypole) has eavesdropped on Nancy's conversation with Rose Maylie and Mr Brownlow, by London Bridge. Nancy informs on Monks, but is careful not to implicate Sikes (whose surname she studiously avoids mentioning) and specifically refuses to give up Fagin. Her reason is 'thieves' honour'. She will betray Monks, because he is gentry, but she will not 'peach' on one of her own. 'I'll not turn upon them who might—any of them—have turned upon me, but didn't, bad as they are.'

Claypole duly tells Fagin what he has heard. The Jew sees danger for himself. He knows too much about prostitutes to trust Nancy's 'honour'. When, just before dawn, Sikes arrives to drop off some swag, Fagin plies him with a series of hypothetical questions about what he would do to someone who 'peached' on him. The robber gives predictably blood-curdling answers as his temper flares at the thought. Fagin climaxes his provocative catechism with the insinuation that 'NANCY' has betrayed him (Fagin cunningly does not say as much, he leads Bill to jump to the conclusion). Bolter, meanwhile, is roused from sleep and is prompted to spill the beans by Fagin:

'Tell me that again—once again, just for him to hear,' said the Jew, pointing to Sikes as she spoke.

'Tell yer what? asked the sleepy Noah, shaking himself pettishly.

'That about—NANCY,' said the Jew, clutching Sikes by the

wrist, as if to prevent his leaving the house before he had heard enough. You followed her?'

'Yes.'

'To London Bridge?'

'Yes.'

'Where she met two people?'

'So she did.'

'A gentleman, and a lady that she had gone to of her own accord before, who asked her to give up all her pals, and Monks first, which she did—and to describe him, which she did—and to tell her what house it was that we meet at, and go to, which she did—and where it could be best watched from, which she did—and what time the people went there, which she did. She did all this. She told it all every word without a threat, without a murmur—she did—did she not?' cried the Jew half mad with fury.

'All right,' replied Noah, scratching his head. 'That's just what it was!' (pp. 380–1)

All this is, as it happens, quite true. Nancy 'did' all that Fagin and Claypole say here. What she did *not* do, and what neither Fagin nor Claypole claim she did, is 'peach' on 'Bill' by surname—which would, of course, lead to his immediate arrest. She specifically refused to do that. Fagin's report is malicious but accurate.[3]

In what follows, it is not clear whether Fagin is trying to restrain Sikes's homicidal rage, stoke it up still further, or direct it into a devilishly cunning act of blood:

'Let me out,' said Sikes. 'Don't speak to me; it's not safe. Let me out, I say.'

'Hear me speak a word,' rejoined the Jew, laying his hand upon the lock. 'You won't be—'

'Well,' replied the other.

'You won't be—too—violent, Bill?' whined the Jew.

The day was breaking, and there was light enough for the men to see each other's faces. They exchanged one brief glance; there was a fire in the eyes of both, which could not be mistaken.

'I mean', said Fagin, showing that he felt all disguise was now
useless, 'not too violent for safety. Be crafty, Bill, and not too bold.'

Sikes made no reply; but, pulling open the door, of which the
Jew had turned the lock, dashed into the silent streets. (p. 382)

Fagin's parting words could be seen as incitement
('Goading the Wild Beast', as the running head puts it).
They could also be interpreted as a coded instruction—
don't use your pistol (which Sikes, with an uncharacteristic prudence, avoids doing, apparently heeding Fagin's
advice). But in his defence Fagin could argue that he never
actually stated that Nancy had informed on Bill, he was
simply advising him to make inquiries in his usual direct
way—beat her up if you have to, but don't kill her. Nor did
he, Fagin, commit the subsequent awful deed, and moreover, he specifically cautioned Sikes against 'violence', in
the presence of a witness. He might be seen as an accessory before the crime, but hardly an accomplice to it. Nor
does he give Sikes refuge after the murder. Above all,
everything that he told Sikes was perfectly true.

Why, then, is the populace so enraged against Fagin?
Why the 'peal of joy' when they learn that he is to be
hanged in forty-eight hours' time, without any hope of
reprieve? It seems rather excessive for a receiver of silk
handkerchiefs, silver snuff-boxes, and gold watches. (And,
to be snobbish, the mob outside Newgate do not seem to
belong to the silver snuff-box-owning class; why do they
care if 'swells' are relieved of some of their surplus finery?) Had Fagin personally bludgeoned Nancy the lynch-
mob jubilation outside the court would have been
comprehensible.

We have to assume that London's blood-lust has been
fanned by sensational accounts of Sikes's crime in the
newspapers, and with Sikes already dead the crowd's rage
has discharged itself on his nearest henchman. Dickens
does not describe the trial, and we do not know what

charges and what evidence were brought against Fagin, but it must, from the outcome, be conspiracy to murder. From one of his more sanguinary ramblings in his cell ('Bolter's throat, Bill; never mind the girl—Bolter's throat as deep as you can cut. Saw his head off!') we deduce that Fagin was shopped by Claypole. This is confirmed in the epilogue, which flashes forward to give us the apprentice crook's future career:

Mr Noah Claypole: receiving a free pardon from the Crown in consequence of being admitted approver against the Jew: and considering his profession [i.e. pickpocket] not altogether as safe a one as he could wish: was for some little time, at a loss for the means of a livelihood, not burthened with too much work. After some consideration, he went into business as an Informer, in which calling he realises a genteel subsistence. (p. 438)

As Kathleen Tillotson suggested in her notes to the World's Classics edition, we may assume that Noah has 'improved on' his evidence—perjured himself, that is. To whip up sufficient wrath in the newspapers, and through them the London populace, Claypole must have laid the main responsibility for the murder squarely on 'the Jew'. In point of fact, as any competent defence counsel could have elicited, Claypole was as much an inciter to the killing as Fagin. It was Claypole's gratuitously sneering report that Nancy had duped Bill by dosing him with laudanum that drove him to an uncontrollable pitch of fury. Claypole is, we assume, a perjurer—and a very culpable perjurer, in that his tainted evidence sends a man to the gallows. He is also a thief (after his first day Fagin congratulates him on making 'six shillings and nine-pence halfpenny'). A good defence counsel could discredit him very easily. At the very least, Noah should spend a little time in clink. Instead, his reward is perfect freedom to pursue his pickpocketing and informing trades for many years to come—presumably under the protection of the police. He suffers the lash of Dickens's sarcasm, but no ill comes to him in the future.

Seen in this light, the rush to execute Fagin—for a murder someone else committed, on the basis of perjured evidence from a petty criminal—is akin to the hysteria that sent Derek Bentley to the gallows in 1952—for allegedly 'inciting' Christopher Craig to kill a policeman (Bentley was in custody at the time of the murder). Londoners did not behave very well on that occasion, either. And many readers, I suspect, feel as I do a kind of savage pleasure (a reverberation of the populace's 'peal of joy') at the thought of Fagin's being hanged. Why, when even by the stern standards of pre-Victorian justice he does not merit the punishment? Because—if I am honest with myself on the subject—Fagin is presented to me in the novel as old, ugly, racially alien, and is monotonously associated with dirt, grease, and physical uncleanliness. I want the world to be rid of him. The reader is, I think, prejudiced by Dickens's rhetoric. He knew what he was doing. In his various revisions of the scene of Fagin in the cell, Dickens judiciously interchanged 'Fagin' and 'Jew', so that the loaded word echoes most effectively in the reader's ear. In as much as we concur with the crowd's 'peal of joy', it is not the trial verdict we are responding to so much as the indelible first impression we received of Fagin on his introduction in Chapter 8:

The walls and ceiling of the room were perfectly black, with age and dirt. There was a deal table before the fire: upon which were a candle, stuck in a ginger-beer bottle: two or three pewter pots: a loaf and butter: and a plate. In a frying-pan which was on the fire, and which was secured to the mantelshelf by a string, some sausages were cooking; and standing over them, with a toasting fork in his hand, was a very old shrivelled Jew, whose villanous-looking and repulsive face was obscured by a quantity of matted red hair. He was dressed in a greasy flannel gown, with his throat bare. (pp. 60–3)

A throat which we already itch to put into a noose. Fagin, we are made to feel, is the unclean denizen of an unclean lair. It complicates one's response that Dickens is at gratuitous pains to make the point that Fagin is not even a good Jew—no need to ask if the sausages are pork.

If one worries about equity in *Oliver Twist*, it seems wrong that Fagin should be so over-punished. It also seems wrong that 'respectable' offenders with clean linen round their clean-shaven chins get off scot-free in the novel. Losberne and the Maylies knowingly harbour a criminal and obstruct police officers investigating the burglary in which Oliver is wounded and left behind. They foil the Bow Street–Runners from the kindest of middle-class motives. But their act—which is plainly felonious—has serious consequences. If the Runners had been able to question Oliver immediately after the crime and had their wits about them they might have arrested the whole gang, including Fagin, Crackit, and Sikes. Nancy's murder would have been prevented. Many London houses would have been spared Sikes's nocturnal visits. It is, however, as unthinkable that Losberne should answer for his actions in court as that Fagin should come to any other end than the rope.

Middle-class gentlefolk harbouring criminals also figure in *Great Expectations*. The novel's climax hinges on Magwitch's melodramatic utterance to Pip in volume III, chapter 20:

'Caution is necessary.'
   'How do you mean? Caution?'
   'By G——, it's Death!'
   'What's death?'
   'I was sent for life. It's death to come back.' (p. 318)

Magwitch was initially sentenced to fourteen years' transportation for the crime of putting stolen notes into circulation. The sentence, already severe, was subsequently increased to transportation 'for the term of his natural life' for the offence of escaping (the episode which led to his first encounter with Pip in the churchyard, twenty years before). Any attempt to return to England, even after he is a free man in Australia, will result in a very unnatural ending to Magwitch's life (he indicates what it will be to an appalled Pip by 'giving his neck a jerk with his forefinger'). Transportation to Australia began in the 1760s and continued to the mid-1840s. As the editor calculates in the World's Classics edition, the narrative of *Great Expectations* opens in the early years of the nineteenth century (around 1805), and at this point we are in the 1820s—certainly not earlier. As Philip Collins points out, Magwitch's apprehensions are historically ungrounded:

Magwitch ends up under sentence of death, of course, not for killing Compeyson (though they were ready enough to kill each other, and Compeyson certainly died through trying to arrest him), but for returning from Transportation. He dies while awaiting the Recorder's Report and the result of Pip's appeals for mercy. As it happens, he need not have feared hanging, though Dickens conceals or ignores the fact that this offence had notoriously ceased to be *de facto* capital by the time when the action of the novel takes place.[4]

As Robin Gilmour points out, 'The last returned transport to be hanged was in 1810, though the crime remained technically a capital offence until 1835.'[5]

In the world of Dickens's novel the law is not disposed to be lenient to illicitly returned convicts from New South Wales—even when they have reformed themselves into model capitalists. The judge picks Magwitch's case out of the thirty-two death sentences he is delivering that day as

the most 'aggravated' and most deserving of the extreme
penalty. In the circumstances, Magwitch was quite right to
be 'cautious'. But so should those inclined to help him
have been cautious. Assisting criminals in the commission
of their capital crimes is no light thing at any period of
history—and never more so than when the 'Bloody Code'
held sway. Pip is specifically warned on this matter, by
Jaggers:

'Now, Pip,' said he, 'be careful.'

'I will, sir,' I returned. For, I had thought well of what I was
going to say coming along.

'Don't commit yourself,' said Mr Jaggers, 'and don't commit
any one. You understand—any one. Don't tell me anything; I
don't want to know anything; I am not curious.'

Of course I saw that he knew the man was come. (p. 331)

On his part, Jaggers is certainly 'careful' to give himself
deniability. So too, although he is more directly helpful to
Pip, is Wemmick (who uses such circumlocutions as
'gentlemen of a not uncolonial nature' to avoid direct
'knowledge' of who Pip's 'Uncle Provis' actually is). Pip
and Herbert are anything but careful. They shelter Magwitch, they give him concealment, they help him evade
agents of the law, after he has been denounced to the
authorities by Compeyson. It must surely be a serious
offence. And Pip's explanation—if he told 'nothing but
the truth'—would stand up very weakly in court: 'I am not
related to the man; he disgusts me; but I have taken huge
amounts of money from him over the years; I knew perfectly well that he was a wanted criminal; I none the less
helped him escape.' A prosecuting counsel would slash
such a witness to pieces.

When Magwitch is arrested, on the river, it must be
known to the authorities that Pip is aiding and abetting a
known felon in the commission of a most serious offence.
Apart from anything else, by returning to England Mag-

witch has rendered his fortune forfeit to the Crown, and Pip is assisting in a fraud on the Exchequer. Pip's house has been under surveillance, he himself has been tailed. Compeyson would have fingered him, and Herbert as well, as Magwitch's accomplices. The most superficial enquiries by the Bow Street Runners among boatmen, innkeepers, and other witnesses would determine, beyond all reasonable doubt, that Pip was not just accompanying Magwitch—he was arranging the felon's escape down to the last detail and paying for it out of his pocket. And if there were the smallest smidgen of doubt about his involvement, Pip erases it in the self-incriminating petition for mercy which he sends to the Home Secretary, 'setting forth my knowledge of [Magwitch], and how it was that he had come back for my sake'. A wideawake minister would automatically confirm the sentence on the convict and initiate proceedings against the young rogue who assisted the old rogue. Too much of that kind of thing, nowadays. But there is no suggestion before, during, or after Magwitch's trial that any charges will be brought against Pip or Herbert. Incredibly, it seems the police do not even question Mr Pirrip.

Of course, no one will protest this miscarriage any more than we protest the miscarriage of justice which brings Fagin to the gallows—although, as Michael Slater notes, readers occasionally worry about the fickleness of Dickensian law. Why, then, is Fagin hanged and Pip not prosecuted? Because one is a dirty old man and the other is a nice young gent.

The Oxford World's Classics *Oliver Twist* is edited by Kathleen Tillotson with an introduction by Stephen Gill; *Great Expectations* is edited by Margaret Cardwell with an introduction by Kate Flint.

Who gets what in Heathcliff's will?

Heathcliff's death is among the most unusual in Victorian fiction. A man in rude health, 38 years old, dies of inanition. He does not eat or drink for four days (a short period, incidentally for someone in Heathcliff's physical condition to starve to death). Every time he makes to eat or drink, he is interrupted—as we deduce—by a distracting vision of his lost love Catherine. 'I'm animated with hunger; and, seemingly, I must not eat' (p. 328), he observes. Nelly makes him coffee, breakfast, lunch, dinner. But something always comes between him and sustenance. 'I vainly reminded him of his protracted abstinence from food', the housekeeper says in her stilted fashion: 'if he stirred to touch anything in compliance with my entreaties, if he stretched out his hand to get a piece of bread, his fingers clenched, before they reached it, and remained on the table, forgetful of their aim' (p. 331). It is a version of the Tantalus torture. 'By God! she's relentless', Nelly overhears Heathcliff say. And, eventually, the relentless Cathy ('she') succeeds in killing him.

Wuthering Heights, with its enigmatic opening and ending (Lockwood's dream and 'They's Heathcliff and a woman, yonder, under t'Nab') leaves open the issue of whether ghosts exist or not. Assuming they do exist—at least in Emily Brontë's fictional universe—and that they have motives, why does the spectre of Catherine choose this moment to kill Heathcliff? There would seem to be other, more appropriate, occasions. Is it simply that after

all these years she wants to be united with her old com-
rade and lover—that she is lonely and dissatisfied with the
spectral Edgar, as anaemic in death as in life? This is the
interpretation supplied by the MGM film, which ends with
a vignette of the two young lovers (Cathy and Heathcliff)
skipping, as carefree ghosts, over Penistone Crags. But
if it were simply post-mortem sexual union that Cathy
wanted, surely she would have intervened sooner. She is
not a patient woman in life; it is hard to think her so in her
afterlife.

The explanation for Cathy's sudden resolution to haunt
Heathcliff is to be found, I believe, in the fact that she
interrupts not just one activity (his intake of food, drink,
and rest) but two. The trigger for Cathy's return is an
oddly ruminative comment Heathcliff makes to Nelly,
summing up his life's work:

> It is a poor conclusion, is it not . . . An absurd termination to my
> violent exertions? I get levers and mattocks to demolish two
> houses, and train myself to be capable of working like Hercules,
> and when everything is ready, and in my power, I find the will to
> lift a slate off either roof has vanished! My old enemies have not
> beaten me—now would be the precise time to revenge myself on
> their representatives—I could do it; and none could hinder me—
> But where is the use? (p. 323)

This is the only occasion on which Heathcliff indicates his
long-term aim—the dispossession of Hareton and Catherine from the Wuthering Heights and Thrushcross Grange
inheritance. Over the years he has centralized the two
estates in his own hands—by extracting gambling IOUs
from Hareton, by eloping with Isabella, by forcing his son
to marry Cathy, by making his son, on his deathbed, leave
everything to his father. Heathcliff can now stop Hareton
and Catherine from coming into their parents' property by
drawing up a will which specifically disinherits them. This

is what he means by 'now would be the precise time to revenge myself on their representatives'.

Already Heathcliff is, as he tells Cathy, 'half conscious' of some power robbing him of the will to carry through this consummating act of revenge. There is, as he tells Nelly, 'a strange change approaching—I'm in its shadow at present'. The shadowy change will, over the next few days, 'materialize' as the wraith of Cathy. Heathcliff becomes a man possessed under her 'relentless' spell. But still the intention to change his will lurks at the back of his mind. On the evening before his death, in a state bordering on distraction, he tells Nelly, 'When day breaks, I'll send for Green [the solicitor] . . . I wish to make some legal inquiries of him while I can bestow a thought on those matters, and while I can act calmly. I have not written my will yet.' Heathcliff then becomes even more distracted, telling Nelly, 'It's not my fault, that I cannot eat or rest . . . I'll do both, as soon as I possibly can. But you might as well bid a man struggling in the water, rest within arm's length of the shore! I must reach it first, and then I'll rest. Well, never mind Mr Green' (pp. 332–3).

Heathcliff dies intestate, the property descends—as it should—to the young lovers, and the two great houses revert to their dynastic owners. But what if Heathcliff had not been conveniently haunted to death at this juncture? He would have written his vengeful will dispossessing Hareton and Catherine. Why then does Cathy return from beyond the grave at this specific moment? To forestall Heathcliff making his will, I would suggest. Cathy has three characters in the novel: she is Edgar's wife, Heathcliff's lover, and Catherine's mother. It is as the last of these that she returns. Her primary aim is not to starve Heathcliff to death in order that they may be reunited for a spot of posthumous adultery. It is to starve Heathcliff to death lest he do what he is just now threatening to do—

make a will which will evict Cathy's descendants for ever from their ancestral lands. If one were doing a screenplay, it should not (MGM-style) show young Cathy and young Heathcliff idyllically united. It should show an adult, maternal Cathy gloating over a raging and thoroughly tricked Heathcliff. In the last analysis, she reverts to type: she is the mistress, he the outsider at Wuthering Heights. He may have a share of her grave, but not the Earnshaws' family house.

The Oxford World's Classics *Wuthering Heights* is edited by Ian Jack, with an introduction by Patsy Stoneman.

Can Jane Eyre be happy?

Margaret Smith's introduction to the World's Classics *Jane Eyre* summarizes the formative influence of Charlotte Brontë's reading in the Bible, Bunyan, Shakespeare, Scott, and Wordsworth. Smith expertly identifies the Byronic and Miltonic elements which fuse into the mighty conception of Edward Fairfax Rochester. There is, however, a principal source for *Jane Eyre* which Smith does not mention—a 'fairy story' which, one assumes, was read by or to the Brontë children in their nursery years.

The story of Bluebeard ('Barbe Bleue') was given its authoritative literary form in Charles Perrault's *Histoire du temps passé* (1697). Perrault's fables were much reprinted and adapted by the Victorians into children's picture books, burlesque, and pantomime. By the 1840s the story of the bad man who locked his superfluous wives in his attic would have been among the best-known of fables. In the twentieth century the Bluebeard story, with its savagely misogynistic overtones, has fallen into disfavour.[1] It survives as the source (sometimes unrecognized) for such adult productions as Maeterlinck's play, *Ariane et Barbe Bleue* (1901), Béla Bartok's *Duke Bluebeard's Castle* (1911), John Fowles's *The Collector* (1963), and Margaret Atwood's *Lady Oracle* (1976).[2] Among its other distinctions, *Jane Eyre* can claim to be the first adult, non-burlesque treatment of the Bluebeard theme in English Literature.

Perrault's 'Bluebeard' is the story of a rich, middle-aged gentleman, named for his swarthy chin and saturnine manner, who marries a young woman. They take up residence in his country castle. Mr Bluebeard leaves on a trip, giving his wife the keys to the house with a strict instruction not to go to 'the small room at the end of the long passage on the lower floor'. The wife's curiosity is piqued and she disobeys his instruction. In the little room she finds the butchered corpses of Bluebeard's previous wives. In her shock, she drops the key into a pool of blood. On his return Bluebeard sees the stain on the key and deduces what has happened. She must die too, he declares. She is saved in the nick of time by her brothers, who ride to her rescue. They kill Bluebeard and enrich his young widow with her former husband's possessions.

The echoes of 'Bluebeard' in *Jane Eyre* are obvious. Rochester is a swarthy, middle-aged, rich country gentleman, with a wife locked up in a secret chamber in his house. He wants another wife—like Bluebeard, he is a man of voracious sexual appetite. Bertha is 'saved', after a fashion, by her brother. Ingenuity can find numerous other parallels.[3] But what is most striking is Brontë's inversion of the conclusion of the fable. In *Jane Eyre* we are encouraged, in the last chapters, to feel sympathy for Bluebeard—a husband more sinned against than sinning. The locked-up wife is transformed into the villain of the piece. It is as if one were to rewrite Little Red Riding Hood so as to generate sympathy for the wolf, or Jack and the Beanstalk to generate sympathy for the giant who grinds Englishmen's bones to make his bread.

Not only is sympathy demanded. We are to assume that—after some moral re-education—Jane will be blissfully happy with a Bluebeard who has wholly mended his ways. It is the more daring since (putting to one side the intent to commit bigamy), Edward Rochester is responsible for Bertha Rochester's death. Although he claims that 'indirect assassination' is not in his nature, this is

exactly how he disposes of his superfluous first wife. Why
did he not place her in one of the 'non-restraint' institutions which were transforming treatment of the insane in
England in the late 1830s? The York Retreat (where Grace
Poole and her son previously worked, we gather) and John
Conolly's Hanwell Asylum in Middlesex were achieving
remarkable results by *not* immuring patients in 'goblin
cells' but allowing them a normal social existence within
humanely supervised environments.[4] Bertha Mason, we
learn, has lucid spells which sometimes last for weeks. In
squalid, solitary confinement, with only Grace Poole as
her wardress, what wonder that she relapses? Why, one
may ask, does Rochester not put his wife into professional
care? Lest in one of her lucid spells she divulges whose
wife she is. What 'care' does he provide for her? An alcoholic crone, a diet of porridge, and a garret.[5] And then
there is the business of Bertha's actual death, as related
by the innkeeper at the Rochester Arms: 'I witnessed, and
several more witnessed Mr Rochester ascend through the
skylight on to the roof: we heard him call "Bertha!" We
saw him approach her; and then, ma'am, she yelled, and
gave a spring, and the next minute she lay smashed on the
pavement' (p. 451).

It is clear from the form of words ('I witnessed and several more witnessed') that the innkeeper (formerly the
Thornfield butler) is parroting verbatim his testimony at
the coroner's inquest. As a pensioner of the Rochesters, he
doubtless said what was required. There is no clear evidence that Edward went up to the burning roof to save
Bertha—it could well be that he said something, inaudible
to those below, that drove her to jump. His 'Bertha!' may
have been uttered in a threatening tone. At the very least
Mr Rochester, if no wife-murderer, might be thought
indictable for manslaughter by virtue of persistent neglect. There have been previous warnings that Bertha is a

threat to herself, and to others, under the gin-sodden care of Mrs Poole. Who is responsible for the fire at Thornfield—the madwoman, the drunk woman, or the husband who, despite these warnings, did not dismiss the drunk woman and put the madwoman under proper supervision? Is Edward Rochester a man to whom we entrust Jane Eyre with confidence, should she suffer a *crise de nerfs* later in life?

The main grounds for a reversal of the traditional antipathy towards Bluebeard the wife-killer are stated by Rochester himself in his explanations to Jane after their disastrously interrupted wedding. Edward was spoiled as a child. It is only late in life that he has gained moral maturity. His father and elder brother intended he should marry money, and conspired with the Mason family in Jamaica to unite him with Bertha. He was kept in the dark as to the madness rampant in the Mason line. Besotted by lust he married, only to discover that his much older wife was incorrigibly 'intemperate and unchaste' (less unchaste, perhaps, than Edward Rochester during his ten-years' philandering through the ranks of 'English ladies, French comtesses, Italian signoras, and German Grafinnen', p. 328). But before the aggrieved husband can use her vile adulteries as grounds for divorce, Bertha cheats him by falling victim to the Mason curse. Lunatics cannot be held responsible in law for their acts. Edward is chained to Bertha. He brings her to England, where no one knows he is married. Nor shall they know. Servants who are necessarily aware of her existence assume she is 'my bastard half-sister; my cast-off mistress' (p. 305). He is free to range Europe in search of sexual relief from mistresses not yet cast off. Sexual fulfilment eludes him. Only another marriage will answer his needs. Bigamy it must be.

Is Bluebeard-Rochester justified in his attempted act of

bigamy? Are there mitigating circumstances, or just a middle-aged roué's glib excuses? In answering the question it is necessary first to determine the date of the action: more particularly, whether Rochester's foiled union with Jane takes place before or after the English Marriage Act of 1835. It was this act which clearly stated that marriage with a mad spouse could not be dissolved if the spouse were sufficiently sane at the time of the ceremony to understand the nature of the contract involved. Subsequent lunacy was no grounds for divorce even if compounded with other offences (violence, infidelity, desertion, cruelty). If the marriage in *Jane Eyre* is construed as taking place after 1835, then Edward is clearly guilty of a serious felony (intent to commit bigamy). It would be the responsibility of the clergyman, Mr Wood, to report Rochester (and Mr Carter, the physician, who criminally conspired with him) to the police. It is one of the small mysteries in *Jane Eyre* that Rochester seems to suffer no consequences, nor any visits from the authorities, following the 'bigamous' service.

If the marriage ceremony is construed as taking place before the firmer legislation of 1835, then Rochester may have a case for thinking that his earlier marriage is either null, or dissoluble on grounds of Bertha's premarital deceits, her subsequent adulteries, or the fact that the marriage may not have been consummated. He persistently refers to his wife as 'Bertha Mason', not 'Bertha Rochester', which suggests that he does not regard himself as married to the horrible woman. A good lawyer might fudge the issue for his client—not sufficiently to get him off the hook, but sufficiently to suggest that he honestly felt himself justified in making a second marriage.

When, then, is *Jane Eyre* set? The 1944 Orson Welles film explicitly declares that the central events occur in 1839.

But in the novel dates are a minefield. The editor who has looked into them most clearly, Michael Mason, identifies two conflicting pieces of dating evidence. When she came over from France (a few months before Jane's arrival at Thornfield, p. 106), Adela recalls 'a great ship with a chimney that smoked—how it did smoke!' Steam-driven vessels were plying up and down the eastern coast of Britain as early as 1821. Scott travelled down by one ('the Edinburgh') to the coronation in 1821. Like Adela, he found the vessel exceptionally smoky and he nicknamed it the 'New Reekie'. Cross-channel steam services seem to have started later in the 1820s.

If steam-driven ships are momentarily glimpsed (or smelled) in *Jane Eyre*, steam-engined trains are wholly absent. This is the prelapsarian world of the stage coach. When Jane waits for her coach at the George Inn at Millcote she has leisure to examine the furniture. On the wall there are a number of prints: 'including a portrait of George the Third, and another of the Prince of Wales, and a representation of the death of Wolfe.' Clearly this is some point before the mid-1830s, when Millcote (Leeds) would have been served by the railway. But it would be interesting to know how faded those prints on the wall are. George III died in 1820; his son ceased to be Prince of Wales, and became Prince Regent, in 1811. West's famous picture of the death of Wolfe as engraved by John Boydell was most popular from around 1790 to 1810.

The clearest but most perplexing date-marker occurs late in the narrative when Jane is with St John Rivers at Morton School. On 5 November (an anti-Papist holiday) St John brings Jane 'a book for evening solace'. It is 'a poem: one of those genuine productions so often vouchsafed to the fortunate public of those days—the golden age of modern literature. Alas! the readers of our era are less favoured ... while I was eagerly glancing at the bright pages of Marmion (for Marmion it was), St John stooped to examine my drawing' (p. 390).

Scott's long narrative poem *Marmion* was published in late February 1808 as a luxurious quarto, costing a guinea and a half. The month doesn't fit, although the year might be thought to chime with the earlier 'Prince of Wales' reference. But 1808 makes nonsense of critical elements in the characters' prehistories. It would give Jane, for instance, a birth-date of 1777. It would mean that Rochester impregnated Céline with Adela (if he is indeed the little girl's father) around 1799. We would have to picture him, an Englishman, gallivanting round France during the Napoleonic Wars, crossing paths with the Scarlet Pimpernel and Sidney Carton. Those wars would still be going on in the background of the main action of *Jane Eyre*.

Sea-going steamers aside, Charlotte Brontë's novel does not 'feel' as if it is taking place in the first decade of the nineteenth century. There are numerous incidental allusions which place it at least a couple of decades later.[6] What seems most likely is that the 'new publication' of *Marmion* is the 'Magnum Opus' edition of 1834. This cheap edition (which came out with Scott's collected works) was hugely popular, and cost 6 shillings—more appropriate to the frugal pocket of St John Rivers than the *de luxe* version of 1808. It is quite possible that what Brontë is recalling in this little digression is the excitement which the purchase of the same, Magnum Opus, volume excited at Haworth Parsonage when she was 19.

A 'best date' for the main action of *Jane Eyre* would be the early to mid-1830s—a year or two before the critical date of 1835, which may be seen as foreshadowing but not as yet clearly defining the grounds for, divorce or annulment. This historical setting would not exonerate Rochester's intended bigamy, but in the legally blurred

context of pre-1835 it would not be as deliberately felonious an act as it would be in the film's 1839.

Rochester is an inscrutable man whom we never know
on the inside. If we want to prognosticate whether, in the
years of their marriage, he will make Jane Eyre happy it is
important to extricate his motives for marrying her in the
first place—more particularly the series of events that
lead to his dropping Blanche Ingram in favour of 'You—
poor and obscure, and small and plain as you are'.

When Mr Rochester brings Blanche Ingram and her
grand entourage to Thornfield Hall, there is every expectation of an imminent happy event. 'I saw he was going to
marry her', says Jane (p. 195) and so, apparently, does
everyone else. Negotiations have been in train for some
time. Lawyers have been consulting. It is common knowledge that the Ingram estate is entailed, which is why they
are smiling on a match with an untitled suitor who happens to be very wealthy. It augurs well that Blanche has
the physical attributes to which Rochester is addicted.
Like her predecessor, Miss Ingram is 'moulded like a Dian';
she has the same 'strapping' beauty and jet-black tresses
that captivated Edward in Jamaica fifteen years before.

The visit of the Ingram party calls for unprecedented
preparations at the hall, as Jane observes:

I had thought all the rooms at Thornfield beautifully clean and
well-arranged: but it appears I was mistaken. Three women were
got to help; and such scrubbing, such brushing, such washing of
paint and beating of carpets, such taking down and putting up of
pictures, such polishing of mirrors and lustres, such lighting of
fires in bed-rooms, such airing of sheets and feather-beds on
hearths, I never beheld, either before or since. (p. 172)

The pre-nuptial junketing at Thornfield is interrupted by
the unannounced arrival of Richard Mason from the West
Indies. Rochester is not present to greet him (he is mount-
ing his gypsy fortune-teller charade), but his reaction on

being told of the Banquo visitation at his feast is
dramatic:

'A stranger!—no: who can it be? I expected no one: is he gone?'
  'No: he said he had known you long, and that he could take the
liberty of installing himself till you returned.'
  'The devil he did! Did he give his name?'
  'His name is Mason, sir; and he comes from the West Indies:
from Spanish Town, in Jamaica, I think.'
  Mr Rochester was standing near me: he had taken my hand, as
if to lead me to a chair. As I spoke, he gave my wrist a convulsive
grip; the smile on his lips froze: apparently a spasm caught his
breath.
  'Mason!—the West Indies!' he said, in the tone one might fancy
a speaking automaton to enounce its single words. (p. 213)

There follows Mason's disastrous interview with his
demented sister, uproar in the house, and a new bond of
intimacy between Rochester and Jane. Shortly after
Mason has gone (back to Jamaica, as Rochester thinks,
see p. 223), Jane is called to the Reeds' house fifty miles
away at Gateshead. There she remains a month settling old
scores. After her return, Mr Rochester is then himself
away for some weeks. During this interval 'nothing was
said of the master's marriage, and I saw no preparation
going on for such an event'. It seems from a later conversation with Jane that Rochester has suddenly decided to put
Miss Ingram to the test, and found her wanting in affection. 'I caused a rumour to reach her that my fortune was
not a third of what was supposed, and after that I repre-
sented myself to see the result: it was coldness both from
her and her mother' (p. 267).
  Having found Blanche and her mother lacking in
warmth towards him, Edward proposes to Jane. It is no
fashionable wedding that he offers. Their union will be
private, furtive even. There are no relatives (apart from the
distant Mrs Fairfax) on his side, and as Jane puts it (with

an allusion to the dragonish Lady Ingram), 'There will be
no-one to meddle, sir. I have no kindred to interfere.' There
is a month of courtship—long enough for the banns to be
discreetly called. Three short months after the world supposed Edward Rochester to be affianced to Miss Ingram,
Rochester takes Jane Eyre up the aisle. The difference
between the two planned weddings could not be greater.
After the ceremony with Jane, the newly weds will leave
immediately for London. There is to be no wedding breakfast. The ceremony itself takes place in a deserted church.
There are 'no groomsmen, no bridesmaids, no relatives'
(p. 301) present. The assembled congregation is one
person—Mrs Fairfax (what Rochester is to do for witnesses
is not clear). The proceedings are then interrupted by the
two strangers whom Jane has seen lurking around the
graveyard: 'Mr Rochester has a wife now living', it is pro-
claimed. The strangers are, of course, Rochester's bad-
penny brother-in-law and a London solicitor.

This is the second time that Richard Mason has arrived
to foil Rochester's imminent marriage. On both occasions
his appearance is out of the blue and uncannily timely. At
Thornfield Hall, Rochester evidently thinks his brother-
in-law dead, gone mad like the rest of the Masons, or
safely ignorant of what is going on 3,000 miles away. Why
does Richard turn up at this critical moment in Rochester's life, and what does he say to his brother-in-law about
the law that joins them, and the impending 'marriage' with
the Hon. Miss Ingram? After seeing him off Rochester
clearly thinks that Richard is on his way back to Jamaica.
He refers twice to this fact (pp. 223, 227). But Richard
Mason, it emerges in the Thornfield church, is not safely
in the West Indies. Moreover, during the three intervening
months he has had sent him a copy of Edward and Bertha
Rochester's marriage certificate.

Who informed Mason of details of the forthcoming

nuptials with Jane Eyre? It would have to be some insider
in possession of two privileged pieces of knowledge: (1)
the date, exact time, and place of the clandestine
marriage—something known only to the two principals,
the clergyman, and the three servants at Thornfield
Hall; (2) that Richard Mason was the brother-in-law of
Rochester's still-living wife, Bertha.

As Rochester later discloses, only four people in England are in possession of that second piece of information:
himself, Bertha during her lucid periods, Carter the physician, and Grace Poole (p. 326). There is, however, one
other who may have penetrated the mystery. Rochester
suspects that his distant kinswoman Mrs Fairfax 'may . . .
have suspected something'. Certain of her remarks suggest that this is very likely. Mrs Fairfax, alone of all the
Thornfield household, dismisses out of hand the likelihood that her relative will ever marry Blanche Ingram
('I scarcely fancy Mr Rochester would entertain an idea
of the sort', p. 168). And Mrs Fairfax is very alarmed when
she subsequently learns that Jane is to marry her master
and very urgent in her dissuasions (p. 276): It is also
relevant that, immediately after the wedding débâcle,
Rochester dismisses Mrs Fairfax from his employment at
Thornfield (p. 450). Nor is she called back after his blind-
ing, when her presence would seem desirable as his only
living relative and former housekeeper.

The most likely construction to put on this series of
events is the following. Rochester had every intention
of marrying Blanche Ingram, until the unexpected arrival
of Richard Mason at Thornfield Hall. Who summoned
him? Mrs Fairfax (although Rochester probably thought
at the time that it was an unlucky coincidence). We do not
know what was said between the two men. But Richard,
timid though he is, would hardly give his blessing to bigamy and the threat of exposure would be implied, if not

uttered. His hopes with Blanche dashed, Rochester still longed for a wife. Another marriage in high life, such as the Rochester–Ingram affair, would attract huge publicity. That option was now too dangerous. Having packed Richard Mason back to the other side of the globe, Rochester put his mind to a partner whom he might marry without anyone knowing. He wanted nothing to get into newspapers which might subsequently find their way to the West Indies. Up to this point, Rochester must have thought of Jane Eyre as a potential future mistress. Now, with Blanche Ingram out of play, she was to be promoted. Carter was somehow squared. Poole was no problem; neither was Bertha. But, unfortunately for Rochester, Jane wrote to her uncle in Madeira, who fortuitously conveyed the news to Richard Mason (who happened to be in Madeira for his health). We can assume that it was Mrs Fairfax, again, who alerted Mason as to the exact time and place of the wedding (something that Jane did not know, when she wrote). He in turn took legal advice and came back to Thornfield with his legally drawn-up 'impediment'. At this point, his marriage hopes in ruins, Rochester discerned who had betrayed him and sent Mrs Fairfax 'away to her friends at a distance' (p. 450). Being the man he is, he also settled an annuity on her, presumably with the understanding that she stay out of his presence for ever (she is not mentioned in Jane's ten-years-after epilogue).

Bluntly, Rochester proposed to Jane as a *faute de mieux*—the *mieux* being Blanche Ingram. The notion sometimes advanced that the Ingram courtship was a charade designed to 'test' Jane is unconvincing. There was no need to test her, and if there were a need something much less elaborate might be devised (at the very least, something that might not land Rochester in a breach-of-promise suit). With many of Rochester's amoral acts (his adoption of Adela, for example) there is a kind of careless grandeur. His courtship of Jane Eyre, by contrast, has something sneaking about it. Would he have proposed to the governess had Mason not arrived to foil his courtship of the society beauty? Probably not.

Like Samson, Rochester is ultimately humbled by tribulation and physical mutilation. 'A sightless block', he discovers Christianity and for the first time in his adult life has 'begun to pray' (p. 471). But again, Jane would seem to be a *faute de mieux*. Supposing Edward Rochester had emerged from the blazing ruins of Thornfield with his limbs and organs intact, would it have been Jane he cried for at midnight? Possibly, possibly not. Blind and crippled, no comtesse, Blanche Ingram, or signorina will have him now. Only Jane will. Doubtless if, instead of killing Bluebeard, the wife's brothers had merely blinded him and cut off a hand (with the threat that if he did not behave himself they would come back and cut off some more), the old rogue might have become a tolerably good husband. But what if, like Edward Rochester, after ten years of marriage, his sight were to return and—barring the minor blemish of a missing hand (common enough, and even rather glamorous in these post-war years)—Bluebeard still cut a handsome figure. Could one be entirely confident that his wife-killing ways would not return?

The Oxford World's Classics *Jane Eyre* is edited by Margaret Smith.

How many pianos has Amelia Sedley?

Like other well-brought up girls of her era and class (early nineteenth century, London *nouveau riche)*, Amelia Sedley has been taught to sing and play the piano. She is neither as gifted in this department nor as industrious as her bosom friend at Miss Pinkerton's Academy, Becky Sharp. Miss Sharp, we are told, 'was already a musician' when she was taken in as a non-paying boarder, and she practises 'incessantly' (p. 19). None the less, Amelia can handle the instrument well enough to make a private recital the pretext of flirting with George Osborne in the 'back drawing-room'. It is there that the Sedleys' family piano is situated ('as pianos usually are', the narrator notes on page 39—pianos, incidentally, are omnipresent in *Vanity Fair)*. This back-drawing-room piano makes a later appearance at the auction where Mr Hammerdown disposes of the ruined Mr Sedley's household effects two years later. It is, we are informed as it comes up for sale, a 'state grand piano' (p. 205). Presumably it is as vulgar a piece of furniture as the 'great carved-legged, leather cased grand piano' in the Osbornes' hateful upstairs drawing-room, in their house on the other side of Russell Square.

At the auction, the point is made that there are in fact two pianos in the Sedleys' household. Amelia has, as her private possession in her own room, 'a little square piano'. It is with the changing fortunes of this modest instrument over the years that I am concerned here. It first makes an appearance in chapter 2. Amelia has brought Becky back to stay with her for a week or so at Russell Square, before

Miss Sharp takes up her new position as governess at Queen's Crawley. Becky has clearly never been to the Sedleys' home before. As soon as they arrive, Amelia excitedly shows Rebecca 'over every room of the house, and everything in every one of her drawers; and her books, and her piano, and her dresses, and all her necklaces, brooches, laces, and gimcracks' (p. 21). Guessing from the context, 'her piano' is the little square instrument in her bedroom, not the great monster downstairs.

The little square piano is not heard of again until months later, in chapter 17 ('How Captain Dobbin Bought a Piano'), where it briefly has a starring role. It is the auction following Sedley's bankruptcy and Dobbin, good-hearted as ever, has resolved to buy the little piano and return it to Amelia. But his agent finds that someone else is interested. To the auctioneer's surprise the bids rise to 25 guineas, at which inflated level Dobbin secures the instrument. It emerges that his rival in the bidding has been Becky. She takes her loss with typical good spirits: 'I wish we could have afforded some of the plate', she tells her husband, Rawdon (they are newly wed, and setting up house); 'Five-and-twenty guineas was monstrously dear for that little piano. We chose it at Broadwood's for Amelia, when she came from school. It only cost five-and-thirty then.' As the World's Classics note records: 'John Broadwood, the piano maker, had his business in Great Pulteney Street. In 1782 he patented his hugely successful design for a domestic pianoforte' (p. 914). There is already a small narrative inconsistency, however. Becky's recollection that the instrument was bought 'when Amelia came from school' indicates that it was acquired during that June 1813 holiday she spent at Russell Square, after the girls had left Miss Pinkerton's for good. But, in chapter 2, it is suggested that Amelia already has a piano in her room. Are we to assume that the

Broadwood is a replacement? Or, as seems more probable,
is Becky fibbing?

Dobbin, having secured the piano, makes arrangements
for it to be sent to the 'little house where the Sedley family
had found refuge' (p. 223) after the crash. Tactfully, he does
not accompany it with a note drawing attention to his
generosity. A desperate Amelia, clutching at straws,
assumes that the piano has come from George. Although
their parents have called off the engagement he still loves
her, she deludes herself. At the end of her note to George
accompanying the return of his presents ('made in happier
days'), she adds a postscript: 'I shall often play upon the
piano—your piano. It was like you to send it.' In their
quarters at the barracks, George shows Dobbin this letter,
and he reads all of it. Surprisingly, there is no recorded
conversation along the lines of: 'Who the deuce sent her
that piano? You did, Dobbin? Gad! What a trump you are.'

The next day, Dobbin calls on the Sedleys in their refuge. He finds Mrs Sedley 'greatly agitated by the arrival of
the piano, which, as she conjectured *must* have come from
George and was a signal of amity on his part'. Captain
Dobbin, we are told, 'did not correct this error of the
worthy lady'. And he sets in motion the events that will
lead to the marriage of George and Amelia in defiance of
old Osborne's tyrannic prohibition and his (Dobbin's) own
forlorn hope that Amelia might one day be his.

At this point, we may digress to indicate where Thackeray got the idea for this Broadwood square-piano subplot.
In volume 2, chapter 8 of *Emma*, the heroine learns from
her friend Mrs Cole that Jane Fairfax, who is staying with
her aunt, Miss Bates, has had a mysterious gift:

Mrs Cole . . . had been calling on Miss Bates, and as soon as she
entered the room had been struck by the sight of a pianoforté—
a very elegant looking instrument—not a grand, but a large-
sized square pianoforté . . . this pianoforté had arrived from

Broadwood's the day before, to the great astonishment of both
aunt and niece—entirely unexpected; that at first, by Miss
Bates's account, Jane herself was quite at a loss, quite bewil-
dered to think who could possibly have ordered it—but now, they
were both perfectly satisfied that it could be from only one
quarter;—of course it must be from Col. Campbell.

No, as we later discover, it was not from the colonel, but
from Jane's secret admirer, Frank Churchill. Frank, like
Dobbin, does not enlighten the world, noting only with an
enigmatic smile to Emma (who entirely misinterprets its
meaning), 'It is a handsome present'. Thackeray evidently
thought that this was too good a subplot to be used only
once in English fiction.

After its return to the Sedley household the little square
piano is lost once more in the background of *Vanity Fair*.
It is glimpsed again when, shortly after her wedding,
Amelia makes a trip to her parents, now in a cottage at
Fulham (supported by an annuity from their nabob son,
Jos). Things are going badly for Mrs Amelia Osborne.
George is already kicking over the traces—spending too
much, drinking too much, gambling too much and, as
Amelia dare not admit to herself, consorting adulterously
with other women. She falls down by the maidenly white
bed she slept on as a girl and prays (prayers which, the
narrator sternly informs us, we have no right to overhear).
Then she goes downstairs and, to cheer up her father, 'she
sat down at the piano which Dobbin had bought for her,
and sang over all her father's favourite old songs' (p. 321).

For twelve long years the little square piano disappears
from view while momentous things happen. Napoleon is
defeated, George is killed, Becky is presented to her sover-
eign then taken in adultery, Amelia loses Georgy to the
Osbornes, everyone (including the piano) gets suddenly
middle-aged. When a grizzled Major Dobbin, CB, returns
in 1827 from India he makes his first call on the Sedleys,

now in lodgings at Brompton. At last, he fondly hopes, he
may make his proposals to Amelia. He is admitted into
the Sedleys' drawing-room: 'whereof he remembered
every single article of furniture, from the old brass orna-
mented piano, once a natty little instrument, Stothard
maker, to the screens and the alabaster miniature tomb-
stone, in the midst of which ticked Mr Sedley's gold
watch' (p. 740).

At the auction Becky specifically recalls the instrument's being bought at Broadwood's. Robert Stothard was
Broadwood's great rival. They did not sell each other's
pianos. There is more confusion to come. Dobbin is with
Amelia a few days later, as arrangements are being made
to move her family to Jos's grand new house (he has
returned from India with Dobbin). To the major's pleasure, he sees that she is taking with her the piano:

that little old piano which had now passed into a plaintive jin-
gling old age, but which she loved for reasons of her own. She was
a child when first she played on it: and her parents gave it her. It
had been given to her again since, as the reader may remember,
when her father's house was gone to ruin, and the instrument was
recovered out of the wreck.

Dobbin's hopes are raised by Amelia's special attention to
'this old music box'. He is glad she has kept it, he tells her:

'I was afraid you didn't care about it.'
    'I value it more than anything I have in the world,' said Amelia.
    '*Do* you, Amelia?' cried the major. The fact was, as he had
bought it himself, though he never said anything about it, it never
entered into his head to suppose that Emmy should think any-
body else was the purchaser, and as a matter of course, he fancied
that she knew the gift came from him. 'Do you, Amelia?' he said;
and the question, the great question of all, was trembling on his
lips, when Emmy replied—
    'Can I do otherwise?—did not he give it to me?'

'I did not know,' said poor old Dob, and his countenance fell. (pp. 758–9)

The Indian fevers he has suffered from must have affected the major's brain. He was shown Amelia's letter to George in April 1815 mistakenly thanking him (George) for the gift of the piano. Shortly afterwards he (Dobbin) gallantly declined to correct Mrs Sedley's misapprehension that George was the donor. At that point in the narrative Dobbin clearly did know that Amelia mistakenly thought that the piano came from George, not him. There are other little mysteries swirling about the episode. Did Amelia and George never talk about the piano? Are we to assume he lied on the subject after their marriage, or deliberately left her in the dark? If so, it adds a new and uncharacteristically sly dimension to his villainy.

Shortly after the above exchange at Brompton, a mortified Amelia suddenly realizes the truth: 'it was William who was the giver of the piano.' She now hates the thing: 'It was not George's relic. It was valueless now. The next time that old Sedley asked her to play, she said it was shockingly out of tune, that she had a headache, that she couldn't play.' The instrument is never heard of again in *Vanity Fair*. Perhaps Amelia keeps it, more likely it is thrown into some lumber-room and forgotten.

There are three problems in charting the long career of the little square piano. Did Amelia get it as a little girl, or did she buy it in company with Becky, as a young woman. Is it a Broadwood or a Stothard? Does Dobbin know that Amelia doesn't know who gave it to her? By tying oneself in knots, one can find ingenious solutions. There was more than one (perhaps as many as three) little pianos over the years at Russell Square—in his palmy days, old Sedley was certainly rich and doting enough to shower his daughter with expensive luxuries. Dobbin has hoped so obsessively that Amelia will love him that his memory has warped. Freudian analysis throws up any number of examples of this 'willed amnesia' phenomenon. When she made her remark about 'We chose it at Broadwood's ... it only cost five-and-thirty', Becky is not remembering an event, but prodding Rawdon to take her, that very minute, to the nearby emporium in Great Pulteney Street to buy her an instrument just like the one she has lost to Dobbin at auction.

Attractive as ingenuity is, it would be misplaced here. As Stephen Blackpool would say, 'it's aw a muddle'—but only if we read *Vanity Fair* the wrong way. What we learn from following the story of the piano is something important about Thackeray's writing habits, something to which we must adjust our own reading habits when we come to his novels. He loved long perspectives and the resonant recurrent detail. No author handles such effects better. But Thackeray could not be troubled, or was too hurried, to turn back the pages of his novel to see what he had written earlier. His memory—wonderfully sure in essentials—played tricks with small details, tricks that the reader happily indulges.

The Oxford World's Classics *Vanity Fair* is edited by John Sutherland.

Charlotte Brontë · *Shirley*

Will she ever come back?

Shirley opens with a robustly drawn 'then and now' framework. 'Of late years,' the unidentified narrator tells us, 'an abundant shower of curates has fallen upon the north of England ... but in eighteen-hundred-eleven-twelve that affluent rain had not descended.' *Shirley*'s 'then' is self-evidently 1811–12. Its 'now' (as Brontë's subsequent reference to the Oxford Movement makes clear) is the period of writing and first publication of the novel, 1848–9. The location of the novel is as precisely staked out—the West Riding of Yorkshire, a setting from which the narrative will not stray by so much as a yard into any neighbouring county.

In her opening paragraphs, the narrator (a Yorkshire-woman, as we deduce) promises a story strenuously purged of sensational event:

Do you anticipate sentiment, and poetry, and reverie? Do you expect passion, and stimulus, and melodrama? Calm your expectations; reduce them to a lowly standard. Something real, cool, and solid, lies before you; something unromantic as Monday morning. (p. 1)

This promise is belied by the novel which follows. *Shirley* is passionate, stimulating, and melodramatic: a page-turner; as a modern publicist would say. Much is compressed into the eighteen months of chronological time which the narrative covers (February 1811 to August 1812). Caroline Helstone almost dies for frustrated love of Robert and discovers her long-lost mother in the shape of Mrs Pryor

There are riots, machine-breakings, and an assassination attempt on Robert. Both he and Caroline are fortunate to reach the marriage altar in one piece. On her part, Miss Keeldar fends off several proposals, before defying her guardian's instructions by falling in love with the unprepossessing Louis Moore. On the memorable 'Summer Night' of chapter 19, Shirley and Caroline heroically fight off a workers' uprising. The narrative concludes with festivities for the victory at Salamanca (events in the Peninsula and in Russia are alluded to throughout the novel) and a spectacular double wedding, neatly settling the destinies of all four principal characters. It is, we may conclude, an eventful year-and-a-half in the West Riding of Yorkshire. If we are curious about such things, events in *Shirley* exactly coincide with those at Mansfield Park, some 200 miles away in Hampshire. In so far as such things can be measured, Brontë's novel contains at least twenty times as much narrative matter as Austen's mild comedy.

When Jane Austen finishes a narrative, it is like a door slamming in the reader's face. At the end of *Emma*, for instance, we are blandly told that the union of the Knightleys will be 'perfectly happy'—with the implication 'that is all ye know, and all ye need to know'.[1] In Brontë's fiction the door at the end of the novel is often left ajar, allowing us to see over the edge of the narrative. The most striking such glimpse in *Shirley* concerns the beyond-the-novel fortunes of the Yorke family. They are introduced at full length in chapter 9, 'Briarmains' (the house where the family has lived for six generations). An idyllic portrait is given of the patriarchal Yorkshire manufacturer (whose name is emblematic of his northern county's rugged virtues), his wife, and of the six children happily gathered round his knee. The apple of his paternal eye is young Jessy. Suddenly, the narrator throws a cloud across the sunny group picture of the Yorkes at home. Mr Hiram

Yorke, she confides to the reader, 'has no idea that little Jessy will die young, she is so gay and chattering'. The narrator—now well into her gloomy stride—widens her clairvoyant view to include the fate of the older daughter, stolid Rose. Having made her dismal forecast to the reader she goes on to inform Mr Yorke himself (who presumably hears her words as a cold gust, as when someone—as they say—walks over your grave):

Mr Yorke, if a magic mirror were now held before you, and if therein were shown you your two daughters as they will be twenty years from this night [in spring 1812], what would you think? The magic mirror is here: you shall learn their destinies— and first that of your little life, Jessy.

Do you know this place? No, you never saw it; but you recognise the nature of these trees, this foliage—the cypress, the willow, the yew. Stone crosses like these are not unfamiliar to you, nor are these dim garlands of everlasting flowers. Here is the place; green sod and grey marble headstone—Jessy sleeps below. She lived through an April day; much loved was she, much loving. She often, in her brief life, shed tears, she had frequent sorrows; she smiled between, gladdening whatever saw her. Her death was tranquil and happy in Rose's guardian arms, for Rose had been her stay and defence through many trials: the dying and the watching English girls were at that hour alone in a foreign country, and the soil of that country gave Jessy a grave.

Now, behold Rose, two years later. The crosses and garlands looked strange, but the hills and the woods of this landscape look still stranger. This, indeed, is far from England; remote must be the shores which wear that wild, luxuriant aspect. This is some virgin solitude: unknown birds flutter round the skirts of that forest; no European river this, on whose banks Rose sits thinking. The little, quiet Yorkshire girl is a lonely emigrant in some region of the southern hemisphere. Will she ever come back? (pp. 149–50)

Charlotte Brontë seems to have wandered out of *Shirley* (whose chronological horizons are 1811–12, and whose

geographical boundaries the West Riding of Yorkshire)
into another, wider-ranging narrative set two decades
later in Catholic Europe (presumably Belgium) and, as we
guess, in Australasia. The Yorkes, we apprehend, have
been ruined—how, the reader is not informed. Six generations have ended with penury and exile. Should I store
these details in my mind? the reader wonders. Are they
going to be needed again later in the novel? They are not.
The business about Rose, pining in a far country, is left
hanging. Where she is, and whether she ever comes back,
is left a mystery.

To add to the mystery, a later aside indicates that the
narrator was actually present as one of the 'watching English girls' at Jessy's burial, twenty years later ('and some
years ago' from the time of writing) when the little girl's
remains were laid to rest 'in a heretic cemetery' overseas.
Why was she buried in an alien grave? How did she die?
Where were her parents? Charlotte Brontë does not tell
us. What we can infer is that Brontë's narrative has tres-
passed well beyond *Shirley* (whose recorded events conclude in summer 1812) deep into afterlife territory.

Although Charlotte is inscrutable, the editors of the
World's Classics edition help out with a brief note—
namely, that the Yorkes are 'closely based' on Brontë's
friends, the Taylor family. Investigation in the standard
Brontë lives turns up the information that the head of the
family, Joshua Taylor, was, like Hiram Yorke, a textile mill-
owner who fell on hard times. There were six children. The
Taylors lived, in the years of their prosperity, at the 'Red
House' on which Briarmains is closely modelled. Rose is
based on Mary Taylor. The prematurely deceased Jessy is
based on Martha Taylor, who died in Brussels in 1842 aged
23, and was buried in a Protestant graveyard in the city
(the Taylors were Presbyterians). Given the historical
antedating of *Shirley*, Brontë gets into something of a

muddle with dates here (it wasn't 'twenty years from this night' in 1812—which would make it 1832—but 1842; but then, if Jessy had died aged close on 40, it would hardly be a premature death).

In short, this vignette of the Yorkes in their parlour is a family photograph of the author's particular friends, slipped in from 'the real world'. Charlotte Brontë, as is her wont (though usually not as disruptively as here), has torn a gaping hole in the fabric of her fiction. Fact floods in, and—once we know there are facts to be had—we want more of them. If the novel won't inform us, who will? Not the *Dictionary of National Biography*. Mary Taylor is not listed. In fact, the best place to begin is the *Times Literary Supplement*, in summer 1996. In the issue for 31 May, Juliet Barker (author of a recent group biography of the Brontës) gives a concise pen portrait of Mary Taylor. An old school friend of Charlotte's at Roe Head school, Mary grew up:

a Radical in politics and a Dissenter in religion [who] defied custom and propriety throughout her long and active life. After the death of her father, when she was still a young unmarried woman, she earned her living as a teacher in an all-boys boarding-school in Germany, before emigrating, in 1845 to New Zealand, where she set up shop with such success that, fourteen years later, she was able to retire to her native West Riding of Yorkshire; an intrepid mountaineer and regular visitor to Switzerland, she led an expedition of four young women on an ascent of Mont Blanc when she was almost sixty.[2]

The answer to Charlotte's question, then, is: yes, 'Rose' did return in 1859. And in some style, it would seem. But the author of *Shirley* did not live to welcome her friend home to the West Riding, having died in 1855.

It is safe to say that, until summer 1996, very few people knew of Mary Taylor. And those who did thought her worth nothing more than a passing reference and a foot-

note in the standard lives of Charlotte Brontë. But 103
years after her death Mary Taylor was to get her Warho-
lian moment of world fame. It all revolved around a novel
which Taylor began writing in the late 1840s, parallel in
many ways to *Shirley*, and eventually published as *Miss
Miles*, in 1890, three years before the author's death.
Taylor had corresponded with Charlotte Brontë about her
unpublished novel-in-progress in the early 1850s. Like
Shirley, Taylor's story was set in the West Riding and
could loosely be described as an 'industrial novel'. But
Miss Miles embodied more aggressive ideas about women
and their right to work. *Shirley*, as Taylor pugnaciously
informed her friend Charlotte, was notably 'cowardly' on
this topic, insinuating merely that *'some'* women may
work, 'if they give up marriage and don't make themselves
too disagreeable to the other sex'.[3] Taylor was an absolut-
ist on such matters—a feminist *avant la lettre*. To her mind
all women had a right to work. It was a view she promul-
gated throughout the 1860s and 1870s, in her writings for
the militant *Victoria Magazine*. *Miss Miles* is similarly
downright on the question.

A furore was caused in early 1996 when an Edinburgh
bookseller, Ian Watson King, announced to the world that
he had found a lost work of Charlotte Brontë's. Moreover,
it was no piece of juvenilia (those had been turning up for
years). It was Charlotte's last, major work of fiction, her
masterpiece. And it *was—Sarah Miles* (alias *Miss Miles*).
'Rights' to the new work (since it was long out of copyright, it was not clear what these meant) were rumoured to
have been sold to the American publisher Random House
for a reported six-figure sum. This commercial interest
was shrewd. The reading public has an insatiable curiosity
about 'newly discovered' works by great writers. The
inclusion of the lyric 'Shall I Fly?' in OUP's Shakespeare
edition generated a huge amount of publicity for the book

in the 1980s. The 'new chapters' *of Huckleberry Finn* were published in the *New Yorker* in the 1990s—and very boring they were. A major work by Charlotte Brontë could be a gold-mine for whoever staked the first claim.

King's thesis depended on a number of interlocking hypotheses. First, that Charlotte Brontë wrote *Miss Miles*. Secondly, that all the correspondence from Mary Taylor to Charlotte (of which a large amount survives in different depositories) was forged by the Victorian bibliophile, T. J. Wise, to disguise Brontë's authorship. Thirdly, that Wise and Taylor conspired in 1890 to pass off *Miss Miles* as Taylor's work to the publisher Remington, who duly produced a three-volume edition which was singularly short-lived. King deduced that somehow Remington got wind of what was going on and 'spiked' the edition. King further claimed that computer analysis supported his claims about *Miss Miles* being a lost work by Charlotte Brontë.

King's claims provoked a storm of angry denial from Brontë scholars, and most authoritatively from Juliet Barker. She pointed out the physical impossibility of Wise's having forged those letters between Charlotte and Mary Taylor specifically discussing *Miss Miles*. The notion that Taylor would have conspired to pass off, or allow to be passed off, her friend Charlotte's novel as her own was preposterous and slanderous. And why go through this charade anyway? If *Miss Miles* was by Charlotte Brontë, there was no reason on earth for not proclaiming the fact to the skies and coining money from it. There were, in point of fact, more copies circulated of *Miss Miles* than King realized. The reason the novel failed was that it was irredeemably second-rate. Dull, tendentious three-volume novels were anyway on the way out in 1890.[4]

If one followed King's line of argument, yes, 'Rose Yorke' did indeed come back from New Zealand; and once back she robbed the grave of the author of *Shirley*. Better that Miss Taylor had stayed out there with the exotic birds rather than return to commit such a dirty deed. Few of those without a direct commercial interest in *Miss Miles* did follow Mr King, it must be conceded. But, whatever else, Mary Taylor had at last, a century after her death, become a significant figure on the Victorian landscape. There will now be a long entry on her in the *New DNB*, due out in 2003. Nor, in future, will anyone be able to read the description of the Yorkes and Charlotte's poignant question about Rose in quite the same way. She has returned—from New Zealand, and from oblivion.

The Oxford World's Classics *Shirley* is edited by Herbert Rosengarten and Margaret Smith.

Nathaniel Hawthorne · *The Scarlet Letter*

═══

What are the Prynnes doing in Boston?

═══

The Scarlet Letter's many enigmas have been exhaustively explicated. The novel is a literary-critical battleground (with the feminists probably slightly in the ascendant at the moment). But no one, as far as I know, ever asks what series of events brought Hester Prynne to Massachusetts, where so much obloquy is heaped on her. One is not encouraged to be curious on this score. Hawthorne's text is studiously inscrutable about events antecedent to Hester's being branded adulteress. The fullest account of her past life is given in sketchy flashback, as she endures her three hours of public shame in the Boston pillory:

Standing on that miserable eminence, she saw again her native village, in Old England, and her paternal home; a decayed house of gray stone, with a poverty-stricken aspect, but retaining a half-obliterated shield of arms over the portal, in token of antique gentility. She saw her father's face, with its bald brow, and reverend white beard, that flowed over the old-fashioned Elizabethan ruff; her mother's, too, with the look of heedful and anxious love which it always wore in her remembrance, and which, even since her death, had so often laid the impediment of a gentle remonstrance in her daughter's pathway. She saw her own face, glowing with girlish beauty, and illuminating all the interior of the dusky mirror in which she had been wont to gaze at it. There she beheld another countenance, of a man well stricken in years, a pale, thin, scholar-like visage, with eyes dim and bleared by the lamplight that had served them to pore over many ponderous books. Yet those same bleared optics had a strange, penetrating power, when it was their owner's purpose to read the human soul. This figure of the study and the cloister, as Hester Prynne's womanly fancy failed not to recall, was slightly deformed, with the left shoulder a trifle higher than the right. Next rose before her, in memory's picture-gallery, the intricate and narrow thorough-fares, the tall, gray houses, the huge cathedrals, and the public edifices, ancient in date and quaint in architecture, of a Continental city; where a new life had awaited her, still in connection with the misshapen scholar; a new life, but feeding itself on time-worn materials, like a tuft of green moss on a crumbling wall. Lastly, in lieu of these shifting scenes, came back the rude market-place of the Puritan settlement, with all the townspeople assembled and levelling their stern regards at Hester Prynne,— yes, at herself,—who stood on the scaffold of the pillory, an infant on her arm, and the letter A, in scarlet, fantastically embroidered with gold thread, upon her bosom! (p. 58)

It seems that Hester (whose maiden name we never know) was the only child of a genteel but impoverished English family. She married an elderly scholar for money as a self-less act of duty to her parents. Her mother has since died. Her father may be living. Further fleeting details emerge in Chillingworth's conversation with onlookers, as Hester stands at the pillory. She is, Chillingworth learns, 'the wife of a certain learned man, English by birth, who had long dwelt in Amsterdam, whence, some good time agone, he was minded to cross over and cast in his lot with us of the Massachusetts. To this purpose, he sent his wife before him, remaining himself to look after some necessary affairs.' Hester Prynne, a new American, has only been some two years in Boston. Since Pearl is, at the time of her mother's pillorying, three to four months old we can calcu-late that Hester succumbed to the Reverend Dimmesdale ten or so months after arriving in the colony. Or perhaps he succumbed to her. From various hints, it seems that the couple only committed adultery once. 'Once in my life I met the Black Man!', Hester tells Pearl. 'This scarlet letter

is his mark!' On his part, we are told, Arthur Dimmesdale
'had never gone through an experience calculated to lead
him beyond the scope of generally received laws;
although, in a single instance, he had so fearfully trans-
gressed one of the most sacred of them'.

Meanwhile no word was heard of Mistress Prynne's
husband who was considered 'most likely . . . at the bottom
of the sea'. If the lovers really believed this, Hester might
have pleaded with her judges to have the scarlet letter
commuted to 'F', for 'fornication'—a lesser, non-capital
crime. Of course, Roger is not at the bottom of the ocean
but has been captured by Indians in the south. He is
brought back by his captors, on the very day of Hester's
public punishment, to be exchanged for ransom (whether
he will pay it, or the community, is not clear—if Roger
Chillingworth is paying, one would like to know how he
gets access to Roger Prynne's funds in his disguised identity). During their interview in prison (where he visits
Hester in his guise as physician) more details of the
Prynnes' marriage emerge. He married her as a 'book
worm of great libraries—a man already in decay'. He
hoped, like many a bookworm, that his 'intellectual gifts
might veil physical deformity'. They did not. 'Thou
knowest', says Hester, 'that I was frank with thee. I felt
no love nor feigned any.' She married him for his
money—not to enrich herself, but to relieve her parents'
wants.

There remain a number of puzzles. What was Roger
Prynne, an Englishman, doing in Amsterdam? He is, as he
frequently says, an 'alchemist'. He is addicted to libraries,
'ponderous books', and dabbling in potentially criminal
arts. Why does he subsequently leave Amsterdam? Above
all, why does Prynne decide on Massachusetts, a colony
not well supplied with ponderous books or the where-
withal for an ambitious scholar. Nor—as a place where

they like to burn witches and wizards—is it somewhere that a prudent alchemist would choose to set up his stall. Roger Chillingworth is not religious—his remarks on his Puritan neighbours indicate scorn for their fanaticism. 'He knew not that the eye and hand were mine!' he says of Dimmesdale's sufferings; 'With the superstition common to his brotherhood, he fancied himself given over to a fiend.' Clearly Chillingworth does not share that superstition although at one point he recalls that he was religious in his distant youth. As we know him, Roger has more in common with the pagan Indians, from whom he has learned many valuable herbal secrets during his period of captivity.

Nor is it poverty that drives Roger Prynne to emigration. When he dies, 'by his last will and testament . . . he bequeathed a very considerable amount of property, both here and in England, to little Pearl, the daughter of Hester Prynne'. Why did he send Hester ahead of him to Massachusetts? Why was she not accompanied by a servant, or at least a maid? (Had she been, the servant might well have recognized her master Roger Prynne, confounding his scheme of revenge.) Apparently, Mistress Prynne was sent to Massachusetts without funds, or access to funds. If Roger Prynne has a 'considerable amount of property . . . here', why is his wife so poor that she has, from the beginning apparently, to earn her living by her needle? Why—in the seven years that Roger is assumed dead—does she receive no money from his estate?

To summarize: the reader may reasonably assume that the Prynnes' marriage was mercenary on her side and over-optimistic on his. Perhaps his optimism had a scientific origin. Like other alchemists Prynne has been searching for the fabled 'elixir' which will change lead to gold. The same elixir also serves as the bodily restorative and aphrodisiac which Epicure Mammon apostrophizes in

Jonson's *The Alchemist* (II. ii). With the elixir's aid he
intends:

> To have a list of wives and concubines,
> Equal with Solomon, who had the stone
> Alike with me; and I will make me a back
> With the elixir that shall be as tough
> As Hercules, to encounter fifty a night.

Once he discovered the elixir, Roger doubtless expected to
be able to satisfy his beautiful young wife.

Although his substantial property is in England,
Prynne pursued his studies in Amsterdam—presumably
because of its better libraries and a more tolerant attitude
towards alchemy. So much the reader may legitimately
suppose. It is with the subsequent events—between the
Prynnes' marriage and Hester's punishment—that mysteries
multiply. Why did the Prynnes decide to emigrate to
Boston? Not because of religious persecution or religious
attraction. It is more feasible that things became too hot
for Roger Prynne in Europe—his experiments may have
attracted official disapproval. Perhaps he was delayed in
accompanying Hester by the need to get his laboratory
together, or to clear himself with the authorities, or to
transfer his property to England.

Or perhaps the reason lay in the marriage bed. From the
name she chooses for her child, it is feasible that Hester
lost her 'Pearl above Rubies', her virginity, not to her husband, but to Arthur Dimmesdale. It may be that Prynne
sent his wife ahead, without servant or adequate money,
to an excessively puritanical community as one might
send a daughter to a convent. The Prynnes' marriage, this
is to say, may not have been consummated. Prynne sends
his spouse to Massachusetts for the same reason that
Wycherley's Pinchwife keeps his wife in the country, so no
one gets to her first. This might also explain Roger

Chillingworth's morbid fear of being revealed as Hester's husband, since his impotent inability to enforce his conjugal rights might emerge as well.

This is deeper into hypothesis than most readers will find it useful to go. But the questions are relevant if we are to balance mitigating circumstance against innate evil (or female rebelliousness) in Hester Prynne's great act. She does not 'belong' in the Boston that judges her so cruelly. She was neither born nor brought up in that peculiar environment. It was not her choice to be in Massachusetts, one assumes. Had she remained in the bosom of her English family, among her own folk, making the kind of marriage normal for a beautiful girl of her class, there would have been no scarlet letter. It points towards a central question in *The Scarlet Letter*. Have the extraordinary conditions of Puritan Boston stripped away external trappings to reveal the 'true' Hester within; or, is she, like the Salem 'witches', the victim of distorting institutionalized paranoia?

The Oxford World's Classics *The Scarlet Letter* is edited by Brian Harding.

What happens to Mrs Woodcourt?

During the libel trial which entertained the nation in July 1996, cricketer Ian Botham was asked under cross-examination if it was true that he had said after a tour of Pakistan, 'it is the kind of place where you would send your mother-in-law for a week's holiday—all expenses paid'. No, the great sporting hero replied, he would never say such a thing. What he had said was that Pakistan was the kind of place you would send your mother-in-law for *two* weeks—all expenses paid. When the laughter died down, Botham was pressed by the cross-examining counsel on whether this was not a racist slur—a kind of verbal Paki-bashing. No, Botham replied, it was a slur against mothers-in-law.

No one likes mothers-in-law, and they are fair game for any basher. It is to Esther Summerson's advantage that she brings no maternal appendage to her marriage. Lady Dedlock would not make an easy in-law. Esther does, however, acquire a mother-in-law at the end of *Bleak House* in the shape of the first Mrs Woodcourt. And her relationship to this lady, if we read the text for its symptomatic silences, shows an unexpected strand of cruelty in the otherwise tender-hearted Dame Durden.

Mrs Woodcourt is a fringe character in *Bleak House* but the centre of an interesting subplot. She is presented through the lens of Esther's retrospective narrative which is written, we can deduce, some five to seven years after the main events of the novel. Written not by Miss Summerson but by Mrs Woodcourt the second, that is. The older Mrs Woodcourt is introduced to the reader in chapter 17. Allan himself we know to be a doctor. He has been in practice in London three or four years but has not prospered. He has resolved to go 'to China, and to India, as a surgeon on board ship'—the resort of second-rate physicians. Esther is already attracted to Allan, although she has not apparently admitted the fact to herself. 'I believe—at least I know—that he was not rich', she says. The lapse into present tense ('I know') indicates subsequent intimacy. She goes on: 'All his widowed mother could spare had been spent in qualifying him for his profession.' He is her only child, we gather, and she has made painful sacrifices to help him make his way in the world.

When Allan comes to Bleak House to make his adieu to Esther he brings Mrs Woodcourt with him. Evidently there has been some conversation between mother and son in which he has intimated his hopes. One of the purposes of the visit is to show Esther off. Esther's first impression of Mrs Woodcourt is mixed: 'She was a pretty old lady, with bright black eyes, but she seemed proud.' Since Allan is only in his mid twenties (seven years older than Esther) Mrs Woodcourt cannot be very ancient. But proud she certainly is. Esther describes Mrs Woodcourt's tedious obsession with the blood of Morgan-ap-Kerrig that flows in her and Allan's veins. More to the point, the mother clearly warns Esther off:

Mrs Woodcourt, after expatiating to us on the fame of her great kinsman, said that, no doubt, wherever her son Allan went, he would remember his pedigree, and would on no account form an alliance below it. She told him that there were many handsome English ladies in India who went out on speculation ... She talked so much about birth, that, for a moment, I half fancied and with pain—but, what an idle fancy to suppose that she could think or care what *mine* was! (p. 256)

Allan, clearly embarrassed, changes the subject. The

meeting has gone very badly. There is one other encounter between Esther and Mrs Woodcourt (they meet only twice in the recorded narrative—itself an oddity, given their eventual close family relationship). It takes place during Allan's long absence abroad. Mrs Woodcourt visits Bleak House at her son's request (he evidently wants news of his intended). During the interview that ensues Esther finds Mrs Woodcourt 'irksome' (a uniquely negative term on her lips). What is it, Esther wonders, that so 'irks' her about Mrs Woodcourt? Not her upright carriage, not the general expression of her face (it was 'very sparkling and pretty for an *old* lady'). 'I don't know what it was. Or at least if I do, now, I thought I did not then. Or at least—but it don't matter' (p. 433). This, I believe, is the only grammatical solecism Esther perpetrates in her long narrative. She is clearly under the stress of conflicting emotions.

What so discomfits Esther, as she clearly knows 'now' (i.e. five years later, at the time of writing), is that Mrs Woodcourt is again warning her off. The mother prates interminably about her son's high birth: 'my son's choice of a wife, for instance, is limited by it; but the matrimonial choice of the Royal family is limited in much the same manner' (p. 434). She is even prepared to malign Allan in the cause of deterring Esther, telling the young lady that he 'is always paying trivial attention to young ladies'. Shrewdly, Mrs Woodcourt then predicts that Esther 'will marry some one, very rich and very worthy, much older— five and twenty years, perhaps—than yourself. And you will be an excellent wife, and much beloved, and very happy.' In other words, Esther will marry her guardian, Mr Jarndyce. She may be a snob and callous about a vulnerable girl's feelings, but Mrs Woodcourt has eyes in her head.

The interview leaves Esther with a suspicion that Mrs Woodcourt is 'very cunning' (p. 436). The ladies are not recorded in the novel as meeting again. When Allan comes back he is unmarried and not much richer. He takes up lodgings in London, where he practises medicine among the poor. Surprisingly, he does not install his mother as housekeeper, as would seem normal. She is, after all, an impecunious widow and a doting parent. One gathers there have been words between mother and son. During his first, emotionally charged, interview with Esther (she has been disfigured by smallpox, he has not made his fortune), Allan asks fondly about Miss Flite. The subject of that other old lady, Mrs Woodcourt, does not come up. Esther does not inquire after her, Allan offers no information.

In fact, the subject of Mrs Woodcourt never comes up again, nor does the widow make any appearance, except as a problem for the omnicompetent Mr Jarndyce to dispose of, in chapter 60. Dickens's working notes for this chapter begin with the entry: 'Mrs Woodcourt and Allan. Prepare the way.' More accurately, Allan's mother is to be got out of the way. 'I come to Mrs Woodcourt,' Jarndyce says, and goes on to ask: 'How do you like her, my dear?' Esther finds the question 'oddly abrupt', and replies mechanically that 'I liked her very much, and thought she was more agreeable than she used to be.' Her guardian concurs: 'I think so too ... Not so much of Morgan-ap—what's his name?' (pp. 849–50). When and where Esther has recently found Mrs Woodcourt more agreeable we do not know; as far as the reader is aware, there have been no meetings since Mrs Woodcourt's highly disagreeable visit to Bleak House in chapter 30, when Morgan ap—what's his name was very much to the fore. But clearly Esther and Mrs Woodcourt have subsequently met, and the older lady has been bested.

Mr Jarndyce then tells Esther that, since the lady has mended her snobbish ways, he intends to 'retain Mrs

Woodcourt here'. There are a number of deductions which we make from this apparently impulsive act of charity. Jarndyce, as we now learn, has arranged for Allan to take up a promising practice as 'medical attendant for the poor . . . at a certain place in Yorkshire'. At last Dr Woodcourt will have income sufficient to set up a home and it would be normal for a dutiful son to install his mother in it. That must not happen. Instead, Mrs Woodcourt is to be 'retained' at Bleak House with Jarndyce's menagerie of dependants, as a kind of female Skimpole.

Jarndyce duly surrenders his claim on Esther, freeing her to marry Allan—now a thriving professional man able to support a family. The courtship and proposal exchanges are missing from the narrative. It would be interesting to know what was said of Mrs Woodcourt, Esther's prospective mother-in-law. We then leap forward to Esther's valediction, written seven years later. She tells us about Ada (much recovered), little Richard (to whom Esther is a second mama), her own two daughters ('my pets'), Charley (prosperous), Caddy (prosperous—but with a handicapped baby), and even Peepy (prosperous). As for Esther herself, life has been very good to her: 'The people even praise Me as the doctor's wife. The people even like Me as I go about, and make so much of me that I am quite abashed. I owe it all to him, my love, my pride! They like me for his sake, as I do everything in life for his sake' (p. 913). Not *quite* everything: she also, it is clear, does much for the sake of her guardian. 'With the first money we saved at home,' she tells us, 'we added to our pretty house by throwing out a little Growlery expressly for my guardian which we inaugurated with great splendour the next time he came down to see us.' As it happens, she continues, 'my darling [Ada] and my guardian and little Richard . . . are coming tomorrow'.

Where is 'the doctor's mother' in all this welter of happy

ever after? It is clear that Mrs Woodcourt is not living
with Allan, his wife, and her grandchildren in Yorkshire.
It is equally clear that she is not coming with the party
tomorrow. If Mrs Woodcourt has died in the interval, it
would surely have warranted half-a-sentence of filial
obituary among the detail of Peepy Jellyby's successful
career in the Custom House or Mr Turveydrop's increasingly worrisome blood pressure.

We assume that Mrs Woodcourt has been left behind, to
languish in Hertfordshire. She is not wanted in Yorkshire.
Given Esther's incessant gush of kindness for all and sun-
dry, it seems wantonly cruel. Whatever her crotchets, Mrs
Woodcourt's snobbery originates in love of her son and a
desire that he shall do well in the world. At no point in the
novel is she shown as wanting anything for herself. She is
a widow who has spent her every mite in the prosecution
of Allan's career, stinting herself so that Esther can eventually be 'the doctor's wife'. If Esther can build a Growlery
for her guardian, why not build an extension for her
daughters' grandmother?

Esther's cuckooing Mrs Woodcourt out of her Yorkshire
nest can be seen as necessary in terms of domestic *Real-
politik*. As 'mother Skipton . . . mother Hubbard . . . Dame
Durden . . . Dame Trot . . . Mistress of the Keys', Esther
cannot, in territorial terms, contemplate any power-
sharing with a mother-in-law (when her daughters grow
up, that will be something else; there will be a subordinate
place for them in the domestic hierarchy). There cannot be
two mistresses of the keys at either Bleak House. Jarndyce
perceived as much, when he made arrangements for Mrs
Woodcourt to live with him. It was not out of kindness to
the older woman, but to make space for Esther that he
took in Esther's mother-in-law (she will, of course, henceforth be a pensioner, and tied to him financially).

There is clearly much of significance between the two

Mrs Woodcourts which is not narrated in the text of *Bleak House*. Interviews and meetings are recorded as having taken place about which we know nothing (it would also be interesting to know what has been said between mother and son on the subject of Miss Summerson). But one thing is clear. If there was a power struggle between mother-in-law and daughter-in-law, Esther has come out on top. Nor is it easy to picture the doting Mrs Woodcourt easily giving up her sovereignty over her wonderful son, the only child who is such a credit to her. If we think about it, Mrs Woodcourt must be wretched as she remains, in solitude, at the southern Bleak House, thinking about the jollifications in Yorkshire. Esther, we surmise, has inherited some of Lady Dedlock's steel. On the whole it augurs well for the marriage. Allan is clearly a spineless kind of fellow—a philanthropic friend to the poor but lacking drive and the ability to rise in his profession. He needs a strong woman, a ruthless woman indeed, behind him. The doctor's wife fits the bill.

The Oxford World's Classics *Bleak House* is edited by Stephen Gill.

The Barchester Towers that never was

Readers attentive to the calendar will be arrested by the opening words of chapter 9 of *Barchester Towers*: 'It is now three months since Dr Proudie began his reign.' The time reference is perplexing. Trollope's novel began vividly with old Bishop Grantly dying 'in the latter days of July in the year 185–'. There follows the magnificent episode of the bishop's son, Archdeacon Grantly, torn between filial grief and ecclesiastical ambition, dispatching a telegram to Downing Street in the hope that it will arrive before the government falls. He is too late (if only his father had died earlier, he thinks—then hates himself for thinking such a thing). A new administration, Palmerston's as we infer, comes in and the Archdeacon's hopes of slipping into his father's *caligulae* are dashed forever. The obnoxiously reforming Dr Proudie is elected Bishop of Barchester. The story of his and his domineering wife's administration will be covered over the massive length of the subsequent Barchester Chronicles (1855–67).

With the above 'July' reference in mind we may make some chronological deductions. They are unsettling. On page 9 we were informed that 'just a month after the demise of the late bishop, Dr Proudie kissed the Queen's hand as his successor elect'. Calculation suggests, therefore, that Bishop Proudie's 'reign' began at the end of August, which means that this new phase of the narrative (marked by the opening of chapter 9) begins 'three months' after the August ceremony, at the end of November and the beginning of December (1854, as we may deduce). But, as a number of specific references indicate, the narrative following on from this point is set in August and the early autumn months thereafter. Three or four months have apparently come adrift. See, for instance, the letter from Mr Harding on page 108, which is dated '20th August, 185–'. Miss Thorne's *fête champêtre* takes place in September following, on a fine autumn day. The end of September sees 'Mrs Proudie Victrix', a week or so after the great affair at Ullathorne. The happy ending of the novel—crowned by the union of Arabin and Eleanor and the final downfall of the Proudie–Slope party—occurs 'in the beginning of October'. So if one is literal about it the Proudies will have returned to Barchester at the beginning of chapter 9 in November 1854 *after* the subsequent events of the novel. When they alight at the station the epic war between Archdeacon Grantly and the Slope faction will be over; Slope and Arabin's personal duel for the hand of Eleanor will have been settled; the wardenship contest between Dr Harding and the Revd Quiverful will have been decided. But, of course, Bishop and Mrs Proudie are principal actors in these contests. They must be in Barchester for the novel which we know as *Barchester Towers* to happen; but, chronologically—if we credit that pesky 'three months' reference—they cannot be.

The easiest way for Trollope to have ironed out the contradictions would have been to pre-date the opening sentence of the novel ('In the latter days of July in the year 185–') to 'In the latter days of April in the year 185–', and make a few minor seasonal adjustments. He did not, probably because he did not notice the anomaly. He was often indifferent to minor inconsistencies in his narratives. Nor should the reader intent on enjoying Trollope linger on such blemishes, unless they point to something interesting in the author's thinking about his novel. Here the confusion about months can indeed lead us to discover something of importance about *Barchester Towers*.

It is plausibly surmised that Trollope began writing *Barchester Towers* in January 1855, and that with eighty-five manuscript pages done he stopped writing.[1] Given Trollope's invariable 235–50 words per handwritten page, and the fact that the whole manuscript came in at 1,018 pages (the manuscript is lost, but we know how long it was), it is very likely that the break occurred between chapters 8 and 9, or chapters 7 and 8. After this first stint of composition there followed an immensely long interval, during which Trollope worked at his anatomy of English society, *The New Zealander*, from February 1855 to April 1856. It was not until 12 May 1856, nearly fourteen months after writing the first eighty-five pages, that Trollope resumed writing *Barchester Towers*. Thereafter, he wrote swiftly, finishing the work on 9 November 1856. It was never, in my experience, Trollope's practice to go back and substantially modify earlier sections of his manuscript once it was on paper. One may reasonably assume that chapters 1 to 8 represent the early, January–February 1855, stratum of composition in its original shape, pristine archaeological evidence of his first thinking about the novel.

The strong presumption is that in the nearly fourteen months' interval during which no work was done on *Barchester Towers* (i.e. between February 1855 and May 1856), Trollope's conception of his novel changed radically. In the early days of January 1855, he had seen *Barchester Towers* as less a proliferating Victorian soap opera (which it becomes) than a 'second part' of *The Warden* (*The Warden II*, as a modern film-maker would call it). *The Warden* had come out in early 1855. *Barchester Towers* was to be in every sense a partnering work, that is, of about the same dimensions and concentrating on precisely the same central issues: the incumbency of the wardenship of Hiram's Hospital (contested between Quiverful and Harding), the wooing of Eleanor (now an eligible widow, as previously she had been an eligible maiden). *The Warden* was, of course, a slim one-volume novel (284 pages in the World's Classics edition). *Barchester Towers*, as it eventually emerged, is a majestically sprawling three-volume novel (553 pages in World's Classics).

In his first mention of the embryonic *Barchester Towers* to his publisher, Longman, on 17 February 1855, Trollope says that: 'I intended to write a second part for publication [i.e. *Barchester Towers*] in the event of the first part [i.e. *The Warden*] taking and the tale was framed on this intention. I have written about one third of the second part.'[2] If eighty-five pages represents 'about one third' of the total manuscript at this stage of conception, the length of the putative whole—some 260 manuscript pages—indicates that *Barchester Towers*, 'the second part', was originally intended like *The Warden* to be a one-volume work. Trollope's first conception, then, was for something only one-third the size of the eventual *Barchester Towers*. And it was to this tight, one-volume scale that he framed the early layer of his narrative which we have as chapters 1–8.

It would seem, from several earlier references, that in the initial one-volume *Barchester Towers* it was intended that the Proudies would spend most of their time in London, off-stage. In the eighty-five-page prelude, Proudie would be a political bishop who made occasional forays into Barchester when the season was over (i.e. in August), when Parliament was in recess, and at important festivals of the year when his attendance at the cathedral was unavoidable. Hence Mr Slope's grandiose musings on page 27: 'He, therefore, he, Mr Slope, would in effect be bishop of Barchester . . . [Mr Slope] flattered himself that he could out-manœuvre the lady. She must live much in London,

while he would always be on the spot.' It would seem that
in his first plans for *Barchester Towers*, and while writing
the first eighty-five pages in January 1855, Trollope fore-
saw a long-distance war lasting three months between the
Proudies in London, and the Grantly faction in Barchester, with Slope as very much a free agent. Trollope set this
up in the early layer of narrative. At the end of chapter 1
Proudie is appointed the new bishop (at the end of August,
as has been noted). The Proudies are introduced in chapter 3 at full length, with heavy stress laid on their attach-
ment to London. Dr Proudie, we are told:

by no means intended to bury himself at Barchester as his predecessor had done. No: London should still be his ground: a com-
fortable mansion in a provincial city might be well enough for the
dead months of the year. Indeed Dr Proudie had always felt it
necessary to his position to retire from London when other great
and fashionable people did so [i.e. in the hot summer months, and
at Christmas]; but London should still be his fixed residence, and
it was in London that he resolved to exercise that hospitality so
peculiarly recommended to all bishops by St Paul. How otherwise
could he keep himself before the world? how else give to the government, in matters theological, the full benefit of his weight and
talents? (pp. 20–1)

Trollopians will find the above passage perplexing. In the
episodes of the Barsetshire Chronicles that follow—
the multi-volume saga that extends through to the *Last
Chronicle* in 1867—the Proudies are wholly resident in
Barchester: provincial through and through. What happened to the plan of having their main base in London? It
is never mentioned again.

In the four chapters that follow we apprehend that the
Proudies are making only a fleeting visit to Barchester—
some three or four days' duration, as we are told, during
which Slope gives the obnoxiously low-church sermon
in the cathedral which sets 'all Barchester by the ears'.

Leaving Slope to fight their reformist battles, the bishop and his wife return to their natural habitat at the end of chapter 7 ('Dr and Mrs Proudie at once returned to London . . . they left Mr Slope behind them'). The next chapter sets up what, in his early conception for the novel, Trollope evidently saw as his main plot-lines. It is entitled 'The ex-Warden rejoices in his probable Return to the Hospital', and at the end of the chapter Slope makes his wooer's visit to Eleanor. Ominously, she is not displeased by his addresses. It leads to some friction between father and daughter. Although he is gratified by the thought of being Warden again, Dr Harding is not overjoyed by the prospect of Mr Slope as son-in-law. All this, of course, is a replay of *The Warden*, where Harding's disputed wardenship and his personal distaste for his daughter's suitor, John Bold, are the novel's main plot elements.

There follows, at the beginning of chapter 9, the 'impossible' dating reference: 'It is now three months since Dr Proudie began his reign.' I surmise that just before this point the fourteen-month hiatus occurred. When Trollope picked up his manuscript again there was a momentary confusion in his mind in which two schemes for the novel conflicted. In the first of those schemes the Proudies were to be absent in London from August to October—while all the manœuvring for the wardenship and Eleanor's hand took place at Barchester, with Slope centre-stage. The Proudies would reappear from the wings in early winter. The second scheme was what we now have as *Barchester Towers*: with the Proudies prominently and permanently installed at the Palace—meddling indefatigably—during those same August-to-October months. The mark of the temporary confusion, like the jolt of a train as it couples itself to new carriages, is that 'three months' anomaly.

The main reason why Trollope did not persist with *Barchester Towers* in February 1855, dropping it for many months, is because Longman blew very cold on the project. *The Warden* (first published in January 1855) had not been an immediate sales success although during the course of 1855 it began to attract attention and to build up what was to become a huge popularity with the British reading public. But all this was in the future in February 1855, when the first edition of *The Warden* was still hanging fire. Had Longman presciently encouraged Trollope in February 1855, posterity would very likely have had a short, one-volume, stripped-down 'Barchester Towers' by the middle of the year: something markedly different from what we now have. But, as I say, they did not encourage him and the project was put into cold storage.

For the fun of it we may hypothesize in detail what this ghostly one-volume 'Barchester Towers' would have been. As I have speculated, it would not have featured the Proudies, except as absent potentates in London—dispatching haughty missives, probably, but not involving themselves directly. The narrative would have centred on a head-to-head struggle about the disposal of the wardenship (Harding or Quiverful?) between the contenders' champions, Archdeacon Grantly and Chaplain Slope.[3] The amiable Mr Harding would once again be caught painfully in the middle. From early references in the first chapter, the *Jupiter* and Tom Towers would have grossly interfered, as they did in *The Warden*. Trollope evidently killed off John Bold (whom he never liked very much, as he confessed) so as to make Eleanor marriageable and a main prize in the ecclesiastical in-fighting. Conceivably Slope would have tried to blackmail her into giving him her hand, with the promise of her father's return to Hiram's Hospital—if he were also Mr Slope's father-in-law. The unwritten (or uncompleted) 'Barchester Towers' would have been altogether more plot-driven and less episodic. The Stanhopes (for whom there is no early foundation),[4] the Thornes (first introduced in chapter 22), and Mr Arabin (first introduced in chapter 14) would probably not have made any appearance in the short 'Barchester Towers'. The widowed Eleanor might well have been married off, but to whom is not clear. Trollope might conceivably have left her in young widowhood.

One admires Trollope's deft changing of the scale and focus of his manuscript novel and there is pleasure to be had in speculating about the 'Barchester Towers' that never was. There is another, larger consideration. As he makes clear in his *Autobiography*, the gradual success of *The Warden*, and the Barchester Chronicles it inaugurated, marked Trollope's belated entry into the ranks of the great British novelists. He was 40 years old in 1855, the author of six novels, and at best a respected middle-rank author. *The Warden* and *Barchester Towers* changed all that. By 1860 he was at the top of the tree—the new Thackeray. In the change from the short 'unwritten' 'Barchester Towers' to the full-sized novel we have, Trollope crossed a significant threshold. He moved away from novels of tight plot, to a kind of fiction *sans frontières* which creates not a story but a world. This new style of fiction-writing—what we think of as the essentially Trollopian style—emerged with the expanded sequel to *The Warden*. Between the 'Barchester Towers' that never was, and the *Barchester Towers* that was finally written, the mature Anthony Trollope came into being.

The Oxford World's Classics *Barchester Towers* is edited by John Sutherland.

George Eliot · *Adam Bede*

Why doesn't the Reverend Irwine speak up for Hetty?

When the Reverend Irwine informs Adam Bede that Hetty has been charged with infanticide, the young man reacts with understandable violence. Adam's first response is an explosive 'It *can't be!*' (p. 408), by which the honest fellow means that, for all he has done, Hetty is still a virgin. Of course, as her intended husband in a couple of weeks (the very day she goes to the gallows, as it turns out), the general scurrilous assumption may well be that he is the father of Hetty's murdered baby and that she ran away and smothered it rather than spend the rest of her life as Mrs Adam Bede.

When Irwine persuades him—by means of the magistrate's letter—that the awful news from Stoniton is probably true, Adam extracts from the parson an assurance that he will inform the Poysers that he, Adam, is innocent of seducing Hetty. Adam's other reactions are equally constructive—if vehement. He apprehends that Captain Donnithorne, his once-idolized 'friend', lied to him when he said that the affair with Hetty had not gone beyond harmless flirting. 'It's *his* doing', Adam mutters:

if there's been any crime, it's at his door, not at hers. *He* taught her to deceive—he deceived me first. Let 'em put *him* on his trial—let him stand in court beside her, and I'll tell 'em how he got hold of her heart, and 'ticed her t'evil, and then lied to me. Is *he* to go free, while they lay all the punishment on her . . . so weak and young? (p. 409)

Irwine does not answer. Tacitly, yes, he intimates: Hetty
is to bear all the blame and the heavy legal consequence.
Adam continues: 'I'll go to him—I'll bring him back—I'll
make him go and look at her in her misery . . . I'll fetch
him, I'll drag him back myself' (p. 410). Arthur, of course,
is serving his country in Ireland (an active-service post-
ing) with the Loamshire Militia. When Adam threatens to
'fetch' Arthur, Irwine at last responds. 'No, Adam, no,' he
counsels. He (Adam) must stay here (in the Hayslope area)
for *her* (Hetty). 'Besides', Irwine adds, reassuringly:
'[Arthur] is no longer in Ireland: he must be on his way
home or would be, long before you arrived; for his grandfather, I know, wrote for him to come at least ten days ago. I
want you now to go with me to Stoniton.'

This is the first we have heard of the old squire's
summons—presumably it concerns the removal of the
Poysers from Hall Farm. It is no life-and-death matter. And
since the Loamshires were posted to Ireland only a few
weeks since, there is no guarantee that Arthur will hurry
back. (What would his fellow officers say if—in the face of
the enemy—he turned tail because his grandfather was
having a spot of bother with one of his tenants?) There is
every likelihood that Arthur will take his time in returning to Hayslope.

Suppose, at this point, Irwine had said to Adam something along the lines of:

Yes, Adam, you must indeed fetch Captain Donnithorne back, the
sooner the better. Take the best horse from my stable and ride like
the wind. Here is fifty guineas for your expenses. Stint nothing. I
learn from the commandant of the Loamshires that Arthur's
troop is quartered in Dublin. Gallop post-haste to Liverpool.
Leave a message there, and at every coaching inn on the
road, telling Arthur *to make all speed to Stoniton: It is a matter of
life and death!* If you have to, hire a ketch to cross the Irish
channel. On my part, I will request the commandant to dispatch a

regimental courier, as fast as may be practical, to fetch Captain Donnithorne back. I will also petition the judge at Stoniton to delay the trial until the arrival of this most material witness. With God's help, we can still avert this awful tragedy. What are you waiting for, Adam? Be off!

And supposing Arthur, having been brought back in time, had addressed the court with remorseful demeanour, clad in his regimentals, as follows:

My lord and gentlemen of the jury. Miss Sorrel was the ward of one of my grandfather's tenants. She was a very guileless girl, of previously excellent character, but easily impressed and perhaps too vain of her beauty. I selfishly seduced her and (unknowingly) left her with child. I lied to the honest man of her own class she was engaged to marry. He trusted me, and I callously betrayed him. I was called away to serve my country. It was in Miss Sorrel's vain attempt to follow me and in a desperate condition—for which I hold myself entirely responsible—that this terrible thing happened. I entreat you to be merciful with her, and reserve your just recriminations for me.

Would any jury, faced with such testimony, convict for murder?

Irwine, however, seems determined not to let the above scenario happen. He persuades Adam to do nothing, and on his own part does nothing to hurry Arthur back. Why should Irwine claim that Adam Bede is needed at Stoniton? As it turns out, Hetty will not see her intended husband, nor is Adam permitted to give evidence in court. The carpenter is wholly out of his depth in all this legal business. Why does Irwine want Adam to cool his heels for ten days, doing nothing?

After the interview with Adam in which he learns that Arthur is Hetty's seducer Irwine returns home to discover that the old squire has suddenly died. Arthur is now squire-elect of Hayslope. A messenger has already been sent to await his arrival at Liverpool, with the news of his grandfather's death. It is Wednesday. The trial is set for Friday week.

Given the uncertain nature of the post in the early nineteenth century, it would seem more than ever urgent to dispatch a courier to speed Arthur on his way. But Irwine does not even send a letter to Liverpool for Arthur to find on his return from Ireland, so that he might come directly to Stoniton. One of the things that goes hard with Hetty in the trial is that she at first refuses to give her identity and obdurately denies that she ever had a baby, let alone killed it. Her motives for this disastrous plea are never clearly explained, but evidently she wants to protect Arthur. If she denies having a baby, no cross-examining counsel can ask who the father was.

On the eve of the trial, Irwine tells Adam, that 'Arthur Donnithorne is not come back . . . I have left a letter for him: he will know all as soon as he arrives.' But, it now seems clear, Donnithorne will not arrive in time to take part in the trial. When Adam again protests about the author of all this misery getting off scot-free, Irwine again counsels patience and forgiveness: 'he *will* know—he *will* suffer, long and bitterly . . . why do you crave vengeance in this way?' (p. 422). The parson goes on to deliver an eloquent sermon on Christian acceptance. As always, he is preparing Adam for the worst—Hetty must hang. Had he been less distraught, Adam might well have replied that it is not Captain Donnithorne's blood he wants so much as his truthful testimony.

The morning session of the trial itself is given obliquely through Bartle Massey's account to Adam. There has been damaging evidence from the doctors. Martin Poyser has been called by the prosecution to identify his niece. But, Massey adds reassuringly, 'Mr Irwine is to be a witness himself by-and-by, on her side'. He adds, 'Mr Irwine'll leave no stone unturned with the judge'. Fortified by the prospect of Irwine telling all, Adam attends the afternoon session where he hears further evidence from various witnesses—one of whom testifies conclusively to the birth of the babe, the other to its murder. The prosecution case is, as Adam perceives, wholly damning. Then comes the Revd Irwine's testimony, about which Bartle was earlier so hopeful. But by now Adam is beyond hope: he

heard no more of the evidence, and was unconscious when the case for the prosecution had closed—unconscious that Mr Irwine was in the witness-box, telling of Hetty's unblemished character in her own parish, and of the virtuous habits in which she had been brought up. (p. 435)

The narrator adds: 'This testimony could have no influence on the verdict, but it was given as part of that plea for mercy which her own counsel would have made.'

What, one may ask, happened to the 'leaving no stone unturned with the judge'? Why does not Irwine—once he has the ear of the jury—thunder out the truth: 'Hetty was seduced and abandoned by a man she trusted and whose duty was to protect her virtue, not debauch it.' He knows the facts of the case, why does he not utter them? And why, as the fiancé of Hetty and the possible father of the dead child in the eyes of the world, is Adam not called—if only to clear his name? His nobility of character would surely deflect judicial severity from Hetty to her culpable seducer.

Irwine's feeble character-witness ('she was a very good girl until she murdered her baby') has no effect. The judge dons his black cap and Hetty is sentenced to hang on Monday. Meanwhile, on the same Friday as the trial, Arthur finally makes his way to Liverpool. There he opens the letter informing him of his grandfather's death. There is no accompanying letter from Irwine on the more serious matter at Stoniton. Had there been, it being early Friday morning, Arthur might conceivably, by fast galloping, have intervened.

Instead he wends his happy way by coach to 'dear old Hayslope', fantasizing all the way about how wonderful his tenure as squire will be. He arrives home in the 'late afternoon'. He finds the servants oddly subdued (they have been talking to the Poysers). Arthur bathes and refreshes himself. At last he reads Irwine's letter and its awful announcement, 'Hetty Sorrel is in prison and will be tried on Friday for the crime of child-murder.' Eliot breaks off the report of Irwine's letter at this point, so we do not know what advice, if any, Irwine went on to give ('Come at once'? 'Do nothing till you hear further from me'?). Arthur rushes to the stables, instructing the butler to 'Tell them I'm gone—gone to Stoniton'. He springs into the saddle 'and sets off at a gallop'. Stoniton is twenty miles distant, and he will be there in an hour and a half.

It is, of course, too late now to give evidence. Sentence has been passed. The trial is over by sunset (as we are told) and the March days are short. It is not clear what Arthur does at Stoniton when—around six or seven o'clock presumably—he gallops into town. What he should do is secure an interview with the judge and crave a stay of execution. He does not, apparently. He does not visit Hetty nor contact Adam, who remains unaware that Arthur is back in the country (had the men met at this moment, Adam might well have killed him—as Irwine constantly fears). Of course there must be a meeting between Arthur and Irwine, but we do not know what the two men say to each other. What seems likely from subsequent events is that Irwine instructs Arthur not to announce his presence in Stoniton but to ride at once to London and intercede privately with friends in high places for a reprieve. Meanwhile, in a scene which Eliot does narrate at length, Dinah prepares Hetty for public hanging—

a fate which is forestalled by Arthur's dashing reappearance in Stoniton, at the eleventh hour, riding pell-mell through the crowd, 'in his hand a hard-won release from death'.

In the public mind Arthur probably gets credit from this exploit. Most onlookers will see him as a heroic squire saving one of his shiftless tenants from deserved punishment. The circle of people who do know Arthur's culpability in the sorry affair are restricted to the Poysers and their close associates. Arthur's treachery was not bruited in court and will not make the newspapers. The world at large will continue to think that Adam was the father of the murdered infant and obscurely responsible for Hetty's flight from Hayslope by some pre-marital unkindness.

What should the reader make of Irwine's equivocal behaviour in all this? At any one of a number of points he could have been more effective in Hetty's defence, if that had been his primary concern. He could have let Adam fetch Arthur and have made strenuous efforts himself in that direction. He could have sent a letter to Liverpool, rather than leaving one to be found, eventually, at Hayslope. He could have given frank evidence as to Arthur's misconduct at the trial—or have had defence counsel put Adam on the stand to do it. He could have told Arthur, when he finally arrived at Stoniton, to make a public proclamation of his responsibility for the girl's pregnancy and request a stay of execution so that his evidence might be considered by the authorities. He did none of these things.

One assumes that Irwine is trying to maintain an awkward balance. Of course he wants to mitigate Hetty's punishment if he can, but he is also obliged to preserve as much of Arthur's reputation as he can. It is not just partiality. These are dangerous times. Britain is at war. Jacobinical principles are abroad. Methodism is attacking the very foundations of the Anglican Church. It could be very dangerous if Arthur were publicly disgraced. The crowd who come to witness the hanging might well become an angry mob and Stoniton gaol their Bastille. Apart from anything else, if the fact that he had lied to one of his most loyal retainers came out—what regiment would ever offer Arthur Donnithorne a commission? Rogering peasant girls might possibly be blinked at. But a squire who would cold-bloodedly betray a loyal retainer like Adam Bede will not make an officer to whom men can trust their lives in battle. The whole English squirearchy and the complex mutual fealties which go with it, would be tainted at a time when it needed to be upheld. A loophole *must* be left for Arthur's redemption.

Irwine, we may assume, methodically limits the damage to Arthur. He does so partly for selfish reasons: his living is in the Donnithornes' manor (it may be in their gift) and it is his duty to protect his protectors. There are also reasons of state. The trustworthy parson and the trustworthy squire are the twin pillars of rural life. Shake them, and Britain may experience what France went through a decade before. There are three prongs to Irwine's strategy in the matter of Hetty's trial. First, he must rein in and neutralize Adam—which he does by confining the violent young man to Stoniton and keeping him out of the witness box. Secondly, he must if possible keep Arthur out of the way. He must also prevent his name coming up in court. And when the young man finally turns up in Stoniton, he is bundled away to London. The 'release from death' (commutation to transportation) carries no public stigma for Arthur, as his self-incriminating evidence in court or in judge's chambers would have done. And the last, sharpest, prong of Irwine's strategy is that Hetty must be sacrificed.

Irwine's strategy works. Adam obediently ends up shaking hands with Arthur, instead of becoming an English

Defarge. Whatever political fire there is in his belly will be extinguished by Dinah and her Methodism. Arthur goes off to win glory in the Peninsula. As Colonel Donnithorne he is, on his return, a rather melancholy old dog—but a true English hero. Conceivably he will still be around to play his part at Waterloo. A respectable cousin will take over as squire if 'the colonel' dies in action. If he survives Arthur will return to take up his squire's duties, purged of all scandal by his feats on the battlefield. The old order is thus preserved by Irwine's manœuvres. He has done his small bit to avert revolution. The loser in all this, of course, is Hetty.

Had the full story of Arthur's seduction, mendacity, and abandonment come out—particularly if it had been reiterated in court by Irwine, Adam, and Arthur himself— she might have won a full pardon, or at least a light cus- todial sentence in England. What actually happens to her is politically necessary (if one shares Irwine's politics) but horribly unjust. As an attractive young woman with the reputation of a hardened trull, she will be subject to sex- ual molestation from her male guards and, all too likely, from other convicts.

As Robert Hughes points out, the lot of the 24,000 women convicts transported to Australia in the early nineteenth century was not enviable:

Convict men might in the end redeem themselves through work and penance, but women almost never. It was as though women convicts had passed the ordinary bounds of class and become a fiction, not far from pornography: crude raucous Eve, sucking rum and mothering bastards in the exterior darkness, inviting contempt from her social superiors, rape rather than help from men.[1]

Thank you, Reverend Irwine, thank you, Captain Donnithorne.

Hetty in fact lives only a few years in Australia, and wretched years we can imagine them to be. It seems a hard fate for a girl whose main fault was a fondness for glass earrings. But, as Irwine would doubtless point out, sorrowfully but firmly, the security of England's institutions is more important than the fate of a light-headed milkmaid.

The Oxford World's Classics *Adam Bede* is edited by Valentine Cunningham.

═══

How good an oarswoman is Maggie Tulliver?

═══

For all his admiration of its author, Henry James did not like the ending of *The Mill on the Floss* one bit:

The story is told as if it were destined to have, if not a strictly happy termination, at least one within ordinary probabilities. As it stands, the *dénouement* shocks the reader most painfully. Nothing has prepared him for it; the story does not move towards it; it casts no shadow before it. Did such a *dénouement* lie within the author's intentions from the first, or was it a tardy expedient for the solution of Maggie's difficulties? This question the reader asks himself, but of course he asks it in vain. For my part, although, as long as humanity is subject to floods and earthquakes, I have no objection to see them made use of in novels, I would in this particular case have infinitely preferred that Maggie should have been left to her own devices.[1]

On his part, Leslie Stephen (writing in 1909) could 'not help wishing that the third volume could have been suppressed'.[2] F. R. Leavis concurred with James, if less dismissively:

The flooded river has no symbolic or metaphorical value. It is only the dreamed-of perfect accident that gives us the opportunity for the dreamed-of heroic act—the act that shall vindicate us against a harshly misjudging world, bring emotional fulfilment and (in others) changes of heart, and provide a gloriously tragic curtain. Not that the sentimental in it is embarrassingly gross, but the finality is not that of great art, and the significance is what I have suggested—a revealed immaturity.[3]

One could multiply examples and it is difficult to find a
critic of weight prepared to commend the last chapter of
The Mill on the Floss. The principal objections are that
the drowning of Tom and Maggie is arbitrary (no fore-
shadow is cast, as James puts it) and that it is sentimental.
It is odd that so few of the critics who dislike the climax of
The Mill on the Floss adduce another objection—namely,
that the scene of the Tullivers' drowning is, by any understanding of the laws of hydrodynamics and the lesser science of river-boating, incredible.[4]

The final chapter of *The Mill on the Floss* (volume
III, chapter 5) is entitled 'The Last Conflict'. It opens
with Maggie's life in ruins. She is estranged from her
stern brother, Tom, who is living again at the Dorlcote
Mill. Stephen Guest, just returned from Holland, cannot understand why Maggie will not see him. He has
written her a violently passionate and hurtful letter. As a
woman to whom public scandal attaches following her
unchaperoned escapade in the boat with Stephen, Maggie
has been advised by the friendly local minister, Dr Kenn,
'to go away from St Ogg's for a time'. The hoped-for position as governess is now out of the question. 'Gossip and
slander' have condemned her. Before taking this step she
has found refuge at good-hearted Bob Jakin's humble
house, by the riverside.

Outside, the equinoctial storms of mid-September are
raging. The rain is incessant. The Floss (which Eliot based
on the Trent, although the St Ogg's region is clearly in
Warwickshire) is running ominously high. A tidal river, its
current is swollen both from the teeming heavens and from
the surging ocean. The old men of St Ogg's shake their
heads and talk 'of sixty years ago, when the same sort of
weather, happening about the equinox, brought the great
floods, which swept the bridge away, and reduced the town
to great misery'.

It is 'past midnight'. While Bob, his wife, and their child sleep upstairs a sleepless Maggie sits in 'her lonely room'. Later called a 'parlour', this room is on the ground floor with a window looking out to the river. Foreseeing the wretched life that lies ahead of her ('how long it will be before death comes! I am so young, so healthy'), Maggie fights down a brief temptation to suicide. But she tacitly pleads that God will end her misery soon. 'At that moment' she feels 'a startling sensation of sudden cold about her knees.' The Floss has broken its banks. She wakes Bob, who is upstairs.

They must get to the two boats belonging to the house, she shouts (this is an error, of course; the sensible thing to do would be to go quietly to the upper storey of the house, and wait until the deluge subsided). As Maggie gives the alarm there is a 'tremendous crash'. One of the rowing-boats has banged through the parlour window. (Was it not moored? Apparently so—how then has it risen so high in the water?) The boat remains, 'with the prow lodging and protruding through the window'.

It turns out that both boats are conveniently jammed against the window, ready for the house's occupants to embark. Bob, who now has a lantern, gets his wife and baby into one boat. Maggie boards the other—no easy task, one would have thought, given the rocking boat and the awkwardness of clambering through the broken window-frame wearing a full-bodied, ankle-length dress (see the illustration at the end of this chapter). But Maggie contrives to do it. Once in the boat she 'gets possession of an oar' and pushes off. We are given a vivid vignette of her by Bob's fitful lantern flare, 'as she stood in the rain with the oar in her hand and her black hair streaming'. The boat is, we apprehend, a narrow-beam, shallow-draft rowing-boat or skiff, designed for river and estuary work close to the land. Lacking a keel, such craft are inherently unstable (as anyone who has been in one on a river will know). Standing up in such a boat would be risky at any time and suicidal in the eddying turbulence of a flash flood which has been violent enough to raise the water-level many feet in a few minutes. But things are moving fast. Suddenly 'a new tidal current' catches Maggie's little vessel, and she finds herself alone on the broad expanse of the swollen Floss in the pitch black. The stream carries her along although she has her oar with which to scull (or possibly two with which to row—the detail is not clari-fied), as she drifts at some speed downstream to St Ogg's.

Maggie's first thought is the Mill ('which is the way home?' she cries). She is now in smooth water 'perhaps far on the over-flooded fields' (St Ogg's is in low-lying Fen country). Day is at last breaking. Maggie seizes her oar again, and paddles 'with the energy of awakened hope' (if she paddles, presumably she is sitting down again, but it is not clear that with one oar she could direct the boat where she wants it to go. Possibly she is sculling, like a gondolier, with the oar secured on a stern rowlock). Her every thought is bent towards her brother and his safety.

Soon the 'dark mass' of St Ogg's looms up. The Mill is at the junction of the faster-flowing tributary, the Ripple, and the main channel of the Floss. Maggie is obliged to navigate her little craft through the swirling crosscur-rents to get to Tom: '*now*, she must use all her skill and power to manage the boat and get it if possible out of the current ... With new resolution, Maggie seized her oar, and stood up again to paddle.' What 'skill', one may ask? The point was made earlier in the text that it was only a few months earlier that Maggie had—for the first time in her life—learned how to handle an oar.

During a summer outing on the river with Lucy and Stephen, 'she thought she would like to learn how to row' (p. 336). The young man gallantly instructed her in the

rudiments of rowing (taking the opportunity to clasp her
hand when her foot slips getting out of the boat). Those
few minutes of tuition from Stephen on still water represent the sum total of Maggie's experience of handling a
boat. Although, as G. S. Haight notes, she has been
brought up as something of a tomboy in a water-mill
alongside a river, neither boatcraft nor swimming seem to
have featured in her childhood.

Now, in the midst of the most turbulent flood stream for
sixty years, Maggie can balance herself, encumbered by a
wet, full-length dress and petticoats, and vigorously ply a
single oar in such a boat as we see in the illustration.
Stephen must, we assume, be a teacher of genius and
Maggie a similarly gifted pupil. How else could she stand
up, on a rocking craft, and 'paddle' (scull, using the rowlock? Or direct her strokes strategically on one side then
the other?). Grace Darling herself would be proud of
Maggie's boating feats on the Floss. George Eliot, one
assumes, has fallen into the landlubber's common error of
thinking that rowing is as easy as it looks.

By energetic 'paddling' Maggie successfully directs her
boat to the mill. The flood is now at a level with the
'upstairs windows' (the water must have risen some twenty
feet in six hours). Fortuitously, Tom is stranded in the
house by himself. Leaving, as Maggie did, by a window, he
'steps into the boat' (wiser, one would have thought, to
have lowered himself into it). Once on board he takes the
'oars' (there are now two). They push off, and Tom rows
'with untired vigour'. Their plan is to row downstream to
Tofton, and Park House, which 'stands high up out of the
flood'. Then comes the tremendous climax:

Nothing else was said; a new danger was being carried towards
them by the river. Some wooden machinery had just given way on
one of the wharves, and huge fragments were being floated along.
The sun was rising now, and the wide area of watery desolation

was spread out in dreadful clearness around them—in dreadful
clearness floated onwards the hurrying, threatening masses. A
large company in a boat that was working its way along under the
Tofton houses, observed their danger, and shouted, 'Get out of
the current!'

But that could not be done at once, and Tom, looking before
him, saw death rushing on them. Huge fragments, clinging
together in fatal fellowship, made one wide mass across the stream.

'It is coming, Maggie!' Tom said, in a deep hoarse voice, loosing
the oars, and clasping her.

The next instant the boat was no longer seen upon the water—
and the huge mass was hurrying on in hideous triumph.

But soon the keel of the boat reappeared, a black speck on the
golden water.

The boat reappeared—but brother and sister had gone down in
an embrace never to be parted: living through again in one
supreme moment the days when they had clasped their little
hands in love, and roamed the daisied fields together. (p. 521)

It is magnificent, but as Gordon Haight points out, it is
not realistic fiction. First, the meteorology is wrong. Flash
floods, of the kind which suddenly and without warning
inundate a whole town under many feet of swirling water,
only occur in mountainous areas or where dams break
creating a tidal wave. This is flat fen-country As Haight
neatly puts it: 'the water could not have risen above the
hedgerows of Dorlcote if the whole twenty-five-inch rain-
fall of Lincolnshire had dropped there in one night'.[5]

As unconvincing as the flash-flood-in-the-fens is the
business about the 'huge fragments' of 'wooden
machinery'. The adjective 'wooden' was an afterthought
added by George Eliot to the second edition of *The Mill on
the Floss*, when it occurred to her that metal machinery
does not float. But 'wooden machinery' is an oxymoron
that strains the imagination. It certainly strained the artist's imagination (see the details on the 'huge fragment'
above). The notion that in 1839, with Britain well into the

'It is coming, Maggie!' Tom said, in a deep hoarse voice, loosing the oars, and clasping her

Industrial Revolution, in a go-ahead place like St Ogg's (substantially Coventry), dockside factories would be using wooden cog wheels six feet in diameter beggars belief.

Most bewildering, as Haight points out, is the depiction of these large masses of wood 'rushing' at a much faster speed than Tom and Maggie's wooden boat, when both are in the same line of the current. These 'fragments' will, like icebergs, have most of their bulk beneath the water, and— dragging on the bottom—will be moving much slower than the shallow-draft rowing-boat. Unless their vessel is snagged on something the Tullivers are in no danger whatsoever. But in contravention of the laws of hydrodynamics, the 'huge mass hurries on' to its 'hideous triumph' and crushes Tom and Maggie's boat. If the illustrator is to be credited, brother and sister stand up to embrace for the last time. At this point, one supposes, it hardly matters if they capsize.

George Eliot was addicted to tremendous scenes of women in little boats. But although the pictorial, poetic, and dramatic aspects of women drifting attracted Eliot, the practical business of navigating boats was clearly unknown territory. Nor, although she undertook laborious research for her novels, did she make any investigation into boating matters. An hour with the oars would have prevented much of the implausibility in 'The Last Conflict'. George Eliot compares poorly in this respect (though in few others) with Wilkie Collins, who loved to mess about in boats and is very accurate about boating details.

The Oxford World's Classics *The Mill on the Floss* is edited by Gordon S. Haight with an introduction by Dinah Birch.

━━━

How good a swimmer is Magwitch?

━━━

Great Expectations has the most vivid of all Dickensian openings, designed to burst explosively on the first page of *All the Year Round*, where it was initially serialized. Pip mournfully regards the graves of his parents and five little brothers, 'who gave up trying to get a living exceedingly early in that universal struggle'.[1] The narrative halts for a paragraph to depict the dreary marsh landscape on a late winter afternoon. It is all too much for the 7-year-old orphan, who begins to cry:

> 'Hold your noise!' cried a terrible voice, as a man started up from among the graves at the side of the church porch. 'Keep still, you little devil, or I'll cut your throat!'
>
> A fearful man, all in coarse grey, with a great iron on his leg. A man with no hat, and with broken shoes, and with an old rag tied round his head. A man who had been soaked in water, and smothered in mud, and lamed by stones, and cut by flints, and stung by nettles, and torn by briars; who limped, and shivered, and glared and growled; and whose teeth chattered in his head as he seized me by the chin.
>
> 'O! Don't cut my throat, sir,' I pleaded in terror. 'Pray don't do it, sir.' (p. 4)

It is not until much later in the novel (II.3), and sixteen years later in Pip's life, that we learn the details of how Abel Magwitch, Pip's 'fearful man', escaped from the hulks and came to be hiding behind the gravestone (of Pip's father, as illustrators have felicitously assumed). He tells Pip and Herbert about his criminal intrigues with the villainous Compeyson, their conspiracy to put stolen banknotes into circulation, the grossly discrepant sentences he and his accomplice received, Compeyson's infuriating taunt after the trial. The two men are consigned to the 'hulks' to await transportation:

> I had said to Compeyson that I'd smash that face of his, and I swore Lord smash mine! to do it. We was in the same prison-ship, but I couldn't get at him for long, though I tried. At last I come behind him and hit him on the cheek to turn him round and get a smashing one at him, when I was seen and seized. The black-hole of that ship warn't a strong one, to a judge of black-holes that could swim and dive. I escaped to the shore and I was a hiding among the graves there, envying them as was in 'em and all over, when I first see my boy! (pp. 347–8)

The prison ships, or 'hulks', lie—as Mrs Joe tells Pip (with the unkind prediction that he will one day know them from the inside)—across the marshes. Decommissioned naval vessels, crudely converted, they lay in the Medway estuary (although Dickens seems in *Great Expectations* to put them at the mouth of the Thames). The hulks held prisoners before passage could be found for them to Australia. It might be a long wait—transportation was an expensive business. For security's sake the hulks were moored some way from shore in deep water—floating Alcatrazes. They fell into disuse as transportation fell out of favour, and the last of the hulks was taken out of service in 1858, a couple of years before *Great Expectations*.

By Dickens's own private reckoning, Magwitch is around 45 years old when he leaps on Pip in the graveyard. For a middle-aged man and a heavy smoker, he is in truly excellent physical shape. Diving into the current-ridden Thames estuary in winter and swimming several hundred yards to the shore fully clothed is no mean athletic feat. Doing it weighed down with a 'great iron' suggests superhuman powers. Nor, it would seem, is Magwitch unique.

On his way to the graveyard with the required 'wittles' and file, Pip meets Compeyson, who has also gone overboard from the hulk; 'He was dressed in coarse grey, too, and had a great iron on his leg.' Like Magwitch, Compeyson must be a remarkable swimmer.

When Dickens repeatedly talks of a 'great iron', he intends us to visualize a large, heavy, metal fetter, which serves the same hobbling purpose as the ball and chain beloved by cartoonists. Even Mark Spitz in his heyday would not be able to swim the distance from the hulk to the shore thus burdened down. Magwitch would never break surface from his dive. This nonsense came about, I imagine, because for Victorians of Dickens's generation 'swimming' (as opposed to 'bathing') was an unusual practice. Magwitch's swim to shore was generally unremarked on because Dickens's readers shared his vagueness about what human limits are in the water. At best Victorians could float, dog-paddle, or thrash about a bit. A tonic 'dip' at the seaside or in the Serpentine would be the extent of their knowledge. Most of the readers of *All the Year Round* were, one guesses, non-swimmers.

As it happened, this widespread ignorance was being corrected, especially among the younger generation of Victorians. In the 1850s Muscular Christianity (with its strong vein of latent homosexuality) was popularizing manly sports like boxing and swimming, which required young men to display their naked bodies to each other. The novelist Charles Kingsley was the main propagandist for the muscular cult, and *The Water Babies* (1863) was, among other things, a long advertisement for the manifold joys of water sport.

In the period between the 1850s and Captain Matthew Webb's swimming the English Channel in August 1875 (the period of what has been called the 'Victorian sports mania'), swimming became a popular national exercise in which, for many decades, Britain led the world. In the early 1870s there were two important developments. In 1873 the 'trudgen' or 'crawl' stroke was developed, allowing much higher speeds in the water (if you had asked Dickens what 'stroke' Magwitch used in his magnificent swim, he would, I suspect, have been puzzled how to answer). Also in the 1870s, the newly founded Amateur Swimming Association began establishing a set of 'world records'. They make comical reading. In 1878, for instance, the record for the free-style 100 yards stood at 76 and three-quarter seconds.

A younger novelist like Wilkie Collins would not have made the error that Dickens makes in *Great Expectations*. Nor, as a keen amateur yachtsman, would Collins make the primitive errors about boating that George Eliot makes at the end of *The Mill on the Floss* (see the previous chapter). For older novelists, like Dickens and Eliot, water was something you drown in (like Quilp, Headstone, Riderhood, the Tullivers) or get shipwrecked on.[2] There are many reasons, most of them inarticulate, why Gwendolen, in *Daniel Deronda*, lets Grandcourt drown after she perceives, with surprise, that he can't swim. But even if Gwendolen had wanted to save her husband, it is not certain that she could have done so. It is suggested in the narrative that she could have thrown him a rope (this assumes there was one to hand, and that Gwendolen had the physical strength to fling it far enough and accurately enough). What is clear is that Gwendolen could not do what a young woman of today might do: tear off her clothes, dive in, reach him with a few powerful strokes, turn him on his back, incapacitate him if necessary with a firm blow to the jaw, and bring him back to the yacht with powerful frog-kicks.

For these writers of an earlier generation, the water was not the playground or gymnasium it later became. It is what Conrad called it, 'the destructive element'. Wilkie Collins's *Armadale* is the first novel in English, I think, to be almost entirely based on yachting as a sport; it was written in the first flush of Collins's acquiring his own pleasure-yacht. Similarly R. M. Ballantyne's *The Coral Island* is the first popular novel aggressively to promote swimming as an activity for boys—something 'manly', but also immensely pleasurable (it was to be many decades before girls, or women, would be encouraged to swim rather than 'bathe').

Ballantyne everywhere celebrates the joys of the plunge. Swimming in *The Coral Island* is not merely functional as it was in the novel's prototype, *Robinson Crusoe*. Robinson is, as he tells us, a 'good swimmer' (for practical reasons, sailors saw it as a necessary skill, like knot-tying).[3] He swims from the wreck to the shore of his desert island. Later he swims back to and around the stranded vessel. But once he is established on his island, with his little economy in good order, Robinson hunts for pleasure but never swims for pleasure. The idea would doubtless have struck him as grotesque.

It is different with Ballantyne's castaways. Ralph, as he modestly tells us, is 'really a good swimmer and diver too'. But he cannot 'equal Jack, who was superior to any Englishman I ever saw'. Peterkin, on the other hand, 'could only swim a little, and could not dive at all'. Peterkin is thus cut off from the wonderful underwater world open to the two other boys as, naked (although illustrations in later editions invariably show them decently covered), they dive down to the reef:

As I have before stated, the water within the reef was as calm as a pond; and, as there was no wind, it was quite clear from the surface to the bottom, so that we could see down easily even at a depth of twenty or thirty yards. When Jack and I dived into shallower water, we expected to have found sand and stones, instead of which we found ourselves in what appeared really to be an enchanted garden. The whole of the bottom of the lagoon, as we called the calm water within the reef, was covered with coral of every shape, size, and hue. Some portions were formed like large mushrooms, others appeared like the brain of a man, having stalks or necks attached to them; but the most common kind was a species of branching coral, and some portions were of a lovely pale pink colour, others were pure white. Among this there grew large quantities of seaweed of the richest hues imaginable, and of the most graceful forms; while innumerable fishes—blue, red, yellow, green, and striped—sported in and out amongst the flower-beds of the submarine garden, and did not appear to be at all afraid of our approaching them.

On darting to the surface for breath, after our first dive, Jack and I rose close to each other.

'Did you ever in your life, Ralph, see anything so lovely?' said Jack, as he flung the spray from his hair.

'Never,' I replied. 'It appears to me like fairy realms. I can scarcely believe we are not dreaming.' (pp. 35–6)

Maybe they were. Unless they were wearing goggles, or were in diving-suits, none of this submarine detail would be clearly visible. What Ralph and Jack would 'see' underwater is not a 'fairy realm' in all its magic detail but a polychromatic blur with a few vague shapes. And the salt content of the water would irritate their eyes horribly. This unnatural underwater clarity is a main feature of the subsequent 'Diamond Cave' scenes, which are central to the plot.

Ballantyne was in most respects a fetishist about accuracy. As J. S. Bratton points out, in the interest of getting the details of his novels just right 'he visited lighthouses, rode on fire engines, and tried out diving suits on the bottom of the Thames'. He must, presumably, at some point have opened his eyes underwater. What then went wrong in *The Coral Island*? If not an error on the same scale as Ballantyne's famous unhusked coconuts,[4] the translucent

Pacific water is clearly a high-order inaccuracy. The point, surely, is that whereas in *Great Expectations* Dickens was writing for readers of his own generation (he was in his late forties) entirely indifferent to 'swimming as sport', Ballantyne was writing for much younger readers enthusiastic about swimming but still not very knowledgeable—readers, that is, who would assume that swimming in the lucid Pacific might be entirely different from what they had experienced in the chilly and opaque waters of Margate.

Within fifty years swimming would be a universally familiar recreation. One still, however, encounters what one might call the 'Magwitch Great Iron' paradox in popular narrative—that is, stories which trade on audience ignorance about 'extreme' physical activities. Although most men and women in the Western world will have swum, relatively few have scaled mountains. In the film *Cliffhanger*, Sylvester Stallone is shown catching with one hand the wrist of a falling companion as she hurtles down. This is, I would guess, physically impossible (even with biceps as well developed as Stallone's). Either the grasp would slip, or the climbers' shoulders would be wrenched from their sockets,

Ice tobogganing is another thrilling sport which only an élite of sportsmen practise, although most of us have seen it on TV. In the James Bond thriller *On Her Majesty's Secret Service* a villain dies horribly when he pitches on to a toboggan run and slides to the bottom—by which time he is hamburger. It was later pointed out to Ian Fleming that a human body on a toboggan run would not slither more than three yards before stopping.

As with mountaineering and tobogganing, few members of a film audience have first-hand experience of sky-diving. In a spectacular stunt in *Eraser*, Arnold Schwarzenegger overtakes as he drops from a plane the parachute which was thrown out many seconds earlier. Is this not against the laws of physics? Objects, however heavy, fall at the same rate. Although he can alter his aerodynamic configuration to go faster (by adopting a forward dive position and lessening air resistance), Arnold could never streamline himself into a narrower mass than the parachute—and he would have to spend precious seconds adjusting for the lateral distance created by the time interval between the pack's being dropped and his jumping from the plane. Schwarzenegger would make a sizeable crater in the ground many seconds after the parachute bounced to rest on its surface, some half-a-mile away. Victorian authors, like Dickens, are as free to make use of these pockets of audience ignorance as modern film-makers. But they may well look as odd to later generations as our breath-taking stunts will, a hundred years hence.

The Oxford World's Classics *Great Expectations* is edited by Margaret Cardwell with an introduction by Kate Flint. *The Coral Island* is edited by J. S. Bratton.

═══

What, precisely, does Miss Gwilt's purple flask contain?

═══

Wilkie Collins wrote *Armadale* under an unusual set of pressures. As the follow-up to his all-conquering *The Woman in White*, he had been offered a huge sum by the publisher George Smith for the new novel—£5,000. 'Nobody but Dickens has made as much', he jubilantly told his mother. Smith wanted *Armadale* for serialization in *his* all-conquering *Cornhill Magazine*. Collins would have to be on his mettle to keep company with such works as Trollope's *Framley Parsonage* and George Eliot's *Romola*.

Unfortunately, Collins—whose health was chronically poor and not helped by his addiction to narcotics—suffered a health collapse as he prepared to embark on his new novel. Originally scheduled to start serialization in January 1863, *Armadale* was postponed for almost two years, the first instalment not appearing in *Cornhill* until November 1864. And even when he was in a position to start composition (around June 1864), Collins was not as well prepared as he would have liked to be for such a challenge.

For novelists like Collins and his friend Charles Reade—rising stars of the 1860s—preparation was a crucial phase of work. They wrote what were often called 'matter-of-fact romances'. That is to say, their fiction was underpinned by a more solid foundation of authenticity than a 'domestic' novelist like Trollope or an out-and-out 'sensationalist' like Elizabeth Braddon. Reade, for instance, created mountainous archives in preparation for his work, with newspaper clippings and other research materials. His fiction is constipated with the factual ingredients he stuffed into it. Collins, although not as fetishistic as Reade, took professional pride in the factual accuracy of his fiction. In his 'Appendix' to *Armadale*, for instance, he tells us that: 'Wherever the story touches questions connected with Law, Medicine, or Chemistry, it has been submitted, before publication, to the experience of professional men.' He was careful about such things.

As Collins came up to the last instalments of *Armadale*, he was working against the calendar. The novel was serialized between November 1864 and June 1866, and for the latter sections Collins was evidently running only a month or two ahead of *Cornhill*'s printers (who, as George Smith told the author, were enjoying *Armadale* immensely). It would seem that, in autumn 1865, Collins had not worked out in his mind how to wrap up his fiendishly complex plot—with the murderous, bigamous, *femme fatale* Lydia Gwilt at its centre. Something spectacular was needed.[1]

On 30 November 1865 there appeared in *The Times* a report which must have seemed to Collins a gift from the gods:

POISONOUS GAS—At the Liverpool Coroner's Court yesterday an inquiry was held touching the deaths of three men who were suffocated within a few days of each other while acting as shipkeepers on board the ship *Armadale* lying in the Huskisson Dock. Dr Trench, medical officer of health, and Mrs Ayrton gave evidence to the effect that death had been caused by inhalation of carbonic acid gas, which, in consequence of the prevailing high winds, had been forced back into the deckhouse where the men slept, and where they had kindled fires. The jury returned a verdict: 'That death resulted from suffocation caused by defective ventilation.'

The coincidence of the ship being called *Armadale* was

amazing—more than amazing, it was ominous. For someone like Wilkie Collins, with his belief in 'fate' (a main
theme in *Armadale*), it must have seemed like a clear sign
from his tutelary spirit: 'this is how to end your novel'.
Moreover, the story was in *The Times*—the nation's
'newspaper of record'. What better provenance for a
'matter of fact' romancer looking for a neat way to tie up
the threads of his novel in progress?

Collins duly wove *The Times'* report into the climactic
section of *Armadale*, entitled 'The Purple Flask'. The
denouement is complex in the extreme. Allan Armadale
has inconveniently returned from a watery grave, foiling
Lydia's bigamous plans *vis-à-vis* Ozias. She conspires with
the villainous Dr Le Doux (alias Downward), now the
proprietor of a sanatorium for nerve-racked women in
Hampstead. Between them they intend to do away with
Allan. To this end the guileless young man is lured to the
Sanatorium, and tricked into spending the night there.

Meanwhile Le Doux (careful always to give himself
deniability should the case come to the notice of the
police) hints to Lydia how she may perform the awful deed.
While showing some prospective clients round his establishment, the doctor makes sure that Miss Gwilt is thoroughly familiarized with the workings of the ingenious
'fumigation' device which he has devised for his patients.
Ostensibly he is showing this Victorian air-conditioning
system off to his visitors; in reality he is instructing Lydia
as to how it may be misused:

Epidemic disease, in spite of all my precautions, may enter this
Sanatorium, and may render the purifying of the sick-room
necessary. Or the patient's case may be complicated by other than
nervous malady—say, for instance, asthmatic difficulty of breath-
ing. In one case, fumigation is necessary: in the other, additional
oxygen in the air will give relief. The epidemic nervous patient
says, 'I won't be smoked under my own nose!' The asthmatic

nervous patient gasps with terror at the idea of a chemical explosion in his room. I noiselessly fumigate one of them; I noiselessly oxygenize the other, by means of a simple Apparatus fixed outside in the corner here. It is protected by this wooden casing; it is locked with my own key; and it communicates by means of a tube with the interior of the room. Look at it! (pp. 773–4)

Miss Gwilt, together with the assembled visitors, duly 'looks at it'. The fumigation and oxygenation apparatus comprises a large stone jar with a glass funnel and a pipe leading into the room. There is no pumping apparatus, the gas, vapour, or fumes merely siphon or drift into the adjoining room—according to whether they are heavier or lighter than air. The occupant, as Le Doux points out, will be unaware of what is going on.

A little later Le Doux describes to Lydia the chemical reactions which will produce what we assume to be deadly carbonic gas. An unnamed fluid in a flask (evidently sulphuric acid) is poured on to a 'common mineral substance' (evidently limestone) in six small measured doses, producing a quantity of gaseous bubbles. 'Collect the gas in those bubbles', Le Doux tells Lydia, 'and convey it into a closed chamber—and let Samson himself be in that chamber, [the gas] will kill him in half an hour.' Not only that, the cause of death will appear to any medical examiner or coroner to be wholly natural—'apoplexy or congestion of the lungs'. The perfect murder, in other words.

This, then, is how the deed will be done. Le Doux early in the evening places quantities of limestone (as we assume) in the stone jar connected to Room Number Four. Alongside the jar he places a small 'purple flask', containing acid (as we again assume) with six levels marked on the outside. It is arranged that Lydia shall have a key to the room's fumigation apparatus. Allan arrives at the Sanatorium and is assigned to number four. But, unexpectedly, he is accompanied by Ozias who—anticipating some villainy—switches bedrooms with his friend. At a quarter past one in the morning, Lydia begins her deadly work, unaware of the room-change. After she has poured four doses from her lethal purple flask into the stone jar, at the prescribed five-minute intervals, she discovers to her horror that she has almost asphyxiated the man she loves—it is Ozias, not Allan, in Room Number Four. She drags Ozias out unconscious (but still living), pours in the sixth and final dose from her purple flask, kisses the recumbent Ozias, then enters the chamber of death herself:

'Good-by!' she said softly.
The door of the room opened—and closed on her. There was an interval of silence.
Then, a sound came dull and sudden, like the sound of a fall.
Then, there was silence again. (p. 807)

It is tremendously effective, but it is, I suspect, scientific nonsense. And, as he wrote this last scene, Collins must have become increasingly nervous about its authenticity. It seems clear that he was misled by a scientific error in *The Times'* report. It is evident that the men on the *Armadale* were suffocated by the massive build-up of carbon monoxide from a heating fire in their bunk-room on board the vessel, forced back by wind pressure on the outside vents. (This is still a hazard with such things as charcoal-fired indoor barbecues.) 'Carbonic acid gas' seems to have got into the report by mistake. Dissolving small amounts of limestone with tiny measures of acid (which is what Collins has in mind with Miss Gwilt's purple flask and the stone jar) would produce negligible amounts of carbon dioxide. In very confined chambers (something the size of a goldfish bowl), this could have a narcotic or even a fatal effect—but not diffused in an area as large as a bedroom. A scientist tells me that it would be like trying to poison someone with the emissions from a fizzing Coca Cola can.

Lydia would need gallons of acid and rock-sized chunks of limestone, many hours of chemical reaction time, and a sophisticated powered pumping mechanism to move the resultant gas into a room. With the toxic apparatus at her disposal, she might conceivably kill a mouse in a glass jar.

In a letter Collins admitted to having encountered problems in 'reconciling certain facts with the incidents in the last chapter'. He handled the problem in a way which must have been deeply unsatisfactory to his artistic conscience. In the text of *Armadale* he never specifies what is in the 'purple flask', nor on what substance it is to react in the stone jar. He knew that if he did so ('there is sulphuric acid in the flask, limestone in the jar') he would invite the kind of deadly 'disproof' of his veracity that *The Times* had brought to bear on *The Woman in White*. That episode was deeply embarrassing to him.[2] Ironically, it was the same paper which had got him into the pickle he was now in. With more time, he could doubtless have got it right—although it is not easy to see how you could poison someone with Le Doux's primitive fumigation apparatus. In the circumstances the only resource open to Collins was a smoke-screen of lurid Gothic horror—the kind of Radcliffian rhetoric which, as a 'matter of fact' novelist, he despised. 'What is inside Lydia's purple flask?' Something too terrible to describe, words fail me—don't ask, just shudder.

The Oxford World's Classics *Armadale* is edited by Catherine Peters.

===

Lemon or ladle?

===

Readers of my generation often bemoan the passing of the 'old' World's Classics. They can still be found (although they are becoming increasingly expensive) in second-hand bookshops. Pocket-book sized, with hard covers (stamped prominently with the Oxford University crest and motto) they were beautiful things. Launched in 1906, they marked OUP's entry into the world of general trade publishing.[1] The World's Classics came into their own in the 1920s and ran to 500 titles by the end of the decade.

If the old World's Classics had any introductions at all (most didn't) they were short belletristic effusions by writers such as Virginia Woolf or G. K. Chesterton. Latterly, in the 1960s, the series attempted to rejuvenate itself with bumper-value 'double volumes' and pictorial dust jackets by Lynton Lamb which are, in my opinion, the best modern illustrations of the Victorian novel we have.[2] They were books of an earlier, less transatlantic, less anxious literary culture. And, with a span of sixty years, they lasted longer than most reprint series of their kind.

Nostalgia aside, there is much to be said in favour of the new (i.e. post-1980), soft-cover World's Classics. They are cheaper. The texts are better. The typography is sharper. Most valuably, unlike their predecessors, the new World's Classics have an *apparatus criticus*—introductions, chronologies, textual notes, explanatory notes, select bibliographies, and often appendices of relevant material.

Even in what is usually the most technical section of the apparatus, inquisitive readers can usually find thought-provoking material. In the 'Note on the Text' to *Felix Holt*, for instance, the editor, Fred C. Thomson, records: 'One oversight by George Eliot, which persists in the manuscript and all editions, has been emended by the editor: in chapter 25 (p. 208), Christian is said to have dropped a "punch-ladle", whereas in chapter 7 (p. 85) it was "a lemon".'[3]

Apparently minor, this emendation leads to what I think is an illuminating puzzle. The scene in question is striking and well worth Thomson's running repair—if that repair is really needed. The background is simple enough—although it gets fiendishly complicated later on. When Philip Debarry, heir-apparent to his father's baronetcy, returns to Treby Manor from Oxford he brings with him a 'factotum', Maurice Christian. The omnicompetent Christian is a figure of mystery. He is 50, grey-haired, and distinguished-looking.

Christian serves as Mr Debarry's 'man'—what in modern parlance we would call a 'personal assistant'. He is very much what the Victorians thought of as an 'upper servant'—that is, one who has frequent intercourse with the gentlefolk of the household and partakes of many of their privileges and perquisites. Christian's fellow servants are awed by the rumour that he was once a gentleman himself and fought a duel. He lords it over them. He is also haughty to the point of insolence with his betters, abasing himself only to Philip Debarry (who treats Christian with more deference than he would an equal, we are told). Christian speaks French, takes opium for an unspecified bodily weakness, and has a 'past' that no one knows about.

We are introduced to the mysterious Mr Christian at length in volume I, chapter 7. As the genteel company upstairs relaxes after dinner, the scene shifts to belowstairs, to the even more convivial steward's room:

where Mr Scales, house-steward and head-butler, a man most solicitous about his boots, wristbands, the roll of his whiskers, and other attributes of a gentleman, distributed cigars, cognac, and whisky, to various colleagues and guests who were discussing, with that freedom of conjecture which is one of our inalienable privileges as Britons, the probable amount of Harold Transome's fortune . . . (p. 83)

Present are Scales, Mr Crowder ('an old respectable tenant'), the head-gardener Brent, and the supercilious Christian. A small altercation breaks out among the company when Christian corrects Crowder's French. As it happens, things French (for reasons we will discover later) make Christian uneasy. Scales, an impulsive and foolish man, is in danger of losing his temper. He resents Christian's 'airs', feeling diminished by his presence. Christian moves to lower the temperature: 'Don't be waspish, man', he tells Scales. 'I'll ring the bell for lemons, and make some punch. That's the thing for putting people up to the unknown tongues.' He gets up and slaps Scales's shoulder, with false *bonhomie*, as he walks over to the bell-pull.

Already there are features of this scene which would make any Victorian householder shudder. The sedulous aping of their betters (to the absurd point of ringing for their own servants!) could be thought amusing. Less amusing is the fact that these servants are drinking heavily in their place of work. This is worrying. Moreover, they are not drinking the servant's traditional porter or ale, but 'punch'. The point has already been made, in the description of Treby in chapter 3, that punch is a tipple for the gentry. 'In no country town of the same small size as Treby', we are informed, 'was there a larger proportion of families who had handsome sets of china without handles, hereditary punch-bowls, and large silver ladles with a Queen Anne's guinea in the centre.' Here, it would seem, even the servant's hall has its hereditary punch bowl and large silver ladle.

It would also be noted by a Victorian that lemons were not easily come by in Britain. Those that Christian calls for must have come from the Treby conservatory, warmed laboriously with 'a nether apparatus of hot-water pipes' (p. 43). They would be a luxury, to be used sparingly by the master of the house himself. They would be a fantastic luxury for the servants—lemons, forsooth! Whatever next? Caviare? *En passant*, the Victorian would feel (as in 1866, with the second great 'Bill' on the horizon, George Eliot felt) that 'reform' was getting out of hand; the aristocracy, the ruling classes, have lost their grip. Important social distinctions are blurring.

Punch, as the nineteenth century knew it, was a concoction of wine or spirits, hot water or milk, sugar, and lemons. It was mixed in a bowl, and served piping hot. Best drunk fresh, punch required a series of ritual operations: getting the utensils (heat-resistant bowl, ladle, and special cup-shaped punch glasses), preparing the hot water, fetching the basic alcoholic ingredients, and mixing them carefully. Eliot does not describe the making of the punch in Scales's room and we have to picture it happening in the background while the conversation about how rich or poor the Transomes are continues in its desultory way.

One thing leads to another, and Crowder—apropos of the law-suits which have so impoverished the family at Transome Court—recalls:

'There was the last suit of all made the most noise, as I understand . . . but it wasn't tried hereabout. They said there was a deal O' false swearing. Some young man pretended to be the true heir—let me see—I can't just remember the names—he'd got two. *He* swore he was one man, and *they* swore he was another. However, Lawyer Jermyn won it—they say he'd win a game against the

Old One himself—and the young fellow turned out to be a scamp.
Stop a bit—his name was Scaddon—Henry Scaddon.'

Mr Christian here let a lemon slip from his hand into the
punch-bowl with a plash which sent some of the nectar in to the
company's faces.

'Hallo! what a bungler I am!' he said. (p. 85)

The little accident is vivid (we can almost feel the hot
liquor scalding our cheeks). The vividness is an effective
device for 'fixing' the episode, like a snapshot, in the
reader's memory. It is, of course, Eliot's intention that we
should recall it a hundred matter-packed pages later, in
chapter 21, when Jermyn drops his bombshell on Christian: 'A—your name—a—is Henry Scaddon.' It's fair to
say that very few first readers of *Felix Holt* will have
already guessed that Maurice Christian is Henry Scaddon
(nor, at this point in the narrative, will they guess the
further twist to come). It is equally fair to say that most
readers will vividly recollect the episode of the splashing
punch, as if it were the page before. 'That's why he was so
clumsy,' we think, as the detail slides pleasingly into place.

There are, however, some things not quite right with the
punch-making scene, closely examined. For one thing, the
timing isn't right. We are in continuous real time—that is
to say there are no breaks in the narrative—and only a
page-worth (mid-84 to mid-85 in the World's Classics edition) passes, all of it dialogue, between Christian getting
up to ring the bell and subsequently dropping the lemon in
the punch. If one speaks the dialogue at the speed it would
have been spoken, the time elapsed is a bare four minutes.
This is insufficient time for the lemons to have arrived.
The servant's servant would come in, having been
summoned by the bell; he would be told to go and fetch
the fruit. It would be some way away—perhaps still in the
conservatory, perhaps in a cold store. Certainly such precious objects would not be left around in the kitchen for

anyone to help themselves to and keys would have to be used.

It would be several minutes (probably more than four) before the servant could make the return trip with the fruit. Meanwhile, the punch-making apparatus has to be assembled, the bottles uncorked, measured, poured out and so on. Water needs to be heated (although possibly there is a kettle steaming on the hob). Clearly Christian is presiding over all this complicated procedure himself (he is described, a couple of pages on, 'ladling out the punch'). Nor, if one is petty-minded enough to think about it, would a lemon (or half a lemon, if Christian is so far forward as to be squeezing the juice out) make a considerable enough 'plash' to spatter the faces of the assembled company—unless they had their noses virtually in the bowl. It's a fine scene, but nigglingly off centre in a few important details.

The reader remembers the episode, and so does George Eliot. She refers directly to it again at the end of the second volume (p. 208). Christian has just had his interview with Rufus Lyon, who mistakenly thinks he has discovered an appalling secret about Esther's parentage. What is going on is by no means clear to Christian, and he is increasingly anxious. He is also keen to provide for his retirement with some judicious blackmail. Eliot writes:

He held various ends of threads, but there was danger in pulling at them too impatiently. He had not forgotten the surprise which had made him drop the punch-ladle [the World's Classics edition has 'lemon'], when Mr Crowder, talking in the steward's room had said that a scamp named Henry Scaddon had been concerned in a lawsuit about the Transome estate. (p. 208)

'Punch-ladle' is clearly a mistake, but why did Eliot make it? Because, I surmise, her artist's mind was trying, retroactively, to get the lemon-in-the-punch business right.

There was a timing readjustment. In Eliot's subconscious rewriting of the scene the splash was pushed further along the mixing process, from the stage when lemons are appropriate to the later point at which Christian is stirring and ladling out the drink.

This left the rather more serious avoirdupois problem. Something heavier than half-a-lemon (which would make little more than a feeble plop) was needed to drop into the steaming liquid so that it might splash several feet on to the expectant faces. Why not one of those massive silver ladles, described so graphically in chapter 3? If this is what happened, Eliot's subconscious mind (what elsewhere she called the 'not self' that took over in her most inspired passages of writing) solved the problems rather neatly. Unfortunately, it neglected to inform its conscious colleague, and the revision, made so effectively in the mind, was not made on the page.

Clearly, no entirely satisfactory solution can be found now without gross interference in the text of *Felix Holt*. But, as a record of George Eliot's unrealized intention, I would rather like the anomalous punch-ladle to remain as a mark of her artistic, unsleeping, conscience.

The Oxford World's Classics *Felix Holt, the Radical* is edited by Fred C. Thomson.

Anthony Trollope · *Ralph the Heir*

Why 'Captain' Newton?

The names in *Ralph the Heir* are very confusing—no less
than four 'Ralph Newtons' figure in the plot, for instance.
But the romantic story at the novel's centre is straight-
forward enough. Ralph Newton ('the heir') is parentless
and has been looked after by the lawyer Sir Thomas
Underwood in the office of guardian. Underwood—a
superannuated widower—has two daughters. Patience,
the elder, is her father's housekeeper and is 'certainly not
pretty'. The younger, Clarissa, is 'a beauty' and the family
pet. Underwood also has another ward living in his Fulham villa, Mary Bonner, a surpassingly beautiful young
orphan from the West Indies. Ralph opens proceedings by
lightly proposing marriage to Clarissa ('Dear, dear
Clary,—you know I love you') during a summer's day loun-
ging by the Thames, dressed fetchingly in his straw hat
and Jersey shirt. She tacitly accepts his offer. Clarissa,
meanwhile, is loved faithfully by Ralph's younger brother,
Gregory, a dutiful clergyman. Gregory glumly knows that
his suit has no hope against that of his dashing brother.
Ralph (who disdains work) subsequently attempts to stave
off his increasingly pressing creditors by borrowing from
his breeches-maker, Neefit, and is persuaded by the
socially aspirant tradesman to propose to his jolly young
daughter, Polly. Polly Neefit—although an eminently
sensible girl (more so than her besotted father)—is flattered sufficiently by Ralph's addresses to turn down the
son of a bootmaker, Onty Moggs. Onty knows that he cannot compete with a West End swell, even if that swell is a

'butterfly' and he, Onty, an honest working man. Without clearly cancelling either of these earlier proposals, Ralph goes on to propose marriage to yet a third young woman, Mary Bonner, who is beloved by another Ralph Newton (an illegitimate cousin). Bastard Ralph, who is no heir, feels that he cannot stand in the way of legitimate Ralph. Finally, at the end of an eventfully romantic year, Ralph proposes to a fourth young lady, Gus Eardham, for whom in truth he does not much care. Thus, the great question posed by the novel is 'who will Ralph the heir marry?'

It is, to be honest, not a very exciting question. Looking back on *Ralph the Heir* in his autobiography, Trollope marked it down as one of his failures, noting bleakly that 'a novelist after fifty should not write love stories' (he was 54 when he wrote *Ralph the Heir*). The great weakness in the love plot of the novel, as Trollope perceived, was that Ralph the Heir is so chronically and incurably 'weak'. Moral weakness is demonstrated by his reckless proposals of marriage to every attractive woman who crosses his path and—more significantly—his disinclination to work, or do anything useful. He is a drone, and there is no lower order of life in the Trollopian universe than idlers.

Although *Ralph the Heir* was not one of Trollope's great successes, everyone liked the vulgar breeches-maker, Neefit (it was Neefit's character that was exploited in the dramatic adaptation of the novel).[1] Trollope catches the tradesman's breezy cockney dialect with great skill. There is, however, an oddity in the breeches-maker's patronizing mode of address to Ralph—the young man whom he fondly thinks he has 'bought' as Polly's husband. On being told, for instance, that Ralph is having difficulty with a bill owing to Moggs, the bootmaker, Neefit

told Ralph to come to him when Moggs's 'bit of stiff' came round. Moggs's 'bit of stiff' did come round, and 'the Captain' did as he had been desired to do. Neefit wrote out the cheque without

saying a word about his daughter. 'Do you just run across to
Argyle Street, Captain,' said the breeches-maker, 'and get the
stuff in notes'. For Mr Neefit's bankers held an establishment in
Argyle Street. 'There ain't no need, you know, to let on, Captain,
is there?' said the breeches-maker. (p. 225)

Why does Neefit repeatedly apostrophize Ralph as 'Captain'? If readers register it as something odd, they probably assume it is a Victorian cockneyism along the lines of
'Squire' ('Right you are, Squire'), 'moosh' ('Watch it,
moosh'), 'mate' ('don't you worry your head about it, mate')
or cock ('Wotcher, cock'). But, unlike these others, 'Captain' has not survived in popular usage.

This explanation is plausible but wrong. 'Captain' is not
a cockneyism. Its origin can be found in cancellations in
the manuscript of *Ralph the Heir*. Up until chapter 8, the
manuscript reveals, Ralph was a captain in the Cold-
stream Guards. Trollope subsequently changed the early
part of his novel extensively so as to write out this detail,
rendering Ralph nothing more than an unemployed heir-
expectant. Neefit's 'Captain' survives as an enigmatic
hangover from this earlier conception of the novel. Either
it crept in as a lapse of memory, or Trollope allowed it to
stand as a private joke.

The protrusion of 'Captain Newton' into the revised
text is an interesting but not very significant detail—like
those earlier designs that X-ray photography sometimes
finds under the surface of old master paintings. But why,
one may go on to ask, did Trollope make the change? It
was not his habit to alter what was written and there are
other examples of his going to some lengths not to rewrite,
even where it might be advisable.[2]

There are, I think, two answers to the puzzle 'why did
Trollope demobilize Captain Newton?' The first of these is
that at some point, well into his novel, the novelist remembered, or someone pointed out to him, an awkward article

in Queen's Regulations. Junior officers in the British army require their commanding officer's permission to marry or they are obliged to resign their commission. A well-disposed colonel in the Household Brigade might permit Captain Newton to marry Miss Underwood, Miss Bonner, or Miss Eardham (although only one at a time). He would never permit one of his junior officers to marry the daughter of the regiment's supplier of breeches. Captain Newton would not merely be required to resign his commission, he would be hooted out of the service, never to lift his head again in the company of officers and gentlemen.

There was another objection to Ralph's being a serving officer in a crack regiment. *Ralph the Heir* was written in spring and summer 1869—the same period that the novel's action is set. This was the time of Prussian expansionism, culminating in the overrunning of France in 1870. It was also a period of general alarm in Britain about the readiness and competence of the country's armed forces—particularly its soldiers. It was this mood of alarm which set the scene for Colonel Chesney's phenomenally successful invasion fantasy, *The Battle of Dorking* (1871), in which the Prussians are shown doing to London what they have just done to Paris. *Ralph the Heir* completed its serial run and the three-volume edition was published in June 1871, when British war panic was at its height. Trollope did not want one of his 'domestic' novels to get embroiled in all this (what did he, Anthony Trollope, know about the army?), so he demobilized Captain Ralph Newton. It was a prudent move, but it fatally weakened the 'hero' of the novel by making him, like Othello, a man without 'occupation'.

The Oxford World's Classics *Ralph the Heir* is edited by John Sutherland.

Thomas Hardy · *A Pair of Blue Eyes*

What is Elfride's rope made of?

One of the zanier stories in the American press in 1993 told of an inmate in a high-security prison who had escaped using a rope made out of the dental floss which his custodians had thoughtfully provided over the years. It is the kind of article that sticks in the mind (was it *used* floss? one wonders). There is a similar episode, similarly memorable, in Thomas Hardy's early novel *A Pair of Blue Eyes*. The blue-eyed heroine, Elfride Swancourt, is the daughter of the rector of Endelstow (i.e. St Juliot), whose deserted parish is on the 'sea-swept' Wessex (Devonshire and Cornwall) coast. The nearest town is Castle Boterel (i.e. Boscastle).

Elfride is beloved by two very different men—close friends before they became rivals for her hand. Stephen Smith is a gifted young architect. Born into the Wessex peasantry, he has risen above his origins but remains socially insecure, particularly in his addresses to a genteel rector's daughter with distant connections to nobility. Henry Knight is a man of letters, older, richer, and endowed with the *savoir faire* which Stephen lacks. But Knight is sexually insecure and less physically attractive.

The episode in question occupies chapters 21 and 22. It is an overcast summer's afternoon and Elfride (sadly torn between her suitors, although she is at the moment pledged to Stephen) resolves to walk over the cliffs to catch an early glimpse of the steamer *Puffin* which is bringing her fiancé back to Castle Boterel. She carries with her a heavy old telescope with which to spy the vessel as it rounds the coast-line from Bristol. It is a whimsical 'act of supererogation', as Hardy calls it. But placing Elfride on a headland, watching for the ship carrying her lover, creates a resonance with Tristram and Isolde which forecasts the novel's eventual tragic conclusion.

On her way to the cliffs Elfride meets Henry Knight—a coincidence which provokes a 'rebellious' thrill of pleasure. She is something of a flirt at heart. Knight offers to accompany her; she does not tell him exactly why she is going to the coast, merely that she intends to look for a ship. Perversely, not only do Elfride and Knight see the *Puffin* as it puffs into view, but Stephen standing on the deck, sees *them* outlined against the skyline. It is a sight which can only inflame his jealousy.

It threatens rain and Knight suggests that they hurry back. To shorten the way, he proposes they follow a steep path which will take them to the crest of a towering cliff from where they can walk over the downs to Endelstow. The sheer cliff face is composed of a 'vast stratification of blackish-grey slate, unvaried in its whole height by a single change of shade' (p. 202). With some effort, they reach the summit which looms 650 feet over the ocean below. The path on which they now stand is banked. Beyond the bank on the seaward side is a yard or two of level ground. Beyond the strip of level ground there is a 'short steep preparatory slope' (a one-in-three incline, as we later learn), slaty and with only the sparsest vegetation. Beyond the slippery slope is 'the verge of the precipice'.

Knight, an inveterate pedant, does not make love to Elfride, Instead, he gives her a lecture on the wind's aerodynamic peculiarities in the spot where they are standing. Carried away by his exposition, he leans forward and his hat is sucked off by the updraft. Feeling foolish, he goes over the bank and the level ledge on to the steep slope to

Elfride's attempt to help Knight

retrieve his headgear. Elfride loses sight of him. A couple of minutes pass and it begins to rain.

Finally Elfride goes over the bank herself to see what has happened. Below her, crouching on the slope on his hands and knees, is Knight. His hat is again on his head (a nice touch), but he now has other things to worry about. The rain has made the surface of the shale slimy and he cannot find the purchase on it to clamber back up. There are beads of perspiration on his brow. He is very frightened. Elfride is an intrepid 'new woman' (although she is dressed in high Victorian style, in a long walking-dress). She ventures on to the 'treacherous incline' herself, to give Knight the necessary hand up. We are told she 'propped herself with the closed telescope', although this is hard to picture. Knight, still crouching, takes her hand, but in trying to haul himself up only succeeds in pulling Elfride down. They slip together, until his foot comes to rest on 'a bracket of quartz rock, standing out like a tooth from the verge of the precipice'. They are almost on the brink. As a reminder of what will happen if they slip further, the telescope rolls down and vanishes over the edge 'into a nether sky'.

Knight and Elfride are now lying prone against the incline side by side. 'Hold tightly to me,' he tells her, and she flings her arms around his neck 'with such a firm grasp that whilst he remained it was impossible for her to fall'. Knight is in no condition to appreciate this exciting physical closeness. Their plight is increasingly desperate. No one comes along this path from one week to the next. Knight realizes that, unless they can ascend the slope 'with the precision of machines', they are doomed.

He makes a 'stirrup' out of one of his hands (presumably steadying himself with the other) and instructs Elfride to lever herself up then step on to his shoulder. With 'trembling limbs' she does as he tells her. Knight will have a good view of those trembling limbs because, as she raises herself on to his shoulder, he will be looking directly up her skirt. Elfride lifts herself up as instructed, and with a 'spring' from Knight's shoulder reaches the safety of the narrow strip of level ground above them. But the force of her spring, added to Knight's weight, breaks the tooth of quartz on which he is balanced. It moves. Knight grabs two tufts of sea-pink. The quartz tooth now completely dislodges and tumbles into the void. One of the tufts in his hands comes away by the roots, and 'inch by inch' Knight begins to 'follow the quartz'. He manages to arrest his fall by grabbing 'the last outlying knot of starved herbage ere the rock appeared in all its bareness'.

Knight is now holding on for dear life by his hands on the very edge of the precipice. How long will it take her to run to Endelstow and back, he shouts up. Three-quarters of an hour, Elfride answers. 'That won't do; my hands will not hold out ten minutes', he forlornly estimates. At this point, Hardy closes the chapter. *A Pair of Blue Eyes* was first serialized in *Tinsley's Magazine* (a monthly), and the instalment finished here—a literal cliffhanger. How, *Tinsley's* readers must have wondered over the next four weeks, will Knight get out of this? ('With one bound he was free!'?) Not one in a thousand can have come up with the solution Hardy had in mind.

Chapter 23 spends its earlier pages describing Knight's state of mind as he hangs, Prometheus-like, on the rock. In one of the most effective of Hardy's digressions on evolution, Knight ('a good geologist') contemplates the fossil of a trilobite embedded in the rock in front of his eyes: 'Time closed up like a fan before him', Hardy observes. Knight's metaphysical speculations on his cosmic insignificance are interrupted by gusts of rain which bite into his flesh like 'cold needles'. All the while his hands are weakening. Three minutes have passed (it seems like ten to Knight).

Where is Elfride? Has she fainted? Run away? What can a mere *woman* do, anyway?

Suddenly Elfride reappears to ask 'how much longer can you wait?' Four minutes he replies. And with good hope of being saved? 'Seven or eight,' he hazards. Desperate as he is, Knight notices two oddities: Elfride looks strangely slimmer than she did and the sinuous contours of her body, where the wet clothing sticks to them, are remarkably—not to say voluptuously—visible. And in her arms she has 'a bundle of white linen'.

This linen, we apprehend, is Elfride's petticoat. The three minutes' absence were spent stripping and putting her outer clothes back on. Elfride now sets to work making 'a perfect rope . . . six or seven yards long'. She does so by tearing the linen (of the petticoat, presumably) into long strips, knotting the ends together, twisting them into braid, and binding the twine in place with thinner strings of linen. It takes some time to describe this process; actually performing it would take even longer.

When she has finished Elfride tests the knots one by one, by standing on the 'linen rope' and yanking it. Some repairs are needed. She then ties one end of the rope around her waist and leans forward on the outward edge of the gently sloping bank of the path, holding hard with her hands and feet—like the 'anchor' in a tug-of-war team. On a prearranged signal (three twitches) to indicate she is ready, Knight uses the rope to crawl up the incline (never putting more than half his weight on the rope, as Hardy carefully notes).

When he reaches safety, they impulsively embrace. It is not the usual decorous Victorian encounter. Elfride has 'absolutely nothing between her and the weather but her diaphanous exterior robe or "costume"' (p. 216). Her flimsy outer covering is wet and clings to her like a 'glove'—or a modern body-stocking. While Knight was waiting for death on the cliff face, we are now informed, 'she had taken off her whole clothing, and replaced only her outer bodice and skirt. Every thread of the remainder lay upon the ground in the form of a woollen and cotton rope.'

After their embrace, Elfride runs off 'through the pelting rain like a hare; or more like a pheasant when, scampering away with a lowered tail, it has a mind to fly, but does not'. Her wet dress, without a petticoat to keep it away from her thighs, impedes her. In her modest confusion, she leaves everything behind her. Ever the gentleman, Knight 'gathers up her knotted and twisted plumage of linen, lace and embroidery work' to take back for her (the Rector may have some awkward questions about how he came by this 'plumage', one imagines).

A number of puzzles hover over this episode. Essentially Hardy recycles a Victorian version of the Rapunzel fable ('Rapunzel, Rapunzel, let down your hair'), but unlike Grimm's story, one expects a degree of *vraisemblance* in a novel of 1873. Is it feasible that Elfride could make a seven-yard linen rope, as described, in as many minutes? Probably not. Given an area of two square yards, and strips of nine inches, could a 'walking' petticoat—closely twisted and tightly knotted—supply such a length of rope? Probably not. Could such a rope bear half (or more) of Knight's weight—say six to nine stone? Probably not.

In the interest of a terrific action scene one would not linger on such picayune calculations about measurement and breaking-strain. But one may legitimately ponder just what garments the rope is made of. The description seems oddly contradictory. Hardy's initial and repeated emphasis that it is a 'linen rope' implies the petticoat. That garment alone could supply the lengths Elfride needs. But Hardy explicitly states a little later on that Elfride has shed everything except her 'diaphanous exterior robe'. Every 'thread' of her other clothing has gone into what is later called 'a woollen and cotton rope'.

Linen (derived from flax) is a stout material suitable for sheets, shirts, and petticoats. It is too coarse for underclothes which come into direct contact with the skin—at least for a fine lady like Elfride. The 'wool' which Hardy refers to presumably comes from Elfride's vest. The cotton comes from her long drawers, or knickers (Elfride would not waste her fine silk underclothes on a solitary walk along the cliffs). Finally, still later, the rope is described as a 'knotted and twisted plumage of linen, lace, and embroidery work'. Elfride's corsetry (the lace and embroidered brassiére, what the Victorians would call an 'under bodice') is now also woven into the rope, apparently.

We experience the thrills of the mountain rescue entirely through Knight's perceptions. As he perceives it, the life-line which dangles down to him is a 'linen rope'. Then, when he sees it on the ledge, it has become a 'woollen and cotton rope'. When he eventually picks it up and can examine it at leisure, it is 'linen, lace, and embroidery work'. How does one account for these changes?

There is, I think, a plausible explanation. Modest young woman that she is, Elfride used the petticoat—least intimate of her underthings—for the end which Knight would grab hold of, and indeed for the main part of the rope he would climb. The notion of him hurtling down to his death holding her drawers was not to be thought of. The end of the rope which she tied around her waist was made up of her more intimate undies, her vest, long knickers, and under bodice. No man's hand should touch those. When he gets to the top, and sees the rope's entire length, Knight perceives that more than linen went into its making.

Victorian modesty—even *in extremis*—is the key to this ingenious scene. Just how ingenious Hardy has been in controverting Victorian mores can be demonstrated by a small mind experiment. Suppose one were to get all the great novelists of the age—Dickens, Eliot, Thackeray, the Brontës, Trollope—into a room and set them the following problem: 'I want you each to devise a scenario in which a well-bred young lady allows a polite young man who is neither her fiancé nor her physician (1) to embrace her tightly and feel the outline of her breasts; (2) to look up her skirt at leisure; (3) to hold and examine in the closest detail all her underwear—articles which you will minutely describe. Neither of these young people is to suffer the slightest damage to their moral reputation in the eyes of the world, or the reader.' It would, one guesses, be a tough competition and the wise money would be on young Thomas Hardy.

The Oxford World's Classics *A Pair of Blue Eyes* is edited by Alan Manford.

George Eliot · *Daniel Deronda*

===

Is Daniel Deronda circumcised?

===

The question is posed, and an elegant answer proposed, by
Kenneth Newton in an article in *Essays in Criticism*.[1]
Newton's starting-point is an apparently devastating
objection to the *vraisemblance* of *Daniel Deronda* noted by
Steven Marcus, who in turn was alerted to the anomaly by
one of his sharp-eyed graduate students, Lennard Davis:

> Mr Davis has discovered a detail—or a missing detail—in *Daniel
> Deronda* that throws the whole central plot of the novel out of
> kilter. Deronda's identity is a mystery to himself and has always
> been. It is only when he is a grown man, having been to Eton and
> Cambridge, that he discovers he is a Jew. What this has to mean—
> given the conventions of medical practice at the time—is that he
> has never looked down. In order for the plot of *Daniel Deronda* to
> work, Deronda's circumcised penis must be invisible, or non-
> existent.[2]

As the author of *The Other Victorians*—a study of the
period's pornography—Marcus knows more about the
lineaments of the Victorian penis than most people. Is
Daniel Deronda, then, a narrative built on sand?

Any response to this conundrum must begin from the
position that Eliot would certainly care about such a
detail. She was scrupulous to the verge of fanaticism
about authenticity in her fiction. And circumcision is not
just a minor feature of Judaism but as central to its ritual
as is baptism to Anglicanism. Eliot took expert advice on
the finer points of Judaic practice and Jewish culture for
Daniel Deronda (as elsewhere she took advice on the legal

intricacies in her plots). Gordon Haight outlines her
extensive reading and notes that 'her lively concern with
the idea of Jewish nationalism sprang directly from her
friendship with Emmanuel Deutsch. Born in Silesia,
Deutsch was educated by his uncle, a rabbi, and then at the
University of Berlin before coming to London in 1855 to
work as a cataloguer of books at the British Museum.'[3] In
the period preceding the writing of *Daniel Deronda*,
Deutsch visited weekly to give Eliot lessons in Hebrew.

It is most unlikely that the rite of infant circumcision
(*bris*), symbolizing Abraham's covenant with Jehovah,
would not have been touched on in Deutsch's explanations
of Jewish religious practices. And there were other, closer,
sources of information accessible to Eliot. In her 1996 life
of Eliot, Rosemary Ashton quotes a hitherto unregarded
letter of G. H. Lewes's about *Daniel Deronda*. Writing on
Christmas Eve, 1876, to the palaeontologist Richard
Owen, Lewes alludes to the unpopularity of *Deronda's*
Jewish plot among Gentile readers:

The English public seem to have been amazingly dead to the
attempt to enlighten it about the Jewish race; but the Jews
themselves—from Germany, France, and America, as well as
England—have been deeply moved, and have touchingly
expressed their gratitude. Learned Rabbis, who can alone
appreciate its learning, are most enthusiastic. Is it not psycho-
logically a fact of singular interest that she was never in her life
in a Jewish family, at least never in one where Judaism was still a
living faith and Jewish customs kept up? Yet the Jews all fancy
she must have been brought up among them; and in America it is
positively asserted that *I* am of Jewish origin![4]

Lewes's origins are not entirely clear and the hypothesis
that he was at least partly Jewish still surfaces from time
to time.[5] What one does know is that he had a training in
medicine. And, in the very unlikely event that Eliot was in
some doubt as to what was physically entailed in circum-

cision, Lewes—of all people—would be uniquely qualified
to enlighten her.

In *Daniel Deronda*, as the Princess—the hero's
mother—records, the baby Daniel was given up at 2 years
old, to be raised as an aristocratic gentile, wholly ignorant
of his racial origins. By this age every Jewish male child
routinely would have gone through the *bris*. Why wasn't
Daniel circumcised, and why didn't he—as Marcus puts
it—'look down' and draw the obvious conclusion?

Newton's approach to what looks like a damaging
lacuna in *Deronda's* plotwork is scholarly and methodical.
He starts with the proposition that: 'Circumcision may be
present in the novel even if not specified: literary criticism
would be extremely restricted if it had to confine itself to
what was directly referred to in a text.' This weakens Marcus's damaging syllogism that Eliot does not explicitly use
the 'C' word, therefore Daniel must be uncircumcised,
therefore the novel falls apart. Newton chooses for the
thrust of his refutation Marcus's phrase, 'the conventions
of medical practice at the time'. The 'time' of Daniel's
infancy is the late 1830s (the main action takes place in the
mid-1860s). Infant circumcision, for general sexual
hygienic motives, became a widespread medical practice
in Britain towards the end of the nineteenth century.[6]
But—Marcus assumes—in the early decades of the century only Jewish (and some Muhammadan) babies would
have their foreskins snipped.

Is this true? Not entirely. Newton turns up evidence
that, particularly among surgeons in London, circumcision was a routine intervention. Evidence can be found in
handbooks as early as the 1820s. Robert Hooper's *Lexicon
Medicum* (1839), for example, has a succinct entry which
clearly defines medical thinking and practice on the topic
during Daniel's babyhood: '*Circumcision*: The removal of
the prepuce from the glans penis. This is a religious rite

among the Jews and Mahomedans. It is also practised by
surgeons in some cases of phymosis.' Phymosis is tight-
ness of the foreskin, or preputial orifice. Circumcision was
also recommended as a surgical procedure where the prepuce was excessively long. There is some evidence that
circumcision may also have been practised as a preventive
against masturbation, although it is hard to think of Sir
Hugo being severe on that subject.

Newton builds on the medical evidence that gentile
children were circumcised—particularly upper-class children delivered by qualified physicians rather than mid-
wives or female relatives. As the putative illegitimate son
of Sir Hugo Mallinger, Daniel would have had the best-
available medical attention. A boy in his position could
quite conceivably have been non-ritually circumcised,
were he born with a congenital deformity. If he were circumcised, it would explain why Daniel gives so much cre-
dence to Mordecai's intuitive conviction that his new
friend is 'one of us'. There is, in short, a physical, not a
purely mystical, explanation for the instant sense of
'belongingness' that Daniel experiences with Mordecai
and his family.

Newton's argument is intellectually attractive and his
scholarship is extremely persuasive. Like him, I believe
that an author as attentive to detail as Eliot would have
been at pains to accommodate the circumcision issue in
her novel—reticent although the Victorian writer had to
be on sexual matters.[7] But, on balance, I do not believe
that Daniel was—until his full adoption of his Judaic des-
tiny—circumcised. Curative circumcision in the early
nineteenth century was, as far as one can deduce, as rare
as congenital deformities of the male sexual organs. It
would, one guesses, be fairly rare, even among the upper
classes. A circumcised child would certainly wonder about
why he was different—assuming (1) he was moderately

curious; and (2) he knew what other boys of his age looked like naked.

The point is made early on that Daniel is an intellectually precocious child. It is from reading Sismondi at the age of 13 that he deduces the 'fact' of his illegitimacy. We are told that at the same period he had 'read Shakespeare'. It is hard to believe that he would not have asked his tutor (as he asked him 'how was it that the popes and cardinals always had so many nephews?') what was the meaning of Othello's final words:

> And say besides, that in Aleppo once,
> Where a malignant and turban'd Turk
> Beat a Venetian and traduc'd the state,
> I took by th' throat the circumcised dog,
> And smote him—thus.

Mr Fraser (who seems unusually candid on sexual matters) would doubtless have replied that circumcision was a ritual operation performed on the *membrum virile*, universal among Jews and some Muhammadans—a racially identifying mark.

After he discovers the fact (as he thinks) of his birth, Daniel is sent to Eton. In the school's communal sleeping and bathing facilities he would surely—given his dark, Semitic appearance and tell-tale penis—have been taunted as a Jew, if only in sport. If, that is, he were circumcised. From books, and from the commonplace anti-Semitic jibes of the English public school, he would have had implanted a seed of suspicion in his mind. Yet Eliot nowhere alludes to this, leaving us to suppose that Mordecai's suggestion is a thunderbolt, that never until late in life has it crossed Daniel's mind that he is Jewish.

Does George Eliot, then, leave room and clues for the reader, curious about the matter, to assume that Daniel is uncircumcised? I think she does. Quite early in the novel, after he has introduced Mirah to the Meyricks, Daniel is surprised to hear her confess that she is not a 'good Jewess':

'In what way are you not a good Jewess?' said Deronda.
'I am ignorant, and we never observed the laws, but lived among Christians just as they did. But I have heard my father laugh at the strictness of the Jews about their food and all their customs, and their not liking Christians . . .' (p. 313)

The implication here is that a dissident, or non-conformist, Jewish parent (even one who fathered the ultra-devout Mordecai) might neglect circumcision ('their food and *all their customs*'). There are much broader hints that Daniel's mother might have been similarly inclined to flout Judaic strictness, as it is embodied in her ultra-orthodox and 'iron-willed' father:

He never comprehended me, or if he did, he only thought of fettering me into obedience. I was to be what he called 'the Jewish woman' under pain of his curse. I was to feel everything I did not feel, and believe everything I did not believe. I was to feel awe for the bit of parchment in the *mezuza* over the door; to dread lest a bit of butter should touch a bit of meat; to think it beautiful that men should bind the *tephillin* on them, and women not,—to adore the wisdom of such laws, however silly they might seem to me. I was to love the long prayers in the ugly synagogue, and the howling, and the gabbling, and the dreadful fasts, and the tiresome feasts, and my father's endless discoursing about Our People, which was a thunder without meaning in my ears. (p. 540)

'I saved you from it', she tells Daniel. On the face of it, the 'saving' refers to her giving Daniel to Sir Hugo, to be brought up out of the faith. But it could as well refer to her keeping him intact from the possessive rituals of Judaism as a baby. Her father died three weeks after her arranged marriage to her cousin Ephraim—'the only one left of my father's family that he knew'. Her mother had been long dead. There were no parental constraints on her as a married woman and mother; nor any extended family to impose on her. Ephraim is a poor creature, and wholly subject to his wife: 'he made it the labour of his life to devote himself to me: wound up his money-changing and banking, and lived to wait upon me—*went against his conscience for me*' (p. 543, my italics).

Ephraim would not stand in her way, should she choose not to submit 'her' child to ritual and 'barbarous' mutilation by tribal elders whom she hates. Her father gone, no family to interfere, a weakling husband who suppresses his 'conscience' in deference to her will—why should she have her baby circumcised?

This hypothesis is easier to sustain if one reconstructs the episode. The *bris*, or ritual circumcision, takes place eight days after birth. The child is taken from the mother, and the operation, performed by the mohel, is a predominantly male affair (it is the father's duty to arrange it). The mother is not necessarily present. No anaesthesia is used. For a woman like the Princess, such a ceremony might well seem a vivid assertion of Judaism's patriarchal tyranny—its ruthless appropriation of 'her' child, and its relegation of a mere woman like herself to the inferior status of a procreative vessel. Would she *allow* Ephraim to take the child away to the *bris*, completely under her thumb as the poor fellow was? She would not, one imagines.[8]

This female rebellion on a point of religious ritual would strike a sympathetic chord with Eliot. The critical—and most agonizing—moment in her early progress to intellectual independence was her refusal to attend church with her father. It provoked, as Gordon Haight records, an explosion in the Evans household: 'Mr Evans, after a fruitless outburst of parental authority, lapsed into stony silence, refusing to discuss the question

of religion with his disobedient child. How was he to hold
a plate on Sunday mornings at Trinity [church], the father
of an avowed free-thinker?'[9] The rift was patched but never
mended. The rebellion was, as all biographers agree,
necessary that the woman of letters might emerge. Had
Eliot borne a baby, she would not, I think, have allowed it
to be baptized in the church of her father, however much
pressure were put on her.

Kenneth Newton is right, I think, to assume that circumcision is a significant thread in *Daniel Deronda*'s rich
narrative tapestry. But it seems more likely that Eliot considered the problem, and accommodated it in the subplot
of the Princess's rebellion—her wilful *non serviam* on
points of ritual. This seems both plausible, and in keeping
with Eliot's understanding of female psychology and its
modes of resistance to patriarchal oppression. And if one
assumes that Daniel is not circumcised it gives what seems
like a sly undercurrent of meaning to Sir Hugo's injunc-
tion to Daniel in chapter 16, 'for God's sake, *keep an English cut*, and don't become indifferent to English tobacco'.
'Cut' here means 'style' (as in, 'I like the cut of his jib').
But one would like to think there is an allusion to that
unkinder cut that Sir Hugo alone (at this point in the narrative) knows Daniel has never had inflicted on his private
parts.

The Oxford World's Classics *Daniel Deronda* is edited by Graham
Handley.

Anna Sewell · *Black Beauty*

Is Black Beauty gelded?

If one takes the autobiography of a horse 'translated from the original equine' at face value, it is clear that Black Beauty must be gelded at some point around chapter 5 but, as the World's Classics editor puts it, 'delicacy prevents Anna Sewell from making any reference at all to the painful surgery' (p. xxiv). Clearly, in the series of tasks that Black Beauty is called on to perform during his working life (running in harness with the sprightly mare Ginger, for instance), his masters would not want him distracted by wayward sexual urges. But even the most oblique allusion to how these urges were normally dealt with in the Victorian horse-trade was problematic. When, infamously, Anna Sewell sold the copyright of *Black Beauty* for £20, it was to a publisher, Jarrold's, specializing in books for children—who have traditionally made up a loyal element in the novel's readership. The *pas devant* rule would certainly extend to the castrating shears, however familiar the instrument might be in the stable. Had Miss Sewell included a reference to Black Beauty's removed bodily parts, it too would have been removed. Victorians were as expert at gelding texts ('bowdlerizing') as livestock. It remains a delicate subject, at least in popular entertainment. How many film-goers, for example, could say offhand whether Trigger, Champion, or Silver are stallions, mares, or geldings?

This 'delicacy' evidently offended Tolstoy, who in his autobiography translated from the equine, 'The Romance of a Horse', makes gelding the central and harrowing episode ('On the following day I became what I am now, and left off neighing for ever'). Generations of readers have happily ignored Sewell's delicacy and enjoyed her story none the less. And the Tolstoyan objection only has force if we assume that *Black Beauty* is primarily about horses. There is a good case for thinking that it is not. Victorian society ran on two mighty sources of power— horses were one and servants were the other. In a quite subtle way Sewell runs the two categories together. Black Beauty is a talking, thinking, social horse—like Swift's Houyhnhnms. The difference is that Swift's beasts are masters: Sewell's are servants. That he is born to service (although, if he is well behaved, he may regard himself as destined to be an 'upper servant') is the first lesson that Black Beauty's mother instils into him:

One day, when there was a good deal of kicking, my mother whinnied to me to come to her, and then she said:
  'I wish you to pay attention to what I am going to say to you. The colts who live here are very good colts, but they are carthorse colts, and of course, they have not learned manners. You have been well bred and well born; your father has a great name in these parts, and your grandfather won the cup two years at the Newmarket races; your grandmother had the sweetest temper of any horse I ever knew, and I think you have never seen me kick or bite. I hope you will grow up gentle and good, and never learn bad ways; do your work with a good will, lift your feet up well when you trot, and never bite or kick even in play.' (pp. 3–4)

In his subsequent life, Black Beauty has many masters and mistresses—farmers, fine ladies, 'cockneys', hackney-cab drivers. Some are good, some careless, some sadistic. But masters and mistresses there always are. It is Black Beauty's duty, like that of all horses, to work for humans— to serve. That is his 'station'. The moral of the book is as applicable to human as to equine servants: 'We horses do not mind hard work if we are treated reasonably' (p. 155).

As well as in nurseries, it is likely that *Black Beauty* was distributed lavishly below stairs—as were tracts and 'improving' moral tales designed to reconcile Victorian servants to their lot.

As a treatise on what Carlyle called 'servantship', *Black Beauty* makes a plea on two fronts as to what 'reasonable' treatment by masters should be. It can be summed up as: don't treat your horses like beasts, don't treat your servants like slaves. Anna Sewell makes the slavery point by direct allusion to *Uncle Tom's Cabin* (and its polemic against the breaking up of negro families) in chapter 5:

When John went into the stable, he told James that master and mistress had chosen a good sensible English name for me, that meant something, not like Marengo, or Pegasus, or Abdallah. They both laughed, and James said, 'If it was not for bringing back the past, I should have named him Rob Roy, for I never saw two horses more alike.'

'That's no wonder,' said John, 'didn't you know that farmer Grey's old Duchess was the mother of them both?'

I had never heard that before, and so poor Rob Roy who was killed at that hunt was my brother! I did not wonder that my mother was so troubled. It seems that horses have no relations; at least, they never know each other after they are sold. (pp. 17–18)

Not even an advocate as friendly as Anna Sewell would propose that horses' family units should be respected. But the insidious effects of 'service' on the human family members employed in middle-class houses clearly worried her, as it worried other *bien pensant* mistresses.

Another main source of worry was sexuality. Two-legged servants could not, like their four-legged colleagues, be mated to order, operated on to remove troublesome urges, or shot in the head if they proved hopelessly recalcitrant. As elsewhere, Victorian doctrine divided into the physical forcers and the moral forcers. A master or mistress who believed in physical force would enforce virtue, by insisting on a good 'character' (i.e. references), by constant inspection of the servants' most intimate affairs, by minimizing free time, by severe rules about visitors. There is an interesting piece of business in Trollope's *Barchester Towers* when Mrs Proudie (a physical forcer if there ever was one) is complaining to Archdeacon Grantly about the physical dilapidation of the Palace, and notes that the locks on the servants' bedrooms are defective from the outside. It is clear that the Bishop's wife is in the habit of locking her servants in their rooms at night. If English law allowed her to, doubtless she would geld and spay her menials, as freely as she does her other livestock.

Moral forcers would try to control their servants' sexuality by instilling a high level of self-control. This could be done by good example, by frequent family prayers, by precept. A 'good' servant could be trusted to restrain himself or herself from straying sexually. It is clear that in her first lesson to Black Beauty (which, as he says, 'I have never forgotten') his mother is enjoining self-restraint and 'manners' ('I hope you will grow up gentle and good, and never learn bad ways'). As it happens (although Harriet Beecher Stowe, like her sister-novelist, is too delicate to mention it), slaves in America before 1865 could, like other cattle, be gelded if their masters so determined. In *Black Beauty*, at least in its aspect as a treatise on servantship, Sewell argues that such extreme and inhumane measures are not necessary. Well trained by his mother, and with a good master, Black Beauty will be able to control himself without recourse to the dreaded shears. Is Black Beauty gelded? Yes (in so far as he is a four-legged servant) and no (in so far as he represents the two-legged class of servant). Self-control will answer.

The Oxford World's Classics *Black Beauty* is edited by Peter Hollindale.

===

What does Mrs Charmond say to Grace?

===

The Woodlanders is a novel resting sedately on a huge chronological flaw. In a narrative oddly lacking in clear historical markers, there is a stark contradiction between the only two which the attentive reader will find. Perplexingly, Hardy seems to go to some pains to etch the clash of dates on our consciousness. The first is signposted relatively early in the narrative. When Giles meets the strange gentleman at the midsummer festivity who has terrified the local girls ('We saw Satan pursuing us'), he feels justified in asking some close questions of the interloper:

'You come from far, seemingly?'

'I come now from the South of Europe.'

'Oh indeed, sir. You are an Italian or Spanish or French gentleman, perhaps?'

'I am not either.'

Giles did not fill the pause which ensued and the gentleman, who seemed of an emotional nature, unable to resist friendship, at length answered the question: 'I am an Italianized American, a South Carolinian by birth,' he said. 'I left my native country on the failure of the Southern cause, and have never returned to it since.' (p. 151)

The strange gentleman is, we learn, one of Felice Charmond's more importunate lovers (and eventually her assassin). His reference to the 'Southern cause' unmistakably indicates the American Civil War, 1861–5. And if he has since 'Italianized' himself (a process which would take some years), the present date is presumably around the mid-1870s, or later. His reason for leaving his homeland is a superfluous piece of information (we are not usually so open about our personal histories to complete strangers). One must assume that Hardy intends us to take careful note, as we do.

The American's *curriculum vitae* is, however, wholly irreconcilable with Fred Beaustock's excited information to Mellbury later in the novel that Grace may get her release from Fitzpiers by a 'new' divorce law. Under this just-passed ordinance, the former law-clerk tells Mellbury:

A new court was established last year, and under the new statute, twenty and twenty-one Vic., Cap. eighty-five, unmarrying is as easy as marrying. No more Acts of Parliament necessary, no longer one law for the rich and another for the poor. (p. 267)

It used to be held by Hardy scholars that what Beaustock is here referring to is a modification to British divorce law introduced in 1878. But, as Michael Millgate pointed out in 1971, the legal dating jargon (twenty and twenty-one years after Victoria's accession in 1837) makes the reference to 1857 unequivocal.[1] Beaustock is a habitual drunkard, and as the World's Classics editor, Dale Kramer, notes: 'perhaps Hardy intends to suggest that Beaustock is so befuddled that the passing of the recent 1878 Act has jogged his memory of what had been current legal news during his sober years.' But if this were the case, Hardy would surely have made Beaustock's error crystal-clear to the reader. Again, by inserting more information than would realistically be given in casual conversation ('twenty and twenty-one Vic., Cap. eighty-five' hardly rolls off the tongue) Hardy seems set on grinding a specific date into our minds—the year after this legislation, 1858.

What is as odd as the glaring, two-decade (1858/1878), discrepancy between these two bearing points is the

almost total lack of other historical markers. Hardy has
deliberately, as it seems, purged his text of any other clues
as to period. We are not sure whether Grace comes to
Hinstock by train or horse-drawn coach: nor whether Mrs
Charmond travels on the Continent by train or coach.
There seems to be no steam-powered, or mechanized
equipment in the Mellbury sawmill—as there would be in
1878. But we cannot be sure of the point. There is no clear
reference to clothing fashions which would help us date
the action (steel-hooped crinolines, for instance, or bustles;
the 'chignon' which Mrs Charmond has made out of
Marty's hair might, conceivably, be linked to the fashion
of the 1870s, but this is not conclusive). Fitzpiers's late-
night reading is all in 'metaphysical' and 'Idealist' sources
which are more appropriate to a Bulwer-Lyttonish 'student' of the 1830s and 1840s than to a late Victorian physician up-to-date with the latest advances in medical science. But again we cannot be sure. Many books and titles
are mentioned in passing, but none are later than the mid-
1850s (if only Fitzpiers had quoted some late Browning, or
early Swinburne, like Sue Bridehead; his favourite poet,
however, is the pre-Victorian Shelley). The only cultural
marker I note is in the exchange between Grace and
Fitzpiers, when they first meet at Hintock House:

'And now, doctor,' she said, 'before you go I want to put a question
to you. Sit round there in front of me on that low chair, and bring
the candles, or one, to the little table. Do you smoke? Yes? That's
right—I am learning. Take one of these; and here's a light.' She
threw a match-box across. (p. 186)

This seems a clear reference to the 'new' practice of cigar-
ette smoking (a tobacco pleasure in which middleclass
women could indulge for the first time) brought back by
British troops from their Russian foe in the Crimean War,
after 1855.

David Lodge, who has examined the evidence thoroughly for his Macmillan edition, advises that we should not try to hunt down clinching chronological evidence in *The Woodlanders*—although he personally leans to 'an earlier rather than a later dating'. The fact that for a hundred years critics were happy to mislocate the narrative by twenty-odd years (twenty of the most transformative years in nineteenth-century history) is not evidence of the critics' impercipience so much as the novel's inscrutability. As Lodge puts it:

Nobody before Millgate, it would appear, has noticed the contradiction between the divorce law reference and the Civil War reference: they occur at widely separated points in the narrative and the reader is not naturally inclined to check one against the other. This reinforces my own feeling that *The Woodlanders* has a distinctly mythopoeic, dreamlike quality about it. History seems suspended—something that goes on in the world outside the woods.[2]

This is probably as satisfactory a solution to the chronological puzzle in *The Woodlanders* as we shall get. Hintock is like Brigadoon, a village out of historical time. There remains, however, a smaller puzzle on which one has less editorial guidance. It has to do with Fitzpiers's mysterious omnipotence over women, and his predatory sexual habits.

Grace's suspicions about her husband develop soon after marriage and harden into the kind of evidence that would satisfy any modern divorce court as to Fitzpiers's incorrigible misconduct (if not the court set up by 'Vic. 20, 21', which required, on the male side, adultery compounded by gross violence, incest, sodomy or desertion without reasonable cause for over two years). Grace sees Suke Damson furtively leaving Fitzpiers's rooms 'between four and five' and soon discovers that his explanation that she had maddening toothache is a lie. There is only one explanation for a hoyden like Suke spending the night

with a handsome young man like Edred. Night after night
Fitzpiers goes out, sometimes not returning till morning,
on spurious calls that Grace knows are pretexts for visiting Hintock House. One morning, returning asleep on his
horse, he miscalls his wife 'Felice'—Mrs Charmond's
Christian name.

Grace's suspicions explode into accusation when, by
accident, she comes across Mrs Charmond walking in
the woods at twilight. The older woman is astonished at
Grace's unexpected 'toughness'. Grace begins with the
warning: 'You may go on loving him if you like—I don't
mind at all. You'll find it, let me tell you, a bitterer business for yourself than for me in the end. He'll get tired of
you soon, as tired as can be—you don't know him so well
as I!—and then you may wish you had never seen him!'
(p. 236). Warming to her theme, Grace pours scorn on her
patrician rival:

Before I came I had been despising you for wanton cruelty; now I
only pity your weakness for its misplaced affection. When Edred
has gone out of the house in hope of seeing you, at seasonable
hours and unseasonable; when I have found him riding miles and
miles across the country at midnight, and risking his life, and
getting covered with mud, to get a glimpse of you, I have called
him a foolish man—the plaything of a finished coquette. I
thought that what was getting to be a tragedy to me was a comedy
to you. But now I see that tragedy lies on your side of the situ-
ation no less than on mine, and more. (p. 237)

Every reader will apprehend that Grace *knows*. She may
have spent a year with fine folks in town, but she is a
country girl by upbringing and is quite familiar with the
facts of life. Fitzpiers has been unfaithful to her—both
with the low-born Suke, and with the high-born Felice
Charmond. Grace's only consolation is that he will treat
them as callously in love as he has treated his wife. Their
triumph will be short-lived.

A discomfited Mrs Charmond rushes off, loses herself in the wood, and falls exhausted by the way. It is now night, and cold. She is again met by Grace, who is still walking by herself. Out of mere humanity, Grace comforts her rival. And to warm themselves, the women cling close together under Mrs Charmond's furs until she feels strong enough to get to her feet. In this nocturnal intimacy, Mrs Charmond finds herself obliged 'to make a confession'. She *'cannot'* give up Fitzpiers, she tells Grace, 'until he chooses to give me up!' Surely, says Grace, as the partner in the superior station, 'the cut must come from you'. There then occurs the following mysterious exchange:

'Tchut! Must I tell verbatim, you simple child? O, I suppose I must! It will eat my heart if I do not let out all, after meeting you like this and finding how guileless you are.'

She thereupon whispered a few words in the girl's ear, and burst into a violent fit of sobbing.

Grace started roughly away from the shelter of the furs, and sprang to her feet.

'O my great God!' she exclaimed, thunderstruck at a revelation transcending her utmost suspicion. 'He's had you! Can it be—can it be!' (p. 240)

When she next speaks to Mrs Charmond, it is with a voice 'grown ten years older'. At last rested sufficiently to be able to move, they part with the following words:

'I have told you something in a moment of irresistible desire to unburden my soul which all but a fool would have kept silent as the grave,' [Mrs Charmond] said. 'I cannot help it now. Is it to be a secret, or do you mean war?'

'A secret, certainly,' said Grace mournfully. 'How can you expect war from such a helpless, wretched being as me!'

'And I'll do my best not to see him. I am his slave; but I'll try.' (p. 241)

In her earlier strictures on Mrs Charmond's 'coquetting', it is manifest that Grace knew that the affair had gone further than flirting. Whatever it was Felice whispered must have been shocking beyond belief. Grace's lapse into country coarseness, 'He's had you', is amazing in a Victorian novel, recalling as it does the yokel ballad 'Oi had 'er; Oi had 'er; Oi upped and Oi had 'er; Oi had 'er on Saturday noight'.[3] The hyperbole suggests something far exceeding mere adulterous congress, that Fitzpiers has 'had' something more than sexual relations conventionally offer ('Can it be—can it be!').

Mrs Charmond, one reminds oneself, is no *ingénue*. She is a woman of the theatre and a woman of the world who has had a string of lovers. She has travelled widely (disposing her favours wherever she goes, as gossip claims), and has cold-bloodedly married an older man whom she did not love for money. He died soon after. This courtesan-cum-Black Widow is ill-cast as a sexual victim.

Initially Grace accused Mrs Charmond of making a conquest of Edred (he was 'the plaything of a finished coquette'), as she had conquered other men. Now, it seems, she has told Grace something that convinces her that Edred has made a conquest of Felice—a conquest which has reduced this sophisticated *femme fatale* to the degraded condition of a sexual slave. There is only so far one can go along this route, depending as it does on an inaudible whisper, but it seems that what is hinted at here is some 'French practice', some refinement of *Ars Amatoria* picked up on the Continent. When Felice talks of 'war' she may be implying that perhaps, after all, were she to face the horrible publicity, Grace may indeed have grounds for divorce under Vic. 20, 21.

The Oxford World's Classics *The Woodlanders* is edited by Dale Kramer.

Who will Angel marry next?

The bitter ending to *Tess of the d'Urbervilles* is well known and much quoted. Angel Clare and his pubescent sister-in-law, Liza-Lu (Elizabeth Louise Durbeyfield), are standing vigil outside Wintoncester Gaol:

Upon the cornice of the tower a tall staff was fixed. Their eyes were rivetted on it. A few minutes after the hour had struck something moved slowly up the staff, and extended itself upon the breeze. It was a black flag.

'Justice' was done, and the President of the Immortals (in Aeschylean phrase) had ended his sport with Tess. And the d'Urberville knights and dames slept on in their tombs unknowing. The two speechless gazers bent themselves down to the earth, as if in prayer, and remained thus a long time, absolutely motionless: the flag continued to wave silently. As soon as they had strength they arose, joined hands again, and went on. (p. 384)

Went on to what? The image, as critics have noted, evokes the end of *Paradise Lost*: 'They hand in hand with wandering steps and slow | Through Eden took their solitary way.' Adam and Eve are, of course, man and wife, carnally united. Is this what will happen here? Will Angel 'go on' to marry Liza-Lu? Tess, as we learn early in the novel, has six siblings. They are: Liza-Lu (four years younger than Tess), then in descending order Abraham, Hope, Modesty, and two unidentified younger children. At the beginning of the story Liza-Lu was described as twelve-and-a-half, and Abraham is apparently around nine.

Throughout the subsequent narrative the younger offspring of the Durbeyfields remain shadowy characters, Tess, apparently, has no intimate relationship with any of them, and the only recorded conversation between her and a sibling is the exchange about 'blighted stars' with Abraham in which he feeds his older sister ingenuous questions about the human condition. None the less, after her father's death Tess feels obliged to support her family, and her sense of a bread-winner's duty is one of the means by which Alec blackmails her.

The fact that Angel only has Liza-Lu with him at Wintoncester Gaol could imply that the other Durbeyfield children are still too young for such a grisly ordeal. It could further imply that he has taken on the protector's role for the surviving Durbeyfields—he will henceforth be their good Angel. Most likely, of course, is that he and Liza-Lu will form some kind of marital, or sexual, liaison. Hardy endorses this likelihood by offering, in this last chapter, our first clear visual image of Tess's sister: 'a tall budding creature—half girl, half woman—a spiritualized image of Tess, but with the same beautiful eyes—Clare's sister-in-law, Liza-Lu.' The suddenly nubile Liza-Lu, as we can work out from the four-year age gap, must be just under 16 at this point—too young to marry for a month or so, but eligible if Angel is patient.

If Angel does take up with Liza-Lu it might strike the reader as in keeping with the cheerfully callous morality of the English ballad, an ethos which hangs over much of *Tess of the d'Urbervilles*—a case, that is, of 'so I kissed her little sister, awful sorry Clementine'. It would be less hard on Angel to suppose that the union with Liza-Lu was a fulfilment of Tess's fervent wishes: 'Why didn't you stay and love me when I—was sixteen', she complained to Angel, 'living with my little sisters and brothers, and you danced on the green? O, why didn't you, why didn't you?' Liza is now verging on 16—and, we assume, a virgin (the word Tess cannot bring out). Angel is now in a position to rectify his mistake—not with Tess herself but with 'the spiritualized image of Tess'.

So what will happen? Hardy is careful in the last chapter to notate not just that Liza-Lu is the image of Tess, but that the girl is Angel's 'sister-in-law'. No Victorian would have missed the cue: with the hoisting of the black flag Liza-Lu becomes Angel's 'Deceased Wife's Sister'—a phrase heavy with legal baggage. Ever since the Act of 1835, marriage with a deceased wife's sister had been determined by the law of England to be within the degrees of incest. Incest, by this statute, was conceived to extend not just to *consanguinei* (those related by blood), but to certain *affines* (those related by marriage). The dead wife's sister was one (but not the dead husband's brother).

As the eleventh edition of the *Encyclopaedia Britannica* puts it: 'For many years [after 1835] an active and ceaseless agitation was prosecuted on behalf of the legalization in England of marriage with a deceased wife's sister.' Bills to reform the anomaly were brought into the House of Commons from 1850 onwards. There were some twenty-six abortive initiatives between 1850 and 1896. In most cases the bill passed in the Commons but was rejected in the Lords. Finally the 'deceased wife's sister' law was belatedly reformed in 1906, although marriage between such *affines* as adoptive parents and children, and adoptive siblings, remained within the prohibited degrees.

If Angel wishes to marry Liza-Lu, he has a number of options. *Tess* finishes around the early 1880s: he can wait a quarter of a century until, in the fullness of time, the English law changes (Liza-Lu will still be of childbearing age—just). Alternatively the couple can emigrate to one of the many self-governing British colonies, which had already revoked the 'deceased wife's sister' legislation (Australia, New Zealand, South Africa, Canada). Given the stigma attached to being relatives of a hanged murderer, this would be a sensible course of action on other grounds. As a third option, Angel and Liza-Lu can stay in England and enter into an 'open sexual union'—the kind of relationship celebrated in such 'New Woman' novels as Grant Allen's *The Woman Who Did* (1895). They can, in other words, flout Mrs Grundy. This last option is highly unlikely, given Angel's moral fastidiousness and (we may guess) his sexual timidity. It could also be dangerous: Angel could conceivably be prosecuted for incest, the more so if the union begins before Liza-Lu's sixteenth birthday.

The key to the future of the relationship lies probably in the term 'spiritualized'. Angel will love, but not violate, Liza-Lu, as the disincarnate relic of Tess. Liza-Lu will remain an ethereal and virginal version of her sister: the Pure Woman's purer essence. The relationship between Angel and Liza-Lu will be 'blank'—white and sexless. Angel will nobly undertake not to impose his animal appetites on the woman he worships, fulfilling himself with a 'higher' spiritual and intellectual union. One of the favourite conundrums of medieval theologians was whether angels had sexual organs and if so whether they used them. This one has, and doesn't.

The Oxford World's Classics *Tess of the d'Urbervilles* is edited by Juliet Grindle and Simon Gatrell.

What cure for the Madwoman in the Attic?

One of the achievements of feminist literary criticism over the last few decades has been the establishment of a canon enriched with 'rediscovered' works. If you had asked typical American readers of *Scribner's* or the *Century Magazine* in 1897, 'what novelist of the day will "last" and still be read in 1997?' they might well have backed Silas Weir Mitchell, whose historical romance of Quaker pacifism in the Revolutionary War, *Hugh Wynne*, was the best-selling novel of 1897. Few of them, I suspect, would have backed Kate Chopin or Charlotte Perkins Gilman for immortality. But it is one of literary history's ironies that, if Mitchell has any name-recognition in the 1990s, it is as not as a novelist but in his other professional capacity as a physician specializing in women's nervous disorders. Specifically, it is his demonized appearance as the advocate of the 'rest cure' in Chopin's *The Awakening* and—most dramatically—in Gilman's *The Yellow Wall-Paper* that has ensured Mitchell a place in modern consciousness.[1]

With the new literary map drawn by Sandra Gilbert and Susan Gubar's *The Madwoman in the Attic* (1979), two texts have been elevated to supreme status in the feminist canon: *Jane Eyre* (particularly as rewritten from the madwoman in the attic's point of view, in Jean Rhys's *Wide Sargasso Sea)* and *The Yellow Wall-Paper.* Gilman's story features another madwoman locked in 'the nursery at the top of the house'. *The Yellow Wall-Paper*—which has been out of print for most of the twentieth century (and virtu-

ally unavailable in the UK)—is now one of the most studied texts in literature departments across the English-
speaking world.

Gilman's story takes the form of a monologue by a
doctor's wife who has been confined to convalescent
inactivity 'for her own good' by her ostensibly well-
meaning husband. He has taken a short locum position for
three months in an unnamed resort town—it seems that he
is not a particularly successful physician. The house he
has rented for the short period of his stay is grander than
what they are used to, as the woman's opening comments
make clear:

It is very seldom that mere ordinary people like John and myself
secure ancestral halls for the summer.

A colonial mansion, a hereditary estate, I would say a haunted
house, and reach the height of romantic felicity—but that would
be asking too much of fate!

Still I will proudly declare that there is something queer
about it.

Else, why should it be let so cheaply? And why have stood so
long untenanted? (p. 3)

The woman, whose name we never learn, has recently
had a baby and has suffered a breakdown ('a temporary
nervous depression—a slight hysterical tendency'). As the
stylistic flourishes indicate, she has 'literary' pretensions
of which her husband disapproves—'He says that with my
imaginative power and habit of story-making, a nervous
weakness like mine is sure to lead to all manner of excited
fancies, and that I ought to use my will and good sense to
check the tendency. So I try.' John has brought his sister
Jennie (also called 'Jane' at one point[2]) to assist him as
housekeeper during his wife's indisposition. A servant
called Mary looks after the baby.

John is a firm believer in Weir Mitchell's 'rest cure'

therapy, and his wife is accordingly kept in a state of vir-
tual sensory deprivation. She is denied reading materials,
forbidden visitors, and may not even see her baby, because
'it makes me so nervous'. It is clear that, to forestall other
sources of 'nervousness', she and John are not sleeping
together. She is confined to what seems like a nursery at
the top of the house, but which may have served a more
sinister purpose. It is:

a big, airy room, the whole floor nearly, with windows that look
all ways, and air and sunshine galore. It was nursery first and
then playroom and gymnasium, I should judge; for the windows
are barred for little children, and there are rings and things in
the walls. (p. 5)

Over the subsequent weeks, the woman's *idée fixe* about
the room's yellow wallpaper develops into full-blown
dementia. The story, given entirely in her own words,
chronicles her descent into madness, with the implication
that her condition is 'iatrogenic'—caused, not relieved, by
the medical treatment to which she is subjected, medical
treatment which is merely a mask for patriarchal oppression. The cruelties of that oppression are hinted at by the
apparatus of Bedlam ('rings and things in the walls').

I taught *The Yellow Wall-Paper* for ten years, on and off,
to what would seem the least congenial pupils imaginable:
a freshman class composed almost entirely of males, all of
them intending eventually to major in science, and many
of them from non-English-speaking backgrounds. They
were, however, extraordinarily intelligent—all selected for
entry into the California Institute of Technology by virtue
of superior ability in mathematics. Their reactions to *The
Yellow Wall-Paper* were refreshingly heterodox. One of
the objections which they regularly brought to Gilman's
story was that John was no villain. He was applying the
latest scientific theory to his wife's case. This was the

right thing to do—the scientific thing. If you can't trust the latest scientific thinking, what can you trust? Why was Gilman so down on the man? Another objection, typically brought by Asian-Americans, was that the woman was a bad mother, thinking always and only of herself. This censure was even more rigorously applied to Edna Pontellier, whose suicide at the end of Chopin's *The Awakening* was seen as the worst kind of maternal dereliction. All she cared about was her own selfish 'liberation'—what about her two children?

Most perplexing, however, was these students' literalistic reaction to a puzzling feature of *The Yellow Wall-Paper* which more sophisticated students of literature overlook: namely, the change in the status of the document which we are (1) reading, and (2) listening to. *The Yellow Wall-Paper* is a fragmentary narrative, mainly composed of one-sentence, barely grammatical paragraphs, without any apparent internal architecture other than that of the fugue from neurosis to psychosis. There is, however, a significant middle point in the story when the woman declares: 'Well, the Fourth of July is over!' The 'fourth' is, of course, 'Independence Day' in the United States. And independence is marked in the story by a tacit change in the narrative mode of address. Before Independence Day, it is clear that the woman is writing. There are, in fact, four references to this activity, concluding with:

There comes John's sister. Such a dear girl as she is, and so careful of me! I must not let her find me writing.

She is a perfect and enthusiastic housekeeper, and hopes for no better profession. I verily believe she thinks it is the writing which made me sick!

But I can write when she is out, and see her a long way off from these windows. (p. 8)

We have to assume that, up to Independence Day, what

we have is a written record—a text. After the Fourth,
there are no more references to writing. We now understand that what we are listening to is a stream of consciousness which some omniscient author is recording for
us—something more akin to a live broadcast. The narrative is now interior monologue, reporting present sensations and events as they happen:

> I quite enjoy the room, now it is bare again.
> How those children did tear about here!
> This bedstead is fairly gnawed!
> But I must get to work.
> I have locked the door and thrown the key down into the front
> path. (p. 17)

The reader is no longer reading the story as words on the
page (as in the first half of the text) but is 'hearing' it
through the words on the page. Students of literature
make the required epistemological gear-change
effortlessly—so effortlessly that they are unaware of it.
Literalistic readers (as I have called them) worry about the
altered status of the 'data'. There is a difference in credit-
worthiness between what is written and what is merely
thought and transcribed by an intuitive third party. The
woman, that is, loses authority with the surrender of her
authorial role—eyewitness testimony becomes hearsay.
Where there was previously a relationship of two (woman
and reader), there are now three persons involved (woman,
reader, and an unidentified narrator who has stepped in to
take charge). Once this is pointed out, it becomes a troub-
ling detail.

The problem could, I think, be solved if we had one
piece of information which Gilman denies us. The passage
immediately before Independence Day alludes to Jenny's
hostility to the woman's writing ('I verily believe she
thinks it is the writing which made me sick'). Did Jenny

take the woman's writing materials away from her, tipping
her over the edge into madness (as might happen in *A Tale
of Two Cities* with Dr Manette, if you took away his cobbler's last)? Or has the woman simply deteriorated to the
point that she can no longer write, even though she still
has her pen and paper by her? This would be the implication of some earlier references to her writing, in which she
records how increasingly difficult the task has become:

I did write for a while in spite of them; but it *does* exhaust me a
good deal . . . I haven't felt like writing before, since that first day
. . . I think sometimes that if I were only well enough to write a
little it would relieve the press of ideas and rest me.
  But I find I get pretty tired when I try. (pp. 1–7)

This uncertainty relates to an enigma at the heart of
The Yellow Wall-Paper. Is the woman 'everywoman'—more
specifically every wife and every mother in the prison of
the bourgeois home, Ibsen's infernal 'Doll's House'. Or is
she a superior kind of woman— a novelist, deprived of the
means of self-expression, and thus of her sanity? A superficial reading of *The Yellow Wall-Paper* might suggest
that, in reaction to Mitchell's 'rest cure', Gilman is advo-
cating a 'writing cure' (a variant on Freud's talking cure),
particularly necessary to an unusually gifted woman like
herself. Not every woman in the prison of the domestic
home is a frustrated writer. Jenny and Mary, for instance,
clearly aren't—what is their status in the story? Quislings
collaborating with the enemy, or a lower order of
womanhood?

The enigma at the heart of *The Yellow Wall-Paper*
(crudely: is the woman mentally ill or has she been driven
mad by solitary confinement?) relates to Gilman's own
experience, which she describes in a 1913 essay, 'Why I
wrote *The Yellow Wall-Paper*'. It seems that after the birth
of her first child, Gilman suffered severe post-natal

Charlotte Perkins Gilman

depression. Her husband (an artist, not a doctor) referred her to the great Dr Silas Weir Mitchell. He prescribed his famous rest cure. She was sent home, 'with the solemn advice to "live as domestic a life as . . . possible [and] never to touch pen, brush, or pencil again" as long as I lived'. She followed the advice for three months, 'and came so near the borderline of utter mental ruin that I could see over. Her glimpse into this heart of darkness is given literary expression in *The Yellow Wall-Paper*. Gilman divorced her husband (on the grounds that marriage was driving her insane) in 1892—the same year that her story was published. The 'divorce cure' wasn't entirely successful, although it worked better than Mitchell's rest cure. Gilman suffered frequent relapses into depression over the next four decades but was not incapacitated by them. She wrote a large number of aggressively feminist tracts (e.g. *Man-Made World*, 1911) and novels (e.g. *Herland*, 1915).

Even in their heyday, R. D. Laing and Thomas Szasz allowed that some schizophrenics are genuinely mentally ill—not everyone is *driven* mad by external circumstances. But assuming that the woman in the story has been driven mad, how could she be brought back to sanity? Clearly Mitchell's rest cure is a non-starter—a form of torture to rank with the snake pit, pre-frontal lobotomy, and the 'liquid cosh' (the megadose-of-tranquillizer regime, beloved by some prison governors). At times the story suggests that giving the woman more 'rights' within the commonwealth of the family might work: she could tend her baby, have visits from 'Cousin Henry and Julia', take over from the odious Jenny (a lineal descendant of Jane Murdstone) the superintendence of the household. But taken as a whole, *The Yellow Wall-Paper* does not make much of a case for domestic power-sharing. The woman won't be cured by a better pre-nuptial contract. Allowing her a zone of freedom within which to express herself

artistically—Dr Manette's last, leather, and hammer—
might also help; but it, too, would only be a palliative, not
a cure—a re-papering of the prison walls that have to be
torn down or leapt over. Gilman's bleak assertion would
seem to be that of the Scottish peasant: if you want to get
there, don't start from here (marriage, that is); or—to
adapt Mr Punch's advice to young men about to marry—
'Don't!' In answer to the question in the title, if you need a
cure, the condition is already incurable.

The Oxford World's Classics *The Yellow Wall-Paper and Other
Stories* is edited by Robert Shulman.

===

Who is George Leach?

===

The Sea-Wolf opens brilliantly—the fog-bound ferry-boat *Martinez* hooting its way across the San Francisco Bay at night, in an atmosphere shrouded in gloomy foreboding. On board the middle-aged littérateur, Humphrey van Weyden, is mightily pleased with himself—more particularly he is pleased with his literary reputation and power. He idly observes, as an entomologist might look at an unusual genus of ant, one of his fellow passengers—a man with no legs who walks on artificial limbs. During Humphrey's complacent reverie the *Martinez* collides with another vessel, is holed, and rapidly sinks. So 'civilized' is Humphrey that at first he simply watches the spectacle as a disinterested observer. This commotion surely cannot affect *him*—the 'Dean of American Letters the Second'? Why are these women squealing like 'pigs'? He is too refined even to struggle for his life—at least initially. He reacts rather more energetically when he feels the sting of the cold bay water on his limbs. At the point of drowning, that mystical moment when the whole of one's life is supposed to flash in front of the eyes, Humphrey is plucked from his doom by a god-like Wolf Larsen. As Humphrey is drifting towards final oblivion and certain death, the *Ghost* sweeps silently past (it is sail-driven—unlike the noisy steam-powered vessels which collided in the Bay). Humphrey glimpses a man on the boat's bridge,

who seemed to be doing little else than smoke a cigar. I saw the smoke issuing from his lips as he slowly turned his head and glanced out over the water in my direction. It was a careless, unpremeditated glance . . . His face wore an absent expression, as of deep thought, and I became afraid that if his eyes did light upon me he would nevertheless not see me. (p. 9)

Wolf Larsen nevertheless does 'see' Humphrey and brings the *Ghost* about to rescue the nearly drowned man.

It emerges that Wolf Larsen has remarkable powers of vision—second sight, it seems. After he has contemptuously refused Humphrey's offer of $1,000 to transfer him to a passing pilot vessel, Larsen presses the appalled 'Dean of American Letters the Second' (or 'Hump', as he crudely rechristens him) into service as the *Ghost's* cabin-boy on its long voyage to the northern seal-hunting grounds. Cabin-boy is all Hump is good for. Captain Larsen then summons the fellow who previously held the menial post. He is now to be 'promoted' (much against his will—serving as a seaman under Larsen is no picnic). It is clear that the two men have never met before. 'What's your name, boy?', Wolf demands:

'George Leach, sir,' came the sullen answer, and the boy's bearing showed clearly that he divined the reason for which he had been summoned.

'Not an Irish name,' the captain snapped sharply. 'O'Toole or McCarthy would suit your mug a damn sight better. Unless, very likely, there's an Irishman in your mother's woodpile.'

I saw the young fellow's hands clench at the insult, and blood crawl scarlet up his neck.

'But let that go,' Wolf Larsen continued. 'You may have very good reasons for forgetting your name, and I'll like you none the worse for it as long as you toe the mark.' (p. 24)

Larsen has deduced that 'Leach' is on the run from the authorities. So much any astute skipper with a knowledge of the riff-raff on the San Francisco waterfront might have done. But what is very strange—superhuman, it would seem—is that Larsen has divined the seaman's true name. He has 'seen through' Leach's disguise. Later in the voyage Leach realizes that Larsen is going to kill him in reprisal for the failed mutiny he and Johnson have led (Larsen eventually carries out his vengeance in a peculiarly sadistic way, calmly watching the two men struggle in a small boat in a heavy sea, tantalizing them all the while with the possibility that he may heave the *Ghost* to and save them).

Before making his vain attempt to escape, Leach comes to speak to Hump, who has now risen to the rank of mate ('Mr Van Weyden') on the *Ghost:*

'I want to ask a favor, Mr Van Weyden,' he said. 'If it's yer luck to ever make 'Frisco once more, will you hunt up Matt McCarthy? He's my old man. He lives on the Hill, back of the Mayfair bakery, runnin' a cobbler's shop that everybody knows, and you'll have no trouble. Tell him I lived to be sorry for the trouble I brought him and the things I done, and—and just tell him "God bless him", for me.' (p. 139)

London does not draw our attention to it, but there is something very puzzling in this confidential exchange. How did Larsen know earlier that 'Leach' was, in fact, called 'McCarthy?' If it was a shot in the dark, it was uncannily accurate: there are many common Irish names, most of which would come more readily to the tongue.

The mystery is compounded by the fact that London was more careful than most authors about such details, and had his friends look through his manuscript for possible factual errors or anomalies. More than with many authors, one can be sure that he was aware of the 'McCarthy' coincidence.[1]

It seems likely that London intended to leave this teasing detail as a mote to trouble the reader's eye. Leach is a minor character and the fact that Larsen effortlessly penetrated his incognito has no central plot significance. Its effect in the text is to suggest that Larsen has god-like powers of divination that flash out at unexpected moments. It consolidates his image as Nietzschean *über-mensch* and his tyrannical power over the mere mortals under his command.[2]

The Sea-Wolf has been filmed several times. In the most famous adaptation, that by Warner Bros in 1940, the pregnant 'George Leach' detail is exploited to create what is effectively a new story for the taste of a later age. The film was directed by Michael Curtiz, and had a screenplay by Robert Rossen, who had evidently studied London's text with some care.

Warner's cast was star-studded and their apparatus state-of-the-art for 1940. The studio had recently invested in a huge new tank (for scenes at sea) and a fog machine. Both were used in the gloomily atmospheric opening on the ferry. Van Weyden, now 'a novelist', was played in the film by Alexander Knox, an actor fresh from the London West End stage who projected a desiccated, patrician image of his character. On the ferry he is approached by an escaped convict, 'Ruth Webster' (spunkily played by Ida Lupino), who is trying to hide from two detectives. Van Weyden refuses to aid the girl, but just at this point the ferry is rammed by the *Ghost* and sinks.

Wolf Larsen (played by Edward G. Robinson) rescues the couple, but refuses to let them go ashore. Humphrey is made assistant to the cook, Mugridge (played by the Irish character actor Barry Fitzgerald). Ruth is kept for the captain's own nefarious purposes: to warm his bunk on cold nights, as we apprehend. In port Larsen has earlier shanghaied a mysterious young sailor—in fact another escaped convict—George Leach (played by the film's principal box-office star, John Garfield). Ruth and Leach fall in love. The middle parts of Curtiz's *The Sea-Wolf* more or less follow London's, but with the role of Humphrey (lover and bookworm) split between the glamorous Garfield and the rather stuffy Knox. As redesigned for the silver screen,

Leach shares the 'lead' with Larsen, with Humphrey Van Weyden trailing some way behind.

The story's climax is strikingly changed. In the novel, Leach is murdered by Larsen. Van Weyden and the high-born Maud Brewster (very unlike the 'moll' Ruth Webster) escape to 'Endeavor Island', where they spend an idyllic, Crusoe-like couple of years discussing poetry and Darwin and virtuously not making love. Larsen, blind and abandoned by his crew, is eventually washed up on the island and slowly dies of creeping paralysis—watched by a forgiving Humphrey. At the end of the novel Humphrey and Maud sail off to Japan in the rejigged *Ghost*. They will marry and doubtless set up a fine literary salon in San Francisco.

In the film all this is altered to revolve around the heroic character of George Leach, now the central character. Leach is not murdered, but is clapped in irons on the sinking *Ghost* by the blind and vengeful Wolf Larsen. Humphrey engages in a battle of wills and wits with Larsen, and contrives to allow Ruth and Leach to escape to a nearby island. What they will do there, how they will square their accounts with the 'Frisco authorities, we do not know—everything is left in Hollywood's blissfully 'happy ever after'. Humphrey, who has been shot, goes down to Davey Jones's Locker, with Larsen and the *Ghost*. The film ends with a vignette of Leach and Ruth, happily united in their little love boat.

Hollywood traditionally takes liberties with classic texts and the history of film adaptation is one of wholesale travesty. But in this instance, London seems to have anticipated the needs of a youth-centred, more proletarian, more sentimental public for whom his superannuated and Brahminical Humphrey Van Weyden would be insufficiently heroic. In the character of Leach/McCarthy, and the unsolved mystery attached to his character (who is he?

where does he come from?), he deliberately left a niche for other fictioneers to work in. There's a story here, he seems to say with his Leach mystery, fill it in as you will.

The Oxford World's Classics *The Sea-Wolf* is edited by John Sutherland.

———

Wanted: deaf-and-dumb dog feeder

———

Edmund Wilson scored some easy points against *The Hound of the Baskervilles* in his amusing essay 'Mr Holmes, they were the footprints of a gigantic hound!' It is not hard to poke holes in this most Gothic of the great detective's cases. What is more interesting, perhaps, is to see Arthur Conan Doyle himself doing running patchwork on some of those holes, as they became apparent to him while writing and serializing his story in the *Strand Magazine*.

The 'gigantic hound' of the title is built up in the reader's imagination by the horrible legends attaching to it and by the fact that to see it is manifestly to risk death by heart attack (as happens with Sir Charles Baskerville). Holmes and Watson's first physical encounter with the beast does not disappoint:

I sprang to my feet, my inert hand grasping my pistol, my mind paralysed by the dreadful shape which had sprung out upon us from the shadows of the fog. A hound it was, an enormous coal-black hound, but not such a hound as mortal eyes have ever seen. Fire burst from its open mouth, its eyes glowed with a smouldering glare, its muzzle and hackles and dewlap were outlined in flickering flame. Never in the delirious dream of a disordered brain could anything more savage, more appalling, more hellish, be conceived than that dark form and savage face which broke upon us out of the wall of fog. (p. 151)

It is rather an anti-climax to learn, as we do in the last chapter, that this monster is in fact a cross between a bloodhound and a mastiff, and that it was purchased from

Ross and Mangles, the dog-dealers in Fulham Road. Of course, the firm's animals do not come bathed in fiery incandescence. 'The man who called himself Stapleton' (alias Vandeleur, alias Baskerville) daubed it with the phosphorescent paste that had recently become all the rage on Victorian watch-faces.

Painting watches would seem to be an easier option (although, as was soon to become evident with the epidemic of 'fossy jaw', working with phosphorescent substances had dangers that even Holmes did not guess at). The 'demon dog' may not be as big as 300 years of rumour suggested, but it is undoubtedly a fierce canine. Stapleton stokes its savagery by keeping it 'half-starved'. In these circumstances it would be a brave man who dared put the animal's fearsome make-up on, before it ventured out on its night's hunting on Dartmoor. It is good-natured of the dog not to lick the paint off. Since it is suggested that its eyeballs are daubed as well, it is surprising that the animal can concentrate on tracking its prey. As a further quibble, one might wonder how the hound—unlike all the unfortunate ponies that keep getting sucked down to their deaths—avoids the quicksands of Grimpen Mire.

A more serious query is, what exactly does Stapleton intend to achieve by setting his hound on Sir Henry? Clearly Sir Charles Baskerville, with his weak heart and superstitious fears, is an easy prey. But Sir Henry has been brought up on the prairies of North America. He will have faced wolves and bears. He carries a firearm. He is not likely to be frightened to death. Rather weakly, Holmes supposes that Stapleton's motive is to 'paralyze Sir Henry's resistance'. If he is out to murder Sir Henry, all the business with the hound (and stealing one of his shoes in London, for the dog to pick up his scent) would seem somewhat unnecessary. Why not just shoot him and pitch him into the bog?

The most worrying of the loose ends which straggle from the denouement ('A Retrospection') is the explanation of who looked after the hound while Stapleton, in his bearded disguise, trailed the new baronet in London (meanwhile his treacherous wife was locked up in her hotel room—it was a busy week or so). The problem of the hungry dog evidently occurred to Doyle only as he was wrapping the story up. He improvised a solution. In his debriefing session with Holmes, Watson asks, 'What became of the hound when its master was in London?' Holmes replies:

I have given some attention to this matter and it is undoubtedly of importance. There can be no question that Stapleton had a confidant, though it is unlikely that he ever placed himself in his power by sharing all his plans with him. There was an old man-servant at Merripit House, whose name was Anthony. His connection with the Stapletons can be traced for several years ... This man has disappeared and has escaped from the country. It is suggestive that Anthony is not a common name in England, while Antonio is so in all Spanish or Spanish-American countries. The man, like Mrs Stapleton herself, spoke good English, but with a curious lisping accent. I have myself seen this old man cross the Grimpen Mire by the path which Stapleton had marked out. It is very probable, therefore, that in the absence of his master it was he who cared for the hound, though he may never have known the purpose for which the beast was used. (p. 164)

Holmes may have seen him, but this is the first that the reader learns of 'Antonio'. It seems clear that Doyle has invented the South American factotum to cover a little local difficulty which suddenly became apparent to him in the last instalment of the serial. But the insertion of a newly devised character into this late stage of the narrative weakens much of what has gone before. Awkward questions crop up. Is it likely that Antonio would not wonder why his master was keeping a gigantic, half-starved hound in the middle of a marsh, together with a supply of luminous paste, traces of which would still be visible on the animal? Might he not put two and two together upon learning that Sir Charles Baskerville had died—reputedly after seeing a spectral hound? If he knew the 'Stapletons' back in Costa Rica, would he not also know that his master was then called by his birth name? If Anthony is 'not a common name in England', neither is 'Baskerville' a common name in Costa Rica. If he did not know 'the purpose for which the beast was used', why has Antonio fled the country? Was he involved with the dastardly series of robberies by which Stapleton supported himself while he pursued his schemes against the successive heirs to the Baskerville title? Did he side with the remorseful Beryl, or the remorseless Stapleton?

Obviously Doyle was torn between making Antonio a version of the deaf-mute servant, beloved by the villains of Gothic fiction, and making him a co-conspirator—as guilty as his master. Or possibly he might be like Beryl, an unwilling accomplice. It is a small thread which will forever now dangle from the otherwise neat design of Doyle's story.

The Oxford World's Classics *The Hound of the Baskervilles* is edited by W. W. Robson.

====

Whose daughter is Nancy?

====

The Good Soldier is, Eugene Goodheart claims, 'one of the most puzzling works of modern fiction'.[1] It is notoriously hard to make sense of Ford's characters, their backgrounds, and their actions. There is critical dissension on such issues as whether the title (in so far as it refers to Captain Edward Ashburnham's 'goodness') is ironic or not. The narrative is speckled with what look like factual contradictions (about such crucial data as when and where the Dowells first met the Ashburnhams).[2] Close inspection reveals that the chronology is awry at almost every point. 'Is this', Martin Stannard asks, 'Fordian irony or simply carelessness about details?'[3] Should we lay the inconsistencies at the door of an artfully unreliable narrator (John Dowell), or at the door of a slipshod writer (Ford Madox Ford)? Some critics, Vincent Cheng for instance (who has assembled a convincing chronology of *The Good Soldier*), believe that Ford is writing in 'the French mode of *vraisemblance*', and that it is legitimate to ask 'what actually happens?'[4] with a reasonable expectation of getting 'right' answers. Other commentators, such as Frank Kermode, see *The Good Soldier* as the *locus classicus* of modernist indeterminacy. 'We are in a world of which it needs to be said not that plural readings are possible (for this is true of all narrative) but that the *illusion of the single right reading is possible no longer*'.[5]

I want to look at a puzzle recently highlighted by Ian Hamilton, reviewing the latest biography of Ford Madox Ford, by Max Saunders, in the *London Review of Books*.[6] A

number of reviewers felt that the fifty-three pages of close
exegesis which Saunders lavished on *The Good Soldier*
might be too much of a good thing. Hamilton did not. He
was particularly grateful for 'a single right reading' that
Saunders brought to a traditionally difficult text:

Saunders has found a real-life model for John Dowell and argues
persuasively (with biographical support) that Ashburnham's suicide was forced on him by the knowledge that Nancy was actually
his daughter. Has this theory been proposed before? Not that I
know of. All in all, Saunders's *Good Soldier* chapter had the effect
of altering my reading of a book I thought I knew—a book I
thought was marred by Ashburnham's implausible exit. So I for
one am grateful.

The Good Soldier is a text well trodden by critical explica-
tion and a couple of weeks later Edward Mendelson wrote
to the *LRB* (18 July) pointing out that Dewy Ganzel
had contributed a 'persuasive' article to the *Journal of
Modern Literature* (July 1984), arguing that Nancy was
Edward's natural daughter. The insight was not quite as
new as Hamilton thought.[7]

Questions of priority aside, what is the case for thinking
that Edward's relationship with Nancy Rufford is not
merely treacherous and adulterous, but incestuous?
Prima facie it is odd that Edward reacts as remorsefully as
he does to this last of his affairs. He is inhibited, as he tells
Dowell, by a 'tabu' round Nancy. There are very few taboos
in modern life; sleeping with one's daughter is certainly
one of them. In other of his philanderings Ashburnham is
wholly uninhibited. As far as we can make out he is a
sexual addict, incapable of keeping his hands off any
woman who takes his fancy. Prudence counts for nothing
when his carnal pleasures are involved. He compromises
his position in English society by assaulting a servant
('the Kilsyte girl') in a third-class railway carriage. In

India, he seduces brother-officers' wives ('Mrs Major
Basil', 'little Maisie Maidan'), exposing himself to blackmail and possible court-martial. He is prepared to bank-
rupt his estate and publicly humiliate his wife by buying
the favours of a courtesan (La Dolciquita) for an outrageous £60,000. For nine years he callously cuckolds his
best friend, the gullible Dowell (Florence meanwhile
denies Dowell his conjugal rights on the grounds of
'heart'). Florence, as Dowell belatedly discovers, poisons
herself when she believes Ashburnham has thrown her
over in favour of the much younger Nancy.

Why then should a late-life fling with Nancy precipitate
Edward's own suicide, Nancy's madness, and a nervous
breakdown in Leonora? The Ashburnhams, at least, must
be habituated to his incorrigible infidelity by now and it
would seem that the worst (Florence's death, financial
ruin, a court-case, blackmail) has already happened. It is
true that Nancy is Leonora's ward but on past record this
would prove no bar to Edward's making her his mistress.

In explaining the traumatic effects of the Ashburnham–
Nancy affair, Ganzel points to some odd inconsistencies in
the accounts we are given of Nancy's background. First
we are told that Nancy was 'Leonora's only friend's only
child', and that 'she had lived with the Ashburnhams ever
since she had been of the age of thirteen, when her mother
was said to have committed suicide owing to the brutal-
ities of her father'. Later we are told that Nancy was sent
to boarding-school and 'her mother disappeared from her
life at that time. A fortnight later Leonora came to the
convent and told her that her mother was dead.' Finally,
nine years later, we learn that 'Nancy Rufford had a letter
from her mother. It came whilst Leonora was talking to
Edward, or Leonora would have intercepted it as she had
intercepted others. It was an amazing and horrible letter.'
What amazing horrors the letter contains we are not

specifically told—except that she may not be Colonel Rufford's daughter (he has retired from the army, and is now a tea-planter in Ceylon).

There are further mysteries about Mrs Rufford: it is implied at one point that she has descended to the condition of a common street-walker in Glasgow. Then it emerges that she is living reasonably prosperously, with a man whose telephone number Ashburnham knows well. There are, as Ganzel points out, loose ends here, and the explanation he comes to is 'that Nancy is Edward Ashburnham's natural daughter'. Edward knew, Leonora knew, and after receiving the 'horrible' letter from her mother, Nancy knew. The only person who doesn't know is the narrator, Dowell (and the bulk of his readers, one might add). Just as he couldn't see what was going on under his nose with Florence and Ashburnham, Dowell is blind to the relationship between Edward and Nancy.

If, against Kermode's instruction, one believes in 'single right readings', this would seem to be extraordinarily satisfactory. Certainly Max Saunders found it so: 'I had known the novel for nine years', he writes (echoing the nine years the Dowells knew the Ashburnhams), 'before the thought occurred to me, but then immediately details began to fall into place.'[8] Saunders's 'thought' is framed slightly more cautiously than Ganzel puts it: 'the girl with whom Ashburnham has become infatuated might be his own illegitimate daughter'. 'Might' leaves open the possibility that Ashburnham and Leonora cannot be sure—it's a wise philanderer that knows his own daughter. But none the less the 'touch of incest' insight is, for Saunders, the key to *The Good Soldier*, discovered only after years wrestling with the text.

Attractive as it is, the 'Nancy is Edward's daughter' interpretation is flawed. There is, one may note, no physical resemblance. Edward is fair-haired ('golden-haired' as he grows older), with striking porcelain-blue eyes. Nancy has 'the heaviest head of black hair that I have ever come across'. Given recessive genes, hair colour is by no means a clinching factor. Dates are. When the four principals meet at Nauheim in summer 1904, Edward is 33. This gives a birth-date of 1870 or 1871. When Florence kills herself it is 1913, and Nancy is something between 21 and 22, which gives a birth date of 1891 or 1892. When Nancy was conceived (1890 or 1891), Edward was between 20 and 21. It was at the age of 22 that he married Leonora, at which time he was, Dowell tells us, 'almost as pure in mind as Leonora herself. It is odd how a boy can have his virgin intelligence untouched in this world.' Edward's career in extra-marital 'libertinism' begins with the Kilsyte case, in 1895.[9]

Dates are notoriously slippery in *The Good Soldier*. But those I have listed here are among the most reliable we can determine in the novel. They are the pegs on which the narrative hangs. If they are not reliable, nothing is—even the names of the characters and the places they visit. It is hard, almost inconceivable, to picture 'virginal' Edward in his early twenties fathering Nancy, by the wife of a Scottish officer in a Highland regiment. Such acts belong to his later life. Probably like the mad (if she is mad) governess in James's *The Turn of the Screw*, Nancy's paternity will become one of modernism's chewed bones. But the balance of evidence is against its being Edward Ashburnham.

The Oxford World's Classics *The Good Soldier* is edited by Thomas Moser.

═══

Clarissa's invisible taxi

═══

It is not an easy novel to read, but Virginia Woolf's *Mrs Dalloway* is the easiest of novels to summarize. 'A day in the life of a middle-aged upper-class London woman planning her party', is how the *Oxford Companion to Twentieth Century Literature* encapsulates it. The long prelude to the novel is Clarissa Dalloway's morning walk through the West End on a brilliant June morning (the 13th) in 1923 to select the flowers for the entertainment she and her politician husband are giving that evening. One of the pleasures of *Mrs Dalloway* is that you can follow quite exactly the route taken by Clarissa on her morning walk.[1] OUP has helpfully provided a map for pedestrian-minded readers. They should also set their watches. Woolf originally called her novel 'The Hours', and Clarissa Dalloway's early morning peregrination through the London streets is precisely measured by the chimes of two clocks, Big Ben and the slightly belated St Margaret's (the parish church of the House of Commons). It is with Mrs Dalloway's morning excursion that I am concerned—specifically, the puzzle of how she makes her return journey.

The novel opens, 'Mrs Dalloway said she would buy the flowers herself'—the servants are busy preparing the house for the grand evening party. She and her Conservative MP husband, Richard, live in Westminster (within a stone's throw of the House of Commons and Westminster Abbey). As she crosses busy Victoria Street, Big Ben tolls 'the hour, irrevocable' (p. 4). It is not indicated what hour

A Map of Mrs Dalloway's London

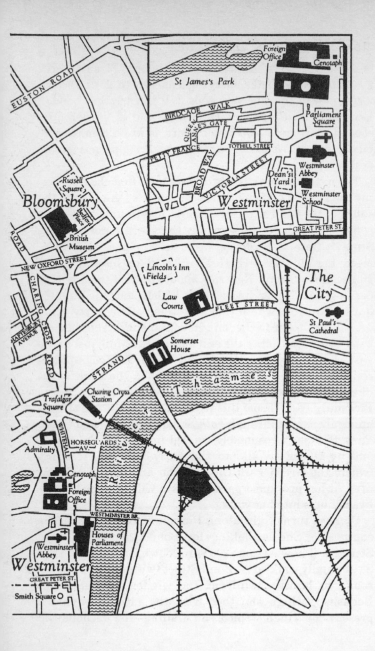

St James's Park

Foreign Office

Cenotaph

BIRDCAGE WALK

QUEEN ANNE'S GATE

Parliament Square

PETTY FRANCE

BROAD WAY

TOTHILL STREET

VICTORIA STREET

Dean's Yard

Westminster Abbey

Westminster

Westminster School

GREAT PETER ST.

Russell Square

Bloomsbury

Bedford Place

British Museum

NEW OXFORD STREET

CHARING CROSS ROAD

Lincoln's Inn Fields

Law Courts

FLEET STREET

The City

St Paul's Cathedral

SHAFTESBURY AVENUE

EUSTON ROAD

ROAD

Somerset House

STRAND

Charing Cross Station

Trafalgar Square

WHITEHALL

HORSEGUARDS AV.

Admiralty

Cenotaph

Foreign Office

WESTMINSTER BR.

Houses of Parliament

Westminster Abbey

Westminster

GREAT PETER ST.

Smith Square

T h a m e s

R I V E R

is sounding but we assume it is ten o'clock.[2] Mrs Dalloway is, we learn much later, carrying a parasol (p. 25), although it is not clear that she yet needs it. It is 'early' but London is already bustling. Mrs Dalloway, who is 'in her fifty-second year' and has a weak heart, is in no condition to bustle with it. We assume that her walking pace is a moderate stroll.

The next landmark the text gives us is that she is 'entering the Park'. This is evidently St James's Park, just to the south of the Mall and Green Park. It is not clear by what route she got here—presumably the short distance along Storey's Gate to Birdcage Walk. In St James's Park she meets her old friend Hugh Whitbread, on his way to the House of Commons. Reveries about the past (mainly concerning her former lover Peter Walsh, and the country house, Bourton, where they had their affair thirty years earlier) bring her to the 'middle of the Park'. The shortest path would lead her to the exit gate on the Mall, just to the east of Buckingham Palace. But the next topographical reference we have is: 'She had reached the Park gates. She stood for a moment, looking at the omnibuses in Piccadilly' (p. 7). From this we deduce that she has absent-mindedly passed through *both* St James's Park, and Green Park. She has, presumably, passed in front of the palace and up Queen's Walk, to the hurly-burly of Piccadilly (where the Green Park tube station and Ritz Hotel now are). At her presumed pace, Clarissa will be some twenty-five minutes into her walk.

Clarissa turns right along Piccadilly, remaining on the south side. She is making for Bond Street (Old Bond Street, as it now is) some 200 yards down, on the other side. She actually walks past Bond Street (without crossing the road), to browse awhile at the window of Hatchard's Bookshop, where she toys with the idea of buying a present for Hugh Whitbread's ailing and menopausal wife, Evelyn (whom she does not much like). Nothing suits, so 'Clarissa ... turned and walked back towards Bond Street'. She is now in the fashionable shopping area of London: 'Bond Street fascinated her; Bond Street early in the morning in the season; its flags flying; its shops; no splash; no glitter; one roll of tweed in the shop where her father had bought his suits for fifty years; a few pearls; salmon on an iceblock' (p. 9). She stops at the fishmongers (to look, not to buy) and the glove shop 'where, before the War, you could buy almost perfect gloves'. Mrs Dalloway proceeds up Bond Street to Mulberry's the florists, 'where they kept flowers for her when she gave a party'. As far as we can make out, this fictional shop is located at the junction with Brook Street—well into New Bond Street (p. 15). Another reverie about her daughter Elizabeth (who is modern and difficult) and about Elizabeth's former governess, the unpleasant Miss Kilman, preoccupy Clarissa in the seconds before pushing through the shop's swing-doors. Once inside she is attended on by Miss Pym ('whose hands were always bright red, as if they had been stood in cold water with the flowers'—the spiteful comment explains why she fictionalizes Mulberry's but not Hatchard's). Clarissa spends some time with Miss Pym, sampling the shop's extensive stock of blooms, relishing the colours and scents. She is uplifted. The sensations are 'a wave which she let flow over her and surmount that hatred, that monster, surmount it all; and it lifted her up and up when—oh! a pistol shot in the street outside.'

Her mood is shattered. It is not, however, a pistol shot. Miss Pym goes to the window and reports that it is merely a car backfiring (Londoners are still jumpy from the Zeppelin raids, we assume). The time elapsed up to this point in the narrative would be some thirty-five minutes easy walking (I timed it myself, on foot, in June 1996) with some ten minutes to a quarter-of-an-hour's conference in Mulberry's with Miss Pym. It is, therefore, around 10.45 to 10.50 a.m.

Up to this point the narrative has been solely attached to Clarissa's consciousness. Now, with the 'violent explosion', it becomes detached. We in fact see little more of Clarissa until she is back at her house in Westminster. Instead, we follow the repercussions of the backfiring motor car. It is no ordinary automobile, but a limousine containing 'a face of the very greatest importance'. Whose face? 'Rumours were at once in circulation from the middle of Bond Street to Oxford Street.' Was it the Prince of Wales, the Queen, the Prime Minister? No one is sure. Septimus Smith, a shell-shocked World War One veteran, overhears people discussing the matter. He too is evidently passing Mulberry's shop, on his way north to Regent's Park with his wife, who has brought him out for his daily exercise. Septimus has heard the report of the car backfiring and it terrifies him (in fact, it sows the seed of the suicide he will commit, later that day). Rezia Smith wonders, with other passers-by, whether the Queen herself is in the car.

After this introduction to the Smiths we follow the mysterious car, which proceeds, 'with inscrutable reserve', south to Piccadilly. Meanwhile, Mrs Dalloway (thinking like others, 'It is probably the Queen') emerges from Mulberry's 'with her flowers'. The car 'glides across Piccadilly', turns left, and then left again down St James's Street, through London's clubland. Gentlemen looking out of the great window at White's 'perceived instinctively that greatness was passing, and the pale light of the immortal presence fell upon them as it had fallen upon Clarissa Dalloway' (p. 16). It passes the sentries at St James's Palace, who salute, then turns right along the Mall to Buckingham Palace (the flag is flying, so it may indeed be the Queen in the car), where a crowd of hopeful onlookers is gathered.

Suppositions about the occupants of the mysterious car ripple among them, as they did among the pedestrians in Bond Street (readers never learn who actually was in the car, although Woolf's working materials indicate it was the Prime Minister, who makes an appearance later at Mrs Dalloway's party). Suddenly, in addition to the great person's limousine, there is another distraction. Above the gawpers clustered outside the Palace an aeroplane is sky-writing a message. It is evidently an advertisement, but no one can quite make out the words. A Mrs Bletchley hazards it is 'Kreemo'; Mr Bowley thinks he sees 'toffee'. As Londoners silently gaze into the sky, 'bells struck eleven times' (p. 18).

Meanwhile, in the time taken by the limousine to get from Bond Street to Buckingham Palace, Septimus and Rezia have reached the fountains at the southern end of Broad Walk in Regent's Park. Given the fact that it is about a mile-and-a-half (it takes me twenty brisk minutes to walk it), they may have taken a bus or a tube from Oxford Circus to Regent's Park Station (which Woolf mentions on page 22) although for one stop it would hardly seem worth it. They too see the skywriting: 'It was toffee; they were advertising toffee, a nursemaid told Rezia. Together they began to spell t . . . o . . . f . . . "K . . . R . . ." said the nursemaid.' Septimus, enclosed in his private psychosis, thinks 'So . . . they are signalling to me'. Evidently this too is happening at eleven o'clock—although Regent's Park is (unlike Buckingham Palace) beyond earshot of Big Ben and St Margaret's. The narrative remains for a few pages with people in the park.

Suddenly, on page 25, the narrative reverts to Clarissa. She is now, we discover, home. 'What are they looking at?' she asks the maid who opens the door to her house in

Westminster. Presumably 'they' are pedestrians, and what
they are looking at is the Kreemo toffee message in the sky.
This would suggest a third simultaneity: Mrs Bletchley's
remarks outside the Palace; Rezia's conversation with the
nursemaid in Regent's Park; Clarissa's return home to her
house in Westminster—all occur with the chimes at eleven
o'clock. This is confirmed, a few pages (but only a couple
of minutes) later, when—hearing that she has a visitor
(her old lover, Peter Walsh, as it turns out)—Clarissa finds
it 'outrageous to be interrupted at eleven o'clock on the
morning of the day she was giving a party' (p. 34).

The question is—how did Clarissa get back from upper
Bond Street so quickly? Although we are given a minute
topographic description of her walk to Mulberry's, we
have no idea how she returned. It is accomplished, we may
calculate, in the time it takes a chauffeured limousine to
make its sedate way from upper Bond Street through the
Mall to Buckingham Palace—ten minutes, fifteen at most
if the traffic is heavy. A good middle-distance runner could
hare down Bond Street and across the parks to Westminster in that time. Doubtless many commuters with trains
to catch at Victoria do it every working day. But if Mrs
Dalloway did it walking (carrying a large bunch of flowers,
a handbag, and a parasol), she should cancel the next
appointment with her heart specialist.

The solution, once one thinks of it, is blindingly obvious. She took a taxi. But why are we not told this fact?
None of the student guides I have seen (*Coles Notes*, for
instance) mentions this invisible taxi. Clarissa's morning
expedition is assumed to be, going and coming, entirely on
foot. But unless those feet are very swift indeed, a taxi
there must be. The taxi hypothesis would also explain why,
until she alights from the vehicle outside her front door,
Mrs Dalloway has been blissfully ignorant of the skywriting that all pedestrian London is looking at.

But even if one inserts the unmentioned taxi, there are still loose ends. The last we saw of Clarissa in the West End was at Bruton Street, watching the queenly limousine. Was it there she got her taxi? Or did she walk down to Piccadilly? What route did her vehicle take (did she, for instance, pass in front of Buckingham Palace, a few feet from Mrs Bletchley and Mr Bowley?) What sights did she see on the way? It is not entirely inconceivable that there was no cab: she walked up to Oxford Circus (possibly alongside Septimus and Rezia) and got the underground to Westminster—although carrying flowers it would not have been an inviting prospect. The taxi seems more likely.

The reason why Woolf does not mention the taxi is to be found, I think, in her and Mrs Dalloway's class habits when in town. For 'upper-middle-class ladies' in 1923 to take a mile's walk to a florist's to save a servant's legs was unusual to the point of eccentricity ('What a lark! What a plunge!' Clarissa thinks as she sets out on her stroll). The wife of Richard Dalloway, MP, would routinely hail a taxi when shopping in Bond Street, or have some shop assistant do it for her. The act is so natural that there is no need to mention it: any more than one need mention that there are pigeons in Trafalgar Square—or that there are underpaid, unidentified servants who keep things shipshape in the Dalloway household. (When she was writing her famous polemic about a room of one's own and £500 a year, the Woolfs had two live-in female servants, Lotte and Nellie, who earned £76 per annum between them. They did not, one suspects, have rooms of their own.)

In his essay on Tolstoy, the Marxist critic Georg Lukacs argues that in reading *Anna Karenina* or *War and Peace*, we should always insert into the narrative 'the invisible serf'. That is, we should visualize (as the novels often do not) the vast servile infrastructure which made the principals' drama possible. Similarly, in *Mrs Dalloway* we should recall the 'invisible taxi'—the fleets of carriages (they used to be called 'horseless'), the armies of servants (now sadly thinned by post-war democracy and insubordination), the attentive shop assistants (only visible when, like the luckless Miss Pym with her cherry-red hands, they are ludicrous or clumsy)—all of which exist to make Clarissa Dalloway's life bearable.

The Oxford World's Classics *Mrs Dalloway* is edited by David Bradshaw.

Notes

Robinson Crusoe

1. Giving Robinson shoes, boots, or moccasins is a very common error, although specifically contradicted by the 1719 illustration, which follows the text closely. See Fig. 1.

2. Stith Thompson's *Motif Index of Folk Literature* (Copenhagen, 1955), contains many entries on the motif of the devil—and sometimes angels—leaving single footprints in rock or soil.

Fanny Hill

1. When, in the 1940s, it was learned that the Cambridge teacher and critic F. R. Leavis was in the habit of referring to James Joyce's *Ulysses* in his classes, he was visited and warned by the police.

2. *Fanny Hill* was prosecuted and banned by London magistrates in the early 1960s. The ban was never formally lifted, although later in the decade Cleland's novel drifted back into print. See J. A. Sutherland, *Offensive Literature* (London, 1982), ch. 3.

3. Joss Lutz Marsh, 'Good Mrs Brown's Connections: Sexuality and Story-telling in Dealings with the Firm of Dombey and Son', *English Literary History*, 58: 2 (Summer 1991), 405–26.

4. See the episode with the sailor in vol. ii, in which Mrs Cole specifically warns Fanny against the dangers of disease ('the risk to my health in being so open-legg'd and free of my flesh', p. 142).

5. Peter Fryer, *The Birth Controllers* (London, 1965), chs. 1–2.

Tristram Shandy

1. Barbara Hardy, 'A Mistake in *Tristram Shandy*', *Notes and Queries*, 207 (1962), 261.

2. On the question of fifth-of-a-second measurements, see David S. Landes, *Revolution in Time: Clocks and the Making of the Modern World* (Cambridge, Mass., 1983), p. 130: 'The growing importance of small unities of time led to the invention in the 1740s of center-seconds watches—that is watches whose second hands ran off the center arbor and tracked the circumference of the dial . . . These watches were customarily fitted with a stop lever, which allowed

the user to freeze the result, the better to make his count . . . By 1770 the logic of this pursuit of ever finer time measurement led to the appearance of the first center-seconds watches with fractions of seconds marked on the dial; the earliest I have seen show fifths. Who cared about fifths of seconds in those days?' Laurence Sterne evidently did.

3. H. K. Russell, 'Tristram Shandy and the Techniques of the Novel', *Studies in Philology*, 42 (1945), 589.

Mansfield Park

1. Tony Tanner, *TLS*, 25 June 1995.

2. The full text reads: 'She had not time for such cares. She was a woman who spent her days in sitting nicely dressed on a sofa, doing some long piece of needlework, of little use and no beauty, thinking more of her pug than her children' (pp. 16–17). Conceivably, it could be the needlework which is of 'little use and no beauty', but I prefer to think Austen meant Lady Bertram.

3. I discuss this question, which remains somewhat ambiguous, in *Is Heathcliff a Murderer?* (Oxford, 1996), 5–9.

Emma

1. *The Review of English Studies*, NS 45: 177 (1994), 70–5.

2. The excellent education Jane has received is described on pp. 145–6 of the World's Classics edition.

Oliver Twist, Great Expectations

1. As many commentators note, there is ambiguity about the historical setting of *Oliver Twist*, and some perplexing pockets of anachronism. The Bow Street Runners who come to the Maylie household, for example, would have been abolished and replaced by modern policemen, around the same time that the Bloody Code was abolished in 1829. In chapter 9, Oliver overhears the Jew musing about five 'fine fellows' who have gone to the gallows—for robbery, one assumes—and never 'peached' on him. They too would seem to be victims of the pre-1829 Bloody Code. It is arguable that we are to assume the execution of Fagin to take place in one of these pockets of anachronism, in the mid-1820s, a decade before other sections of the narrative.

2. As Angus Wilson sardonically notes in his Penguin Classics edition of *Oliver Twist* the murder of a London tart by her ponce

cannot have been all that rare an event in the London underworld of the 1830s.

3. Oddly enough, in *Sikes and Nancy*, the 'reading version' of *Oliver Twist*, Dickens altered the episode, so Nancy does indicate Sikes by surname. See the World's Classics edition *Sikes and Nancy and Other Public Readings*, edited by Philip Collins.

4. Philip Collins, *Dickens and Crime* (London, 1964), 281.

5. *Great Expectations* (Everyman Paperback, ed. R. Gilmour, London, 1992), 442.

Jane Eyre

1. For the popularity of the Bluebeard story in the nineteenth century, see Juliet McMaster, 'Bluebeard at Breakfast', *Dickens Studies Annual*, 8 (1981), 197–230.

2. See Sherrill E. Grace, 'Courting Bluebeard with Bartok, Atwood, and Fowles: Modern Treatment of the Bluebeard Theme', *The Journal of Modern Literature*, 11: 2 (July 1984), 245–62.

3. The 'Sister Anne on the Battlements scene' in the Bluebeard story is alluded to in Jane's visit to the towers of Thornfield Hall with Mrs Fairfax, pp. 111–12.

4. See J. A. Sutherland, *Victorian Novelists, Publishers and Readers* (London, 1995), 55–86.

5. As Michael Mason points out, in his Penguin Classics edition of *Jane Eyre* (Harmondsworth, 1996, p. viii), there is confusion as to whether Bertha is confined on the second or the third floor. She is no madwoman in an attic, or locked in a tower (as the 1944 film suggests).

6. See, for example, the allusions to Byron's *The Corsair* (1814) by the Ingram party (p. 189 of the World's Classics edition).

Shirley

1. According to her nephew, James Austen-Leigh, Jane Austen 'took a kind of parental interest in the beings who she had created, and did not dismiss them from her mind when she had finished her last chapter'. Of *Emma*'s characters she told him 'that Mr Woodhouse survived his daughter's marriage, and kept her and Mr Knightley from settling at Donwell, about two years' (James E. Austen-Leigh, *Memoir of Jane Austen* (1871), ed. R. W Chapman, Oxford (1926), 157).

2. See Joan Stevens, *Mary Taylor: Friend of Charlotte Brontë: Letters from New Zealand and Elsewhere* (New York, 1972).

3. Juliet Barker, *TLS*, 31 May 1996.

4. The British circulating libraries united to boycott three-deckers in 1893–4. See Guinevere E. Griest, *Mudie's Circulating Library* (Bloomington, Ind., 1970), 95.

Barchester Towers

1. As R. H. Super surmises, on 17 Feb. 1855. See *The Chronicler of Barsetshire* (Ann Arbor, 1988), 79.

2. *The Letters of Anthony Trollope*, ed. N. John Hall (Stanford, Calif., 1983), i. 40.

3. The Revd Quiverful has been carefully introduced (on p. 56) and we may expect that if his lover's ambitions are thwarted, Mr Slope will switch his patronage to the other candidate for the wardenship.

4. Between 3 May and 13 June 1855 Trollope travelled in Italy with his wife, meeting his brother Thomas in Venice. This excursion to Italy evidently inspired the Stanhope family. There is one previous mention of Mr Stanhope but it is slight and rather out of character (see for instance 'the unique collection of butterflies for which he is so famous'; there is no subsequent allusion to Mr Stanhope being an amateur entomologist; nor is any mention made in this first appearance of his extraordinary family).

Adam Bede

1. Robert Hughes, *The Fatal Shore* (1986; repr. London, 1987), 244–5.

The Mill on the Floss

1. Henry James, 'The Novels of George Eliot', *Atlantic Monthly* (Oct. 1866), repr. *The Mill on the Floss* (Norton Critical Edition, ed. Carol T. Christ, New York, 1994), 465.

2. Ibid. 480.

3. F. R. Leavis, *The Great Tradition* (London, 1948), 24.

4. An exception is Gordon S. Haight, whose appendix 'A' on the geography of *The Mill on the Floss* in the Clarendon edition of the novel (Oxford, 1980, 463–7) I draw on in this chapter.

5. Ibid. 466.

Great Expectations, The Coral Island

1. 'Universal struggle' is an allusion to the third chapter of Darwin's just published *Origin of Species*. K. J. Fielding informs me that Dickens had the second edition of Darwin's work, published in January 1860. Dickens first makes mention of *Great Expectations* in August of that year.

2. I would guess that like most early and mid-nineteenth-century authors Eliot and Dickens were not much good in the water. There were a few exceptions. Walter Scott, for example, seems to have been a good swimmer. Like Byron (another good swimmer), he was disabled, and had courses of 'water treatment' at the seaside inflicted on him in childhood which probably accounts for his proficiency.

3. Ben Franklin, as his autobiography informs us, was inordinately proud of his ability to swim, and saw it as something extraordinary in the mid-eighteenth century. See the World's Classics edition, *Autobiography and Other Writings*, edited by Ormond Seavey.

4. The most commented-on error in *The Coral Island* (see the notes to chapter 4, p. 340).

Armadale

1. In his epilogue Collins claims that 'the end of the story' was sketched in a notebook in spring 1864—a period when he was recuperating his health in Rome. R. D. Altick, *The Presence of the Present* (Columbus, Ohio, 1991), 86–7, suspects that Collins in fact got the details from the *Times* report, cited below: as do I. See note on the text, *Armadale*, ed. J. Sutherland (Penguin Classics, 1995).

2. See the chapter on *The Woman in White* in *Is Heathcliff a Murderer?*, pp. 117–22, for Collins's apprehensions about being caught out by *The Times*.

Felix Holt, the Radical

1. For the early history of World's Classics see Peter Sutcliffe, *The Oxford University Press* (Oxford, 1978), 140–5.

2. See the Lynton Lamb illustration to *Robinson Crusoe* in the first chapter.

3. The World's Classics edition of *Felix Holt, the Radical* follows the Clarendon text.

230 Notes to pages 157–87157–87

Ralph the Heir

1. See appendix 1, in the World's Classics *Ralph the Heir*, on 'Shilly Shally'.

2. See my chapter on *Barchester Towers*, above.

Daniel Deronda

1. Kenneth Newton, 'Daniel Deronda and Circumcision', *Essays in Criticism*, 31: 4 (1981), 313–27.

2. Ibid. 313.

3. Gordon S. Haight, *George Eliot* (Oxford, 1968), 470–1.

4. Richard Owen, *The Life of Richard Owen*, 2 vols. (London, 1894), i. 231–2.

5. Rosemary Ashton, *G. H. Lewes* (Oxford, 1991), 11.

6. See the entry on 'Circumcision' in the 11th edition of the *Encyclopaedia Britannica* (1910), vi. 390.

7. It is not just Victorian novelists who were inhibited where circumcision is concerned. In her first Lord Peter Wimsey novel, *Whose Body?* (1923), Dorothy Sayers conceived a vivid opening scene. A naked body is found in a bath-tub in Battersea. It is assumed to be that of a Jewish millionaire. Wimsey comes in, and instantly detects it is not said millionaire. How does he know?—in the manuscript, apparently, Sayers used non-circumcision as the tell-tale evidence which keen-eyed Lord Peter immediately perceived. Sayers's publishers demanded she take the scene out. She made the crucial evidence 'dirty fingernails' instead.

8. Female opposition to the ritual of circumcision boiled up in 1995–6, following the broadcast of Victor Schonfeld's Channel 4 programme, *'It's a Boy!'*. In the furore that followed, largely conducted in the *Jewish Chronicle*, it emerged that a number of defiant Jewish mothers were, on principle, refusing to have their children circumcised.

9. Gordon Haight, *George Eliot* (London, 1968), 40.

The Woodlanders

1. Michael Millgate, *Thomas Hardy: a Biography* (London, 1971; repr. 1994), 245–6.

2. David Lodge, *The Woodlanders* (Macmillan: London, 1974), 392.

3. Thomas Hardy had doubts about the propriety of this phrase; see

Dale Kramer's notes to the World's Classics edition of *The Wood-landers*, p. 388.

The Yellow Wall-Paper

1. See, for instance, Dr Mandelet in *The Awakening*, ch. 22. Gilman was treated by Silas Weir Mitchell and the heroine in *The Yellow Wall-Paper* is threatened with 'Weir Mitchell in the fall'. The neurologist-novelist also appears in William Dean Howells's *The Shadow of a Dream* (1890).

2. Jennie is called Jane in the last paragraphs of the novel, which may be an allusion to *Jane Eyre*.

The Sea-Wolf

1. See, for instance, the business of the Bible on board the *Ghost*. Early in the narrative, when the mate drinks himself to death, it is specifically said that there is no 'Bible or prayer-book on board' (p. 20). Later (p. 96), Wolf Larsen is found reading a Bible. Cloudsley Johns (who read the MS for London) pointed out the error, and the author made the necessary correction about a Bible being found in the dead mate's gear.

2. There is another episode, late in the action, when Larsen again shows these god-like powers. Completely blind, on board the *Ghost*, he deduces the hero's silent presence, despite the fact that Humphrey is thought to be drowned.

The Good Soldier

1. Eugene Goodheart, 'What Dowell knew: A Reading of *The Good Soldier*', *Antaeus*, 56 (Spring 1986), 70.

2. Thomas Moser, in the World's Classics edition of *The Good Soldier*, gives a full account of the story's anachronisms.

3. Martin Stannard (ed.), *The Good Soldier* (Norton Critical Edition, New York, 1991), p. xi.

4. Vincent Cheng, 'A Chronology of *The Good Soldier*', *ELN* 24 (Sept. 1986), repr. in Stannard, 385.

5. J. F. Kermode, 'Novels: Recognition and Deception', *Critical Inquiry*, 1: 1 (Sept. 1974), repr. in Stannard, 336.

6. *LRB* 20 June 1996.

7. The editor of the World's Classics *The Good Soldier*, Thomas

Moser, also briefly raises this possibility, only to pass it by as implausible.

8. Max Saunders, *Ford Madox Ford* (Oxford, 1996), i. 422.

9. It is possible to date this episode as 1897, but I follow Cheng in preferring 1895.

Mrs Dalloway

1. The novel began as the short story, 'Mrs Dalloway in Bond Street', which is occupied only with the morning expedition.

2. In 'Mrs Dalloway in Bond Street' the time is given specifically as 'eleven o'clock'. See *The Complete Shorter Fiction of Virginia Woolf*, ed. Susan Dick (London, 1985), 146.